CONTENTS

THE ARDEN SHAKESPEARE

GENERAL EDITORS:

RICHARD PROUDFOOT, ANN THOMPSON

THE ARDEN SHAKESPEARE

* Third Series

THE ARDEN EDITION OF THE
WORKS OF WILLIAM SHAKESPEARE

TIMON OF ATHENS

Edited by
H. J. OLIVER

The general editors of the Arden Shakespeare have been
W. J. Craig and R. H. Case (first edition 1899-1944),
Una Ellis-Fermor, Harold F. Brooks,
Harold Jenkins and Brian Morris (second edition 1946-1982),
Present general editors (third edition)
Richard Proudfoot, Ann Thompson and David Scott Kastan

This edition of *Timon of Athens* by H. J. Oliver,
first published in 1959 by
Methuen & Co. Ltd
Reprinted ten times

Reprinted 1997 by Thomas Nelson & Sons Ltd

Thomas Nelson & Sons Ltd
Nelson House Mayfield Road
Walton-on-Thames Surrey

Nelson Australia
12 Dodds Street South Melbourne
Victoria 3205 Australia

Nelson Canada
1120 Birchmount Road Scarborough
Ontario 1K 5G4 Canada

I(T)P® Thomas Nelson is an International
Thomson Publishing Company
I(T)P® is used under licence

Editorial matter © 1959 Methuen & Co. Ltd

Printed in Croatia

British Library Cataloguing in Publication Data
A catalogue record for this book is available from
the British Library.

Library of Congress Cataloguing in Publication Data
A catalogue record for this book is available from
the Library of Congress

ISBN 0-416-47250-8 (cased)
ISBN 0-17-443476-6 (paperback)
NPN 9 8 7 6 5 4 3 2

PREFACE

THE present edition is not a revision of, or dependent on, K. Deighton's "old" Arden edition of *Timon of Athens*. Deighton's notes have been read with respect and are sometimes quoted, as are those of other commentators, in both agreement and disagreement; but his text was not used as the basis of mine.

In preparing this edition, I have been greatly helped by many scholars, and in particular by the General Editors of the "new" Arden series. It is a privilege to record my indebtedness to the late Professor Una Ellis-Fermor for numerous characteristic acts of kindness and for much good advice, especially on the arrangement of the material in the Introduction; she was able to read that part of my edition in typescript and generously expressed her approval of it. Dr Harold Brooks also has answered questions put to him from time to time and, without imposing opinions in any way, has contributed much that is valuable, particularly to the Explanatory Notes.

Mr J. C. Maxwell, who has collaborated with Professor J. Dover Wilson on the edition of this play for the New Shakespeare series (C.U.P.), generously sent me page-proofs of his work; and although these did not reach me until my edition was in the press, I am glad to have been able to insert mention of his interpretation of I. i. 33–4, III. iii. 34–5, and IV. iii. 451, 457. (Other references to Mr Maxwell's opinions are to his earlier article on the play, listed in my bibliography.)

Dr James G. McManaway and Dr Charlton Hinman, of the Folger Shakespeare Library, were most generous in arranging to send me microfilms of Folio texts of *Timon*; and Dr Hinman added to that kindness by sending me in advance a copy of an address on problems of Folio texts which he was preparing for delivery at the Annual Meeting of the Modern Language Association in Washington, D.C., in December 1956. Dr F. D. Hoeniger, of Victoria College, Toronto (editor of the Arden *Pericles*), was equally generous in drawing my attention to, and copying out for me, Edward Dowden's marginalia in his copy of Deighton's edition of *Timon*, now in the Folger; and Professor Fredson Bowers, of the University of

Virginia, spent valuable time looking through the papers of the late Philip Williams for me, in search of collected evidence on the question of the "copy" for the First Folio text of *Timon*.

I am particularly grateful to them all, and also to Mr John Metcalfe, Principal Librarian of the Public Library of N.S.W., and his Deputy, Mr G. D. Richardson, who arranged for me to have special access to the Library's copy of the First Folio and the fine collection of texts and critical works in its Shakespeare Room.

I also desire to express my thanks to the Oxford University Press for permission to print, as Appendix C of this edition, extensive selections from H. W. Fowler's translation of Lucian's *Timon the Misanthrope*, originally published at the Clarendon Press in 1905.

H. J. OLIVER

Sydney, 1958

NOTE TO 1963 REPRINT

I HAVE taken the opportunity of correcting a few minor errors and misprints; of distinguishing between the first three editions of Rowe and between the various editions of Steevens and Reed, where those editors are mentioned in collations or notes; and of revising or adding to the explanatory notes, at II. ii. 237; III. vi. 114; IV. iii. 2–3, 123, 163; and v. i. 34.

I have tried to profit from the comments of reviewers and other readers of the first edition and am particularly grateful to Professor G. Blakemore Evans (*J.E.G.P.* 59, 1960), Mr J. C. Maxwell, and Mr E. J. Dennis for helpful suggestions.

Since this revised edition was prepared, Professor Charlton Hinman, in *The Printing and Proof-Reading of the First Folio of Shakespeare* (Oxford 1963), has revealed that in different copies of the First Folio *Timon* there are variant states of pages Gg1^v and hh5 (as well as of gg2^v); these variants, however, are insignificant and do not alter the text. (For gg2^v, see pp. xxxi–xxxii of my Introduction; see also p. 26.)

H. J. O.

University of N.S.W., 1963

ABBREVIATIONS AND REFERENCES

The following abbreviations are used for the principal editions cited in the Collations and Explanatory Notes:

Rowe	*The Works*, ed. N. Rowe, 1709 (2 editions), 1714.
Pope	*The Works*, ed. Alexander Pope, 1723-5.
Theobald	*The Works*, ed. L. Theobald, 1733, 1740.
Hanmer	*The Works*, ed. Sir T. Hanmer, 1744.
Warburton	*The Works*, ed. with Notes by Pope and William Warburton, 1747.
Johnson	*The Plays*, ed. Samuel Johnson, 1765.
Capell	The *Comedies, Histories and Tragedies*, ed. Edward Capell, 1768.
Steevens	*The Plays*, with Notes by Johnson and George Steevens, 1773, 1778, 1793.
Malone	*The Plays and Poems*, ed. E. Malone, 1790.
Reed	*The Plays*, ed. Johnson and Steevens, revised and augmented by Isaac Reed, 1785, 1803, 1813.
Singer	*The Dramatic Works*, ed. S. W. Singer, 1826.
Knight	*The Comedies, Histories, Tragedies and Poems*, ed. Charles Knight, 1838-43 (*The Pictorial Shakespeare*).
Collier	*The Works*, ed. J. Payne Collier, 1842-4, 1853, 1858.
Verplanck	*The Plays*, ed. G. C. Verplanck, 1847 (*The Illustrated Shakespeare*).
Delius	*Shakespeares Werke*, ed. N. Delius, 1854.
Hudson	*The Complete Works*, ed. H. N. Hudson, 1851-6 (*The Harvard Shakespeare*).
Dyce	*The Works*, ed. Alexander Dyce, 1857, 1864-7.
Grant White	*The Works*, ed. R. Grant White, 1857-66.
Staunton	*The Works*, ed. Howard Staunton, 1858-60.
Camb. Edd.	*The Works*, ed. W. G. Clark and W. A. Wright, 1863-6, 1891-3 (*The Cambridge Shakespeare*).
Keightley	*The Plays*, ed. Thomas Keightley, 1864.
Globe	*The Works*, ed. W. G. Clark and W. A. Wright, 1864 (*The Globe Edition*).
Rolfe	*The Works*, ed. W. J. Rolfe, 1871-96.
Evans	*Timon of Athens*, Intro. and Notes by H. A. Evans, [1890] (*The Henry Irving Shakespeare*).
Deighton	*Timon of Athens*, ed. K. Deighton, 1905, 1929 (*The Arden Shakespeare*).

Fletcher	*Timon of Athens*, ed. R. H. Fletcher, 1913 (*The Tudor Shakespeare*).
Williams	*Timon of Athens*, ed. Stanley T. Williams, 1919 (*The Yale Shakespeare*).
Ridley	*Timon of Athens*, ed. M. R. Ridley, 1934 (*The New Temple Shakespeare*).
Kittredge	*The Complete Works*, ed. G. L. Kittredge, 1936.
Alexander	*The Complete Works*, ed. Peter Alexander, 1951.
Sisson	*The Complete Works*, ed. C. J. Sisson, [1954].

The conjectures of Dowden are those recorded in his manuscript notes in a copy of the Arden edition of *Timon of Athens* now in the Folger Shakespeare Library; those of Becket, Daniel, Heath, Jackson, Mason, Mitford, and Rann are cited from the collations of the Cambridge editors.

Titles of works mentioned in the Introduction and Appendices are cited in full; the following abbreviations are used in the Explanatory Notes or in footnotes:

Abbott	E. A. Abbott, *A Shakespearian Grammar* (3rd edition, London 1873).
Armstrong	E. A. Armstrong, *Shakespeare's Imagination* (London 1946).
Joseph	Sister Miriam Joseph, *Shakespeare's Use of the Arts of Language* (Columbia U.P., N.Y. 1947).
Kennedy	M. B. Kennedy, *The Oration in Shakespeare* (Univ. of North Carolina 1942).
Kökeritz	Helge Kökeritz, *Shakespeare's Pronunciation* (Yale 1953).
M.L.R.	*The Modern Language Review* (C.U.P.).
M.P.	*Modern Philology* (Univ. of Chicago).
Maxwell	J. C. Maxwell, '*Timon of Athens*', *Scrutiny*, xv, 3 (Summer 1948), 195–208.
N. & Q.	*Notes and Queries.*
Noble	R. Noble, *Shakespeare's Biblical Knowledge* (London 1935).
North's *Plutarch*	*The Lives of the Noble Grecians and Romanes, compared together by that grave learned philosopher and historiographer, Plutarke of Chaeronea: Translated out of Greeke into French by James Amiot . . . and out of French into English, by Thomas North* (4th edition 1676).
O.E.D.	*The Oxford English Dictionary, being a corrected re-issue of A New English Dictionary upon Historical Principles* (1933).
P.M.L.A.	*Publications of the Modern Language Association* (of America).
Painter	William Painter, *The Palace of Pleasure*, 1566.
Partridge	Eric Partridge, *Shakespeare's Bawdy* (London 1947).
Pettet	E. C. Pettet, '*Timon of Athens*: The Disruption of Feudal Morality', *R.E.S.*, xxiii (1947), 321–36.
Phillips	J. E. Phillips, *The State in Shakespeare's Greek and Roman Plays* (Columbia U.P., N.Y. 1940).
R.E.S.	*The Review of English Studies* (O.U.P.).
S.B.	*Studies in Bibliography* (Bibliographical Society, Univ. of Virginia).
S.Q.	*Shakespeare Quarterly* (Shakespeare Association of America, N.Y.).

Schmidt	Alexander Schmidt, *Shakespeare-Lexicon* (2nd edition, Berlin 1886).
Shadwell	*The History of Timon of Athens the Man-Hater* (1678; ed. Willis Vickery, The Bankside-Restoration Shakespeare, N.Y. 1907).
Sisson	C. J. Sisson, *New Readings in Shakespeare* (C.U.P. 1956).
Spurgeon	Caroline Spurgeon, *Shakespeare's Imagery and What it Tells Us* (C.U.P. 1935).
Tilley	M. P. Tilley, *A Dictionary of the Proverbs in England in the Sixteenth and Seventeenth Centuries* (Univ. of Michigan, Ann Arbor 1950).
Wright	Joseph Wright, *The English Dialect Dictionary*, 1900.

Abbreviations used for the titles of Shakespeare's other plays are those of C. T. Onions, *A Shakespeare Glossary* (2nd edition, Oxford 1919), p. x; and the line-numbers cited for these plays are those of the Globe Edition.

INTRODUCTION

I. THE TEXT

A. THE FOLIO

Timon of Athens is one of the eighteen plays now regularly thought of as Shakespeare's which, not having appeared separately in Quarto during his lifetime, were first printed, after his death, in the First Folio of 1623; and before publication it was therefore entered in the Stationers' Register by Isaac Jaggard and Edward Blount, on 8 November 1623, among the "Copies as are not formerly entred to other men".

For this play, then, the Folio is the only text. But *Timon* differs in many important respects from other "Folio plays" and sometimes presents an editor with problems that are unique.

It is known[1] that *Timon* was not originally intended for the position it now has in the Folio, after *Romeo and Juliet* and before *Julius Cæsar*. There survives in some copies of the Folio a leaf (gg3) with the last page of *Romeo and Juliet* (p. 77) on the recto and the first page of *Troilus and Cressida* (p. 78) on the verso. But there were difficulties over the text of *Troilus and Cressida*, which was therefore withdrawn, and printing was resumed with *Julius Cæsar*. At a later stage (not, as was thought until recently, in October or November 1623 after the printing of *Cymbeline*, the last play in the Folio, but, as J. W. Schroeder has shown, at an earlier date "during an interval in the printing of portions of *Hamlet, Lear* and *Othello*"[2]), *Timon* was printed to fill the gap left between *Romeo and Juliet* and *Julius Cæsar*. The original leaf gg3 was cancelled and a new quire signed gg begun[3]; the last page of *Romeo and Juliet* was reprinted on

1. The pioneer conclusions of E. E. Willoughby in *The Printing of the First Folio of Shakespeare* (Bibliographical Society, Oxford, 1932) have now been modified by, particularly, Giles E. Dawson, 'A Bibliographical Problem in the First Folio of Shakespeare', *The Library*, 4th ser., XXII (1942), 25–33; W. W. Greg, *The Shakespeare First Folio* (Oxford, 1955); John W. Schroeder, *The Great Folio of 1623* (1956); and the conclusions of Charlton Hinman from his collations of the First Folios in the Folger Shakespeare Library, Washington, D.C., including those stated in his paper 'Bibliographical Oddities in the Shakespeare First Folio' read to the Modern Language Association in Washington in December 1956.

2. *Op. cit.*, p. 87.   3. The actual signatures are Gg, gg², gg³.

the recto of the new gg1 and *Timon* begun on the verso. (And since the reprinted page was wrongly numbered 79 instead of 77, there were now no pages numbered 77 and 78 in *Romeo and Juliet* and the first three pages of *Timon* were wrongly numbered also as 80–2; the correct pagination did not begin again until 81 was repeated on the new gg3ʳ.) *Timon* proved to be a much shorter play than *Troilus and Cressida*, for which the remainder of the original quire gg and the whole of quires hh and ii had been allowed; *Timon* ended on hh5ᵛ (p. 98). Accordingly an unusual (and inaccurate) list of dramatis personae, headed "The Actors Names", was printed to fill up hh6ʳ; the verso, exceptionally, was left blank; and since *Julius Cæsar* began on quire kk, on p. 109, there are no quire ii and no pages numbered 99–108 in this section of the Folio.

The conclusion that *Timon* would not have appeared at all in the First Folio if there had been no difficulties over *Troilus and Cressida* can nevertheless not be drawn with full confidence, since there is nothing to show that *Timon* was not originally intended for a later place in the volume. But there are many other curious features of the text which lend some weight to the conjecture.

B. "INCONSISTENCIES AND LOOSE ENDS"

Even before the days of modern bibliography, editors and readers of *Timon* were puzzled by what seemed to be loose ends in the play or even false starts, by certain inconsistencies in the naming of the characters or the spelling of their names, and by the exceptional irregularity of the versification, which more often than in any other play by Shakespeare refused to scan according to the regular iambic pentameter pattern.

Under the first head, the appearances of Ventidius in the play were perhaps most often cited as difficulties. In the opening scene,[1] Timon generously redeems him from prison by paying the debt of five talents for which he has been imprisoned (and the name here is spelt "Ventidius"). It was then argued that Ventidius' refusal of help to Timon when Timon was in need of money would mark the climax of ingratitude, be the last straw. And Timon does indeed instruct the Steward to approach Ventidius for help (at II. ii. 224–35, where the name is spelt "Ventiddius"). We do see Lucius and Lucullus refuse assistance, but we only hear casually and indirectly, from Sempronius, of Ventidius' refusal (at III. iii. 4–10, where the spelling becomes "Ventidgius"). But he does refuse; and therefore his earlier offer to repay the money to Timon at I. ii. 1–8 is regarded

1. Here and throughout the Introduction, by "act" and "scene" I refer to the usual modern divisions of the play (found, for example, in the "Globe" edition): in the Folio text there are no act and scene divisions at all in *Timon*.

as an inconsistency or false start (and the name there is "Venti-gius"). Obviously, and to anticipate, the door was wide open for a theory of divided authorship, with one author spelling "Venti-d(d)ius" and the other "Venti(d)gius".

Alcibiades was also regarded as a character whose proper place in the play had not been determined. The scene of his banishment from Athens—because he insists on pleading before an ungrateful Senate for the life of a friend who is neither named nor mentioned anywhere else in the play—was a particular puzzle; and E. H. Wright, for one, proclaimed that it "has not the slightest reference to Timon or the remotest relation to anything whatsoever that takes place in the half of the play preceding".[1] The same critic was worried by the effect of the appearance of Alcibiades at the end of the play as "a kind of Fortinbras in the drama, fighting out the wrongs at which Timon can only curse"[2]; Hardin Craig spoke of "the rather inconsistent Alcibiades" who "appears as a restorer of normal social life—a sort of Richmond or Octavius"[3]; and E. K. Chambers could not make up his mind whether Alcibiades was intended to contrast with Timon or was "merely Timon over again, in a weaker and less clearly motived version of the dis-illusioned child of fortune".[4]

Chambers, again, found the very presence of the faithful steward in the play a further difficulty. "What", he asked, "is the precise dramatic purpose served by the good steward . . . and his senti-mentalities, which seem to give the lie to Timon's wholesale con-demnation of humanity, without any appreciable effect upon its direction or its force?"[5]

Finally, Timon himself seemed an unsatisfactory character. J. W. Draper could not reconcile the Steward's praise of Timon with what seemed to him a lack of common sense in the Timon of the first two acts: "Clearly", he wrote, "Shakespeare intended his audience to admire Timon's very prodigality",[6] but Draper found that he could not admire it himself. More recently, Una Ellis-Fermor has complained that Timon simply does not exist as a person. For a tragic hero he is, in her eyes, curiously "colour-less and neutral"[7]; and this, at least, is a serious charge against the play.

Under the second head, inconsistency in the naming of charac-ters, there was also no lack of material. The Ventidius–Ventigius–

1. *The Authorship of "Timon of Athens"* (N.Y., 1910), p. 44.   2. *Ibid.*, p. 17.
3. *An Interpretation of Shakespeare* (N.Y., 1948), p. 253.
4. *Shakespeare: A Survey* (London, 1925), p. 269.   5. *Ibid.*, p. 269.
6. 'The Theme of *Timon of Athens*', *M.L.R.*, xxix (1934), 21.
7. '*Timon of Athens*: An Unfinished Play', *R.E.S.*, xviii (1942), 283.

Ventiddius–Ventidgius sequence has already been noted; and it may be added that the spellings "Apemantus" and "Apermantus" are both found from time to time in the Folio text, though not necessarily in separate scenes as are the various spellings of Ventidius. Worse, the two women who visit Timon with Alcibiades and are given gold to destroy mankind are called in that scene (iv. iii) "Phrynia" and "Timandra"; but apparently they are also the "Phrinica and Timandylo" who, we are told at v. i. 5–6, "had gold of him". Worst of all, the character who is elsewhere in the play consistently called only "Steward" is apparently the one who in I. ii. 153–202 is temporarily named "Flavius"; but later, at II. ii. 189, while the Steward is on stage, Timon, calling for two servants, names one of them "Flavius", and that one seems to be identical with the "Flaminius" who goes to Lucullus to ask aid for Timon in III. i.

Under the third head, of versification, perhaps the most important features are the extremely free verse of many parts of the play, so free that it has not even the "ghost" of the iambic pentameter behind it as has most of the free verse of, say, T. S. Eliot; the large proportion and irregular occurrence of prose; and the high number of rhymes, often occurring at the most unexpected places. The general impression is perhaps even more important here than any single speech; but particular reference may be made to a speech by Apemantus (I. ii. 38–52) which (so far as one can judge) begins as prose, has three lines of verse in the middle, returns to prose, and ends with a rhymed couplet (though that is also printed as prose in the Folio). Another instance of irregularity is the speech of Alcibiades to the Senate (III. v. 41–59); and still another, perhaps the most frequently cited, is the soliloquy of the Steward at IV. ii. 30–51 which Chambers described as an "alternation of jolting rhymed couplets with lines in which the metre seems suddenly to come to an abrupt stop"[1] while Wright could only call it "little more than prose run mad in the inferior author's manner"[2] (and therefore to be ascribed to a lesser dramatist than Shakespeare).

C. THE BIBLIOGRAPHICAL ANALYSIS

Before proceeding to any such theory of collaboration, the modern reader will want to know whether bibliography can throw any light on the problem and in particular whether any of the peculiarities of the text can be explained as the fault of the compositor (or compositors) who set the play in type or as the result of any abnormality in the "copy" provided. It is not a question to

---

1. *Shakespeare: A Survey*, p. 271.   2. *Op. cit.*, p. 46.

which as yet any final answer can be given, but the following is a tentative analysis of the evidence.

The usual spelling tests[1] suggest that *Timon of Athens* (except, possibly, one or two pages) was set up in type by the more inaccurate of the two main compositors of the First Folio, the so-called "Compositor B". His characteristic spellings "yong", "heere", "deere", "greefe", "do", "go", "divell" and "bin", for example, are far more in evidence than the alternative spellings favoured by his principal colleague, "A"; one also finds his rather exceptional use of apostrophes and, as Hinman has recently pointed out, a preference for one long dash over two short ones to indicate the breaking-off of a speech.[2] Hinman has also added the information that, except possibly for one page, *Timon* is set throughout from the same type cases—and this happens in the Tragedies only when a play is set by one man.

Already, then, one is faced by a likelihood of some textual corruption, for Compositor B has been proved careless. He is likely to omit words and make other errors through trying to carry too many words in his head; and he will sometimes set prose as verse or verse as prose, either to make the layout of the page look more attractive or simply to fit a predetermined number of words into a given space.

The further complication is that alongside the characteristic spellings of Compositor B, there are others, not compositorial, which are probably a "show-through" from the copy he was setting up in type. At this stage, the evidence becomes very difficult to interpret, and bibliography is in danger of completing the vicious circle if it argues that the presence of some spellings suggests a certain compositor and then that the absence of them or the presence of others suggests a characteristic of the copy (rather than a different compositor). But used with care (and particular care when B is involved, since he was more likely to alter spellings in his copy than were his colleagues), the evidence of unusual spellings in a printed play can give presumptive evidence of the nature of the copy from which the compositor worked.

1. See, for example, Willoughby, *The Printing of the First Folio*; Hinman, 'Principles Governing the Use of Various Spellings as Evidence of Alternate Setting by Two Compositors', *The Library*, 4th ser., XXI (1941), 78–94; Alice Walker, *Textual Problems of the First Folio* (Camb., 1953); Greg, *The Shakespeare First Folio*; Williams, 'New Approaches to Textual Problems in Shakespeare', *S.B.*, VIII (1956), 3–14.

2. 'Bibliographical Oddities in the First Folio'. Compositor "E" was not concerned with *Timon*—possibly because he "was not regarded as competent to deal with manuscript copy" (Hinman, 'The Prentice Hand in the Tragedies of the Shakespeare First Folio: Compositor E', *S.B.*, IX (1957), 3–20).

It is certain that the copy for *Timon* was not prompt-copy or any kind of manuscript that had been used in a theatre. The very first stage-direction, for example, says "Enter Poet, Painter, Jeweller, Merchant, and Mercer" although as far as one can determine there is no Mercer in the play. (There are speech-prefixes "*Mer.*" but they apparently stand for the Merchant; and the Poet and Painter discuss the other *two* people on stage, not three.) Such a "ghost-character" would certainly be struck out in a prompt-book but is characteristic of author's "foul papers" (or a transcript of them): the author writes down a list of characters he may require but forgets one of them or changes his mind.[1] The error is all the more likely to remain, of course, if the author has in fact never read through his manuscript but has left it unrevised.[2]

The "false exit" such as one finds at iv. iii. 377–95 is also not likely to stand in a prompt-book. Here, after Timon and Apemantus have indulged in a valedictory exchange of insults, Timon begins what reads like a soliloquy: "Then, Timon, presently prepare thy grave . . ."; yet when he has finished speaking, one is astonished to find Apemantus still on stage. The explanation is not that the lines are misplaced; Apemantus replies to Timon's last words. One can only conclude that the author changed his mind while writing and did not go back to alter.

The stage-directions also are of the kind characteristic of foul papers rather than of prompt-copy. "Ventigius which Timon redeem'd from prison", when the character is re-introduced, reads like an author's reminder to himself; and "Then comes dropping after all Apemantus discontentedly like himselfe" is at the best an indication of what the *author* would like to see on the stage. These fall within the class that Greg has called "descriptive stage-directions"; others, such as "Enter divers Friends at severall doores" (iii. vi. 1), are "permissive" and make no attempt to decide the exact number of characters who are to be on the stage.[3] The calling of servants by their masters' names (e.g. "Varro" and "Isidore" in ii. ii)—a kind of author's shorthand—and the decision *during* the scene to call the Second Stranger of iii. ii "Hostilius" are then further indication that the copy had not been used for theatrical performance. In fact, most of these features and the inconsistency with some of the speech-prefixes provide an exceptionally good parallel to the part of the play of *Sir Thomas More* which is now generally

1. See Greg's interesting examples, *The Shakespeare First Folio*, pp. 111–12.
2. This whole discussion of the "copy" of *Timon* should be related to what is said in Sections 3 and 7 of this Introduction on *Timon* as an unfinished play.
3. See also the directions at i. i. 245, iii. i. 1, iii. iii. 1, iv. ii. 1, v. i. 29 and v. i. 129, and notes on some of them.

believed to have been written by Shakespeare: as Alice Walker has remarked, if Hand D of that manuscript was his, then "it is plain that he left a trail of ambiguities and loose ends in the speech prefixes of minor characters to be solved at a reviser's discretion".[1]

None of the characteristics already mentioned, however, is inconsistent with the copy's having been a transcript of the foul papers. The late Philip Williams, shortly before his death in 1955, announced his belief that *Timon* "was set from a fair transcript made by the same scribe who prepared the manuscript from which the folio text of *Coriolanus* was set", his evidence being apparently largely spellings which he found in both texts and considered not typical of the Folio compositors.[2] I myself think it probable that part of the copy was Shakespeare's own foul papers but that another part was a transcript—and that it was a transcript made by Ralph Crane, the scribe who prepared many dramatic scripts in the early 1620s and whose transcripts are thought to have been the copy for at least five of the other plays in the First Folio.[3] Again the evidence is not easy to interpret,[4] and Crane's habits as a scribe did not remain constant; but his characteristic "ha's" for both "he has" and "has" and "'em" for "them", his curious use of apostrophes in phrases like "I'am" and "ye'have", and his fondness for hyphens, colons and parentheses are all found in the text of *Timon*. Using such cumulative evidence as this, I would suggest that at least the following sections of the copy of *Timon* were transcripts in Crane's hand of those parts of Shakespeare's foul papers which were too "foul" for a compositor easily to read:

> I. i. 176–end
> I. ii
> III. ii, iii, iv and v
> IV. iii parts, including 461–end
> V. i–end

This hypothesis is based on a study of all the spellings in the play

1. *Op. cit.*, p. 97.
2. See his paper 'New Approaches to Textual Problems in Shakespeare', posthumously published in *S.B.*, VIII (1956). Professor Fredson Bowers was kind enough to look through Williams's papers for me but could find nothing further on the problem.
3. For Crane's characteristics as a scribe see, for example, F. P. Wilson, 'Ralph Crane, Scrivener to the King's Players', *The Library*, 4th ser., VII (1927), 194–215; R. C. Bald's edition of Middleton's *A Game at Chesse* (Camb., 1929); and the Malone Society editions of *Demetrius and Enanthe* (1951) and *The Witch* (1950).
4. For example, Crane's favourite spelling "ha's" is also found in the work of Compositor "B" setting from printed copy in *Troilus and Cressida*; and forms like "I'am" are common enough at a slightly later date.

and not on the occurrence of any one in a particular scene. But once having formed from all the available evidence his theory of the copy, the editor must print in his text nothing that is inconsistent with that theory. In practice, it is only rarely that I wish to emend the Folio text of *Timon*; but, to take one example, I do believe that Sempronius' "Has much disgrac'd me in 't" at III. iii. 15 is not, as William Wells argued,[1] an instance of Middleton's alleged dropping of the personal pronoun in the nominative case but an example of the compositor's failure to set up correctly Crane's characteristic "ha's" or "h'as" (meaning "he has").[2]

If indeed the copy was in two hands, in some such division as that very tentatively suggested above, then it may be that there is also a bibliographical explanation of the two spellings of "Ventidius" and "Apemantus": I suggest that Crane wrote "Venti(d)-gius" and "Apermantus" where Shakespeare wrote "Ventid-(d)ius" and "Apemantus". It does seem interesting, for example, that before the entrance of "Apermantus" in I. i, there are spellings which are not like Crane's (such as "vouchsafe") and spellings which are almost certainly Shakespeare's (particularly "saciety" i.e. "satiety"); immediately after his entrance are found the Crane-like "toong" ("tongue") and "whether" ("whither"). Whether this is so or not, it is clear that we shall not understand the occurrence of these various spellings of proper names until we remember that the pages were set up by the compositor not in their present order but by formes; in any set of twelve pages the normal order of setting would be 6, 7; 5, 8; 4, 9; 3, 10; 2, 11; 1, 12.[3] A reader of the Folio text finds on gg2, seven lines from the bottom, "*Enter Apermantus*"; he sees "Gentle Apermantus" and the catch-

1. '*Timon of Athens*', *N. & Q.*, N.S., VI (1920), 266–9.

2. If v. i was in transcript, it may also have been the *scribe* who ailed to notice that one of the two epitaphs on Timon had been, or had to be, deleted; he copied both and the compositor could only follow.

3. Charlton Hinman, 'Cast-off Copy for the First Folio of Shakespeare', *S.Q.*, VI. 3 (Summer 1955), 259–73. Briefly, Folio is quired in sixes: i.e., each gathering consists of three folio sheets placed one inside another, so that sheet 3 forms the third and fourth leaves of the gathering (3ʳ, 3ᵛ, 4ʳ, 4ᵛ: pp. 5, 6, 7, 8); sheet 2 forms the second and fifth leaves (2ʳ, 2ᵛ, 5ʳ, 5ᵛ: pp. 3, 4, 9, 10); and sheet 1 forms the first and sixth leaves (1ʳ, 1ᵛ, 6ʳ, 6ᵛ: pp. 1, 2, 11, 12). Printing proceeds with the sheets unfolded, and of course one side of the sheet (two pages) is printed at a time—either the two pages from the "outer forme" of type or the two from the "inner forme" (sheet 1ᵒ=pp. 1, 12; sheet 1ⁱ=pp. 2, 11; sheet 2ᵒ=pp. 3, 10; sheet 2ⁱ= pp. 4, 9; sheet 3ᵒ=pp. 5, 8; sheet 3ⁱ=pp. 6, 7). What Hinman has shown is that not only did the printing proceed by formes, but also the pages were set up by formes and not in the order in which they appear in the printed volume; the compositor normally began with the inner forme of sheet 3. This was possible because the copy was "cast off": i.e., an estimate was made of the amount of copy that would be needed for each page.

word abbreviation "*Aper*"; then he turns the page and immediately finds "*Ape*" and "*Apemantus*" and wonders how the copy can have changed so suddenly at such an unlikely point. But of course the copy did not change here: the compositor probably set 2^v *before* 2^r; and he used the spelling "Apemantus" on 2^v not because it was in his copy for that page (it almost certainly was not) but because it was the spelling he had been using on the previous page he had set, 4^v (where he changed to it, perhaps, because that part of his copy was in Shakespeare's spelling). When he came to set 2^r (after 5^r, where the word does not occur) he again followed his copy and reverted to "Apermantus".

Perhaps there is one even more valuable service that bibliography can do us in connection with these variant proper names: it can remind us that the problem is not peculiar to *Timon* and that too much reliance cannot be placed on theories which treat them as if it were. If Compositor A, in setting *1 Henry VI*, spells "Burgundy" and later "Burgonie", "Puzel" and later "Pucell", it may be because the spellings in his copy changed and it may be that the copy changed because two authors were involved; but it could also be, as Peter Alexander pointed out years ago, that at one moment Shakespeare was thinking of Grafton and Halle who spelt "Puzel" and at another of Holinshed who spelt "Pusell".[1] Names are spelt differently in *Hamlet* Q2 by one compositor setting direct from Shakespeare's foul papers[2]; there is considerable confusion over characters' names in *The Comedy of Errors*, also presumably deriving from foul papers; in *The Merchant of Venice* Shakespeare seems himself never to have made up his mind about Salanio–Salarino–Salerio; and in *Cymbeline* the names Cloten and Imogen which have come down in history may both be uncorrected errors, the first for Clotten (which does appear in the play) and the second for Innogen (as it ought to be, judging from the sources and the notes of a spectator).[3] It may not be amiss to recall the modern parallel of T. E. Lawrence, who, when the printer of *The Seven Pillars of Wisdom* pointed out to him that "Bir Waheida" was, on an earlier page, "Bir Waheidi", wrote "Why not? All one place" and when told that "Jedha, the she-camel, was Jedhah on Slip 40" annotated it "She was a splendid beast". I suspect that Shakespeare may have

1. *Shakespeare's "Henry VI" and "Richard III"* (Camb., 1929), p. 183.

2. Harold Jenkins, 'The Relation between the Second Quarto and the Folio Text of *Hamlet*', *S.B.*, VII (1955), 81–2.

3. See also the examples cited by Greg, *The Shakespeare First Folio*, p. 114 (*Sir Thomas More*), p. 116 (*Much Ado about Nothing*), pp. 213–15 (*The Taming of the Shrew*), and pp. 252–3 (*King John*). I might add that Elizabethans did not even spell their own names consistently and that both "Ventidius" and "Ventigius" appear in *Antony and Cleopatra*.

had similar retorts for anyone who questioned his spelling of foreign names. But then no Elizabethan compositor would have raised the question. In *Timon* itself, the compositor showed his own capacity: he not only managed "Lucilius" and "Lucillius" within four lines and "Tymon" in the very head-title of the play, but also in the list of "Actors Names", for which there was presumably no author's copy, spelt "Apemantus" yet a third way, as "Appemantus". With Lawrence again, I can only say "Good egg. I call this really ingenious".

2. THE THEORIES OF DIVIDED AUTHORSHIP

Ever since Charles Knight in 1838 argued that *Timon of Athens* was a reworking by another dramatist of a tragedy originally by Shakespeare, there have been theories that the state of the text could be explained if it was held *either* that Shakespeare was working over a play by another (Wilkins, Chapman, Day and Middleton being among those mentioned[1]) *or* that another (such as Heywood, Chapman, Middleton or Tourneur[2]) was revising a play by Shakespeare. Such theories always began with the assumption that the play as it stood was unworthy of Shakespeare and that the poorer parts must be attributed to an inferior hand. Then on the evidence of alleged verbal parallels between *Timon* and the work of the man chosen, the collaborator was identified to the satisfaction of the theorist. Scenes assigned to him almost invariably included I. i, I. ii, III. i–v, IV. ii and v. iii.

It is now clear that such theories defeated their own object. They began with the desire to explain the presence in the play of "inferior" work and almost without exception ended up by assigning to Shakespeare's alleged collaborator some of the best scenes in the play (e.g. the first three of Act III) as well as parts that were crucial in the plot (such as II. ii). Their verbal evidence was in fact capable of a completely different interpretation: the presence in both *Timon* and *A Chaste Maid in Cheapside*, for example, of the phrase "My wounds ache at you" ought to have suggested not that the one author wrote the two plays but that the phrase was in everyday use. The *Oxford English Dictionary* has indeed shown most of this alleged evidence in a new light and has made it impossible to believe any longer that most of the words quoted were in fact characteristic of one dramatist. The various theories identifying the co-author also cancelled each other out, of course. Signi-

1. By Delius, J. M. Robertson and Dugdale Sykes.
2. Verplanck, for example, suggested Heywood; Fleay, Tourneur; and Parrott, Chapman.

ficantly, Sykes had no difficulty in showing that Fleay and Wright had attributed to two different authors parts of the play which contained almost identical phrases; his own division of it was open to the same objections.[1]

Indeed, Sykes unwittingly announced the prejudices from which all such theories began when he wrote: "If we give to Shakespeare the great poetry the play contains and all the good blank verse, and to the 'unknown author' all the irregular, halting verse, jingling rhyme, and uninspired prose, it is clear that the division thus made cannot be far wrong".[2] This is not only, in the famous phrase, treating a play like a plum-pudding and giving Shakespeare only the plums; it is also, in practice, assuming quite falsely that all verse that is irregular is halting,[3] that all rhyme is jingling and that all prose is uninspired. A finer ear is needed if *Timon* is to be appreciated.

A still more cogent objection to most of the theories that posited revision is the one insisted on by Hardin Craig and others: that all our experience goes to suggest that it is precisely the loose ends and the irregular versification of *Timon* that a non-Shakespearian reviser would have "tidied up". Alternatively, if Shakespeare left in this condition a play originally by another, he could equally well so have left his own.

One very special revision theory ought perhaps to be mentioned in passing: that of Dixon Wecter,[4] who maintained that Shakespeare wrote a full five-act play embodying "the Southampton judgment on the crying injustice of the Essex affair, particularly the part played by Francis Bacon"—i.e. a play about a lavish nobleman (Timon=Essex) who was let down by those he befriended (particularly Ventidius=Bacon) and finally rebelled against the sovereign state (the rebellion being "transferred" from Timon to Alcibiades for safety!). The implausible argument then goes that because the play was politically dangerous, it was later deliberately mutilated by another. Just why it should have been mutilated and not destroyed is far from obvious, nor is any parallel between Timon and Essex, let alone between Ventidius and Bacon, at all clear. Nor is there evidence of sufficient interest in Essex in 1605 or later to make a revival of the play then at all probable.

It may safely be said of all the theories of revision and collabora-

1. F. G. Fleay, *Shakespeare Manual* (London, 1878); Wright, *op. cit.*; H. D. Sykes, 'The Problem of *Timon of Athens*', *N. & Q.*, 13th ser., 1 (1923), reprinted in *Sidelights on Elizabethan Drama*.

2. *Ibid.*, p. 84.

3. As Wright clearly does in considering the Steward's soliloquy at IV. ii. 30.

4. 'The Purpose of Timon of Athens', *P.M.L.A.*, 43 (1928), 701–21.

tion that they contradict each other; that they fail to explain such features of the play as are really exceptional, and notably the versification; and that they continually disregard equivalent problems in other Shakespearian plays. Theories of collaboration can be revived, if at all, only on bibliographical grounds, on the argument that different spellings in the text imply different spellings in the copy and *therefore* two authors. I have tried to show both that the theory of transcript as part of the copy is more probable and that too much must not be made of variant spellings of proper names in any Elizabethan play.

Moreover, any theory of divided authorship has to face the evidence of the *imagery*, which throughout the play is of a Shakespearian kind although not perhaps of a Shakespearian intensity: Caroline Spurgeon pointed out in 1935 that such imagery occurred in the play in scenes which on other grounds she might not have wished to attribute to Shakespeare as they stand.[1] I should like to add that certain *repetitions* of imagery and idea in *Timon* argue strongly for a single author. For example, the man who wrote Timon's lines

> But then renew I could not like the moon;
> There were no suns to borrow of   (IV. iii. 69–70)

must surely have written the earlier prediction by Lucius' servant:

> You must consider that a prodigal course
> Is like the sun's,
> But not, like his, recoverable.   (III. iv. 12–14)

—significantly, the one in a scene usually given to Shakespeare, the other in a scene given to the collaborator or reviser. Again, the exchange between Apemantus and Timon at their last meeting:

Apem.   Art thou proud yet?
Tim.   Ay, that I am not thee   (IV. iii. 278–9)

must be an ironical reversal of that at their first meeting:

Tim.   Thou art proud, Apemantus.
Apem.   Of nothing so much as that I am not like Timon

(I. i. 189–90—another allegedly un-Shakespearian section). There is added bitter irony in Timon's begging from the earth's "plenteous bosom, one poor root" (IV. iii. 188) if it is remembered that flatterers once came freely to "gratulate" Timon's own "plenteous

1. *Shakespeare's Imagery and What it Tells Us* (Camb., 1935), p. 344. See also notes on, for example, II. ii. 166 and III. iv. 51–2, scenes invariably given by the disintegrators to the second author.

bosom" (I. ii. 120–1—again attributed to the collaborator); or, to take a final example (but there are others[1]) the linking of false friendship and the summer is found once in a passage that is proved to be Shakespeare's by its train of associations[2] (IV. iii. 252–69), once in a section which is not questioned by the disintegrators (II. ii. 175–6) and again in one which is (III. vi. 28–31). The theory of divided authorship must surely give way before such evidence as this.

3. "TIMON" AS AN "UNFINISHED" PLAY

"I do not doubt", wrote E. K. Chambers of *Timon*, "that it was left unfinished by Shakespeare, and I believe that the real solution of its 'problem', indicated long ago by Ulrici and others, is that it is unfinished still"[3]; and again "The soliloquy of the Steward [IV. ii. 30–51] gives me the impression of being not so much un-Shake-spearean as incompletely Shakespearean".[4]

If, on this hint, one examines the soliloquy, it does indeed seem improbable that any reviser would have left it in its present form; and its series of complete thought units read not like verse that has been broken down from iambic pentameters but like verse that has never been worked up to them. The thought is coherent, the expression sometimes succinct and forceful and not least so when it assumes, as it several times does, the form of the epigrammatic rhymed couplet such as:

> Who would not wish to be from wealth exempt,
> Since riches point to misery and contempt?

and

> Who then dares to be half so kind again?
> For bounty, that makes gods, do still mar men?

If "point to", for example, is not the most cogent phrase possible, it is the kind of phrase that is easily strengthened on revision.

Una Ellis-Fermor, whose article '*Timon of Athens*: An Unfinished Play'[5] is the fullest treatment of the question, has similarly analysed the speech of Alcibiades to the Senate, III. v. 41–59, and has written: "The power both of the language and of the music of individual lines or groups of lines is unmistakable. The speech is a succession of units, sometimes a line and a half, sometimes two, sometimes as many as seven. . . These passages . . . are jottings,

---

1. See, for example, v. i. 30 and note; and compare I. ii. 71 and 130–1 with IV. iii. 23 and 187–98.
2. See note on it.   3. *William Shakespeare* (Oxford, 1930), I, 482.
4. *Shakespeare: A Survey*, p. 273.   5. *R.E.S.*, XVIII (1942), 270–83.

thoughts that form in the writer's mind as prosodic units, but are not yet related prosodically so as to form a verse paragraph or even a continuous succession of blank verse lines. . . [These] prosodic units are . . . simultaneously units of thought or imagery, complete in themselves even when imperfectly related to their neighbours or to the whole speech". She has then added that although "Shakespeare's artistic experience cannot without irreverence be interpreted in terms of any but a very few of those upon record", these jottings are a normal stage in the composition of blank verse.

Nor is the evidence only of this kind. I have pointed out that the imagery met even in some of the scenes where the writing has been thought least satisfactory is typically Shakespearian and that certain repetitions argue strongly for his unaided authorship. The imagery is not, however, always carried through with a Shakespearian thoroughness. Since the work of Caroline Spurgeon, W. H. Clemen[1] and others, we are beginning to understand how much of the effect of *Antony and Cleopatra* comes (without our necessarily knowing it) from the cumulative imagery of worlds and universes, and how *Coriolanus* profits both from the animal and from the body imagery that is woven through the play. But although mention of "dogs" is frequent in *Timon*, and although Shakespeare here as elsewhere thinks of them when he wants an image of fawning or cloying, and although something might have been made of the fact that Apemantus was a cynic philosopher and that "cynic" is derived from the Greek word for "dog", curiously little emerges from all the dog references in this play.[2] Nor can I quite agree with Una Ellis-Fermor that the continual references to "gods" in *Timon* constitute "a recurrent minor theme".[3] They *could* have done so—either, for example, as an ironical undercurrent or as a constant reminder of the eternal norm behind the aberrations of a particular Athenian society—but in my judgment relatively little is added to the meaning of the play as it stands by the mention of gods from time to time. In both these instances, the dramatist has not woven his imagery into a *pattern*; and it is perhaps not too much to assume that while images of a particular type will preponderate even in a first draft, the systematic interweaving of them belongs to a stage of composition later than the first.

The loose ends in the plot are further reason for believing in the theory of *Timon* as an unfinished play.[4] It may be sufficient to men-

1. *The Development of Shakespeare's Imagery* (London, 1951).
2. See, for example, William Empson, *The Structure of Complex Words* (London, 1951), ch. 8.
3. *Op. cit.*, p. 277.
4. See also the discussion of the plot in Section 7 of this Introduction.

tion here the section introducing the Fool (II. ii. 51–127). These lines involve little more than the jesting of Apemantus, certain servants and an unnamed Fool who belongs to an unspecified master and mistress; the Fool does not appear again in the play and there is not much point in his exchange with Apemantus. That the scene is nevertheless Shakespearian is suggested by the similarity with the incident in *Romeo and Juliet* in which an illiterate servant has to ask Romeo to read a letter (I. ii); nor ought one to forget the Clown who appears for so short a time in *Othello* (III. i and iv) that few readers ever remember him and few producers ever include him. In spite of the *Othello* parallel, however, the appearance of the Fool in *Timon* seems to be only a rough start on a possible comic subplot, for the development of which there was ample room, since the play falls far short of the normal Elizabethan and Shakespearian length; and it is tempting to speculate how it could have been developed like the Pompey scenes in *Measure for Measure* which do so much to make the Vienna of that play a real city and build up the background of general corruption against which the main story is played out.

One other small piece of evidence probably clinches the case for incompleteness. J. M. Robertson noticed that the author of *Timon* apparently did not know the value of the Attic talent[1] and that contradictory ideas of its value remain in the play. Robertson, of course, wanted to use this as proof of dual authorship; but Terence Spencer showed that the only possible explanation was that the text of *Timon* was a draft.[2] The Attic talent used to be estimated as equivalent to £243 15s. and would represent much more than this in terms of the modern pound sterling, so that Timon's gift of five talents to release Ventidius from prison is indeed noble, and even a Timon might need to "strain a little" to find three talents for a servant to match a girl's dowry (I. i. 146). Yet elsewhere in the play Timon sends to Lucius, Lucullus and Sempronius for fifty talents each and to the Senate for a thousand. One might like to think that the dramatist was emphasizing the sheer irresponsibility of Timon in all matters financial, and perhaps that was the intention, but the sums in question are almost too absurd even for that. One assumes that when these figures were put in, Shakespeare had forgotten the value of the talent and could not be bothered looking it up; and indeed if he had been reading North's *Plutarch*, it was no wonder his head was spinning, for North says the young Antony ran into a debt of two hundred and fifty talents, that Calpurnia had four

1. *Shakespeare and Chapman* (London, 1917), p. 133.

2. 'Shakespeare Learns the Value of Money: The Dramatist at Work on *Timon of Athens*', *Shakespeare Survey*, VI (1953), 75–8.

thousand after Caesar's death and that Ptolemy promised Gabinius ten thousand for aid in regaining his kingdom.[1] So far, however, the evidence could be interpreted as Robertson interpreted it, as betraying the hands of two men, one a classical scholar, the other not. But Spencer went on to point out that in III. ii, three times, the text reads "so many talents": Servilius even requests Lucius "to supply his [Timon's] instant use with so many talents"—an extraordinary request for a loan. Since Timon had specifically mentioned fifty, the dramatist must either have forgotten the figure or have realized that it was absurd and intended to put in an appropriate one in both scenes. In either case, his work had not reached the stage of completion: it could not have been handed to the acting company in this state.

The bibliographical and what may be called the literary evidence, then, point in the same direction. If only one could be absolutely certain that *Timon* was all Shakespeare's and unfinished, some fascinating conclusions could, of course, follow: it would be clear that, although Heminge and Condell said that "his mind and hand went together: And what he thought, he uttered with that easinesse, that wee have scarce received from him a blot in his papers", Shakespeare like lesser mortals did not always compose spontaneously in perfect blank verse. *Timon* would suggest that thoughts often came to him in a kind of incomplete verse form, sometimes in prose and sometimes (interestingly) in rhyme, and that only on revision did the text evolve into, predominantly, blank verse. It might also suggest, I think, that he wrote scenes as he felt in the mood for them, not bothering to complete one if at the minute he was more interested in another. And while some characters (like Lucius, Lucullus and Sempronius) were conceived from the start as wholes, as individuals, others perhaps received their distinguishing characteristics later, at a second or third stage of composition.

This last conclusion, however, would not be acceptable to those who maintain that *Timon* needs no fuller characterization, being a play of a special allegorical or "morality" kind. It would certainly be well to remember that *Timon* may have been exceptional. Every artist knows the experience of the work which simply refuses to "go well", and *Timon*, apparently, did not "go well" for Shakespeare. It might be unwise, then, to infer from it too much about his methods of composition when subjects proved more readily adaptable into dramatic form.

1. Much the same point is made by Parrott, 'The Problem of *Timon of Athens*', *Shakespeare Association Papers*, x (1923), 12.

4. THE PRESENT TEXT

The hypothesis concerning the textual history of *Timon* outlined in Sections 1–3 above necessarily determines the principles on which I have established my text. The substantive text, that of the First Folio, is treated as a setting by Compositor B of a script that was probably partly the author's unrevised foul papers and partly a transcript of them, possibly by Ralph Crane. The two kinds of textual corruption that must be allowed for are therefore scribal and compositorial, but there is no question whatever of prompt-book alterations, actors' perversions or mishearings.

I submit, however, that the editorial problem in *Timon of Athens* is unique in at least one way. An editor of *As You Like It* will presumably try to decide whether Celia or Rosalind is the taller, because he will probably reason that Shakespeare had at one stage made a decision on the point (and that the present inconsistency in the text comes, for example, from some changing of cast). But there are many things in *Timon* about which Shakespeare had presumably not made up his mind at all (for example, whether the First, Second, Third and Fourth Lords of the closing lines of Act III are identical with Lucullus, Lucius, Sempronius and Ventidius) and I do not myself think it is an editor's business to make Shakespeare's mind up for him. If he is not particularly careful, indeed, the editor of *Timon* will destroy part of the very evidence for thinking the play as fascinating a document as it is. The crucial case is the naming of the Steward who, as has been seen, is called only "Steward" throughout the play except in I. ii where there can be no reasonable doubt that he is the man called "Flavius". It can surely not be said with any confidence that it was Shakespeare's *final* intention to call him "Flavius". (If he elsewhere gave the name temporarily to a servant,[1] it ought perhaps to be remembered that he called both a major and a minor character Jaques in *As You Like It*; and too much ought not to be made of the repetition *alone*.) I have used only "Steward" in my speech-prefixes throughout the play but have, of course, recorded the Folio's "Flavius" both in collation and notes.

It also seems to be desirable, when one is, apparently, so close to Shakespeare in the act of composition, to run the risk of preserving what could be mere scribe's or compositor's mannerism rather than to run the risk of losing what could be a genuine Shakespearian idiosyncrasy or way of writing. On this reasoning I have reproduced the Folio's frequent apostrophe in "th'" before a consonant, because it seems to me that it marks an attempt to indicate a casual-

---

1. See Section I.B. above, p. xvi, and note on II. ii. 189.

ness or colloquialism of tone and so could even be said to be part of the characterization. (It *could*, of course, on my own admission, merely be Ralph Crane's fondness for the apostrophe; but significantly it appears in Shakespeare's own script—Hand D—in *Sir Thomas More*.)

On the same reasoning, I have normally preserved not only the wording but also the placing of the stage-directions. Some entrances may seem to occur a line or two early; but while Crane, for one, was capable of advancing them, we must not forget that a dramatist familiar with the stage and particularly one writing for a stage unusually deep, as was the Elizabethan one, will rightly mark an entrance when a character appears and not merely when he first begins to speak. The General Editors of the New Arden series have also agreed to my omitting all the conventional locations of scene; if Shakespeare ever did worry much about such things (I am convinced, of course, that most of his scenes are unlocalized), it was clearly not at the stage of composition reached in *Timon*. Readers accustomed to these directions will, however, find them recorded in the collation. Purely to facilitate reference, I have preserved the traditional Act and Scene divisions, in square brackets; but there are no such divisions in the Folio *Timon*, even though they were put into the Folio in some plays, at the time of printing, and often in inappropriate places. The conventional break between "Act IV" and "Act V" is particularly absurd—comparable with the division between "Act I" and "Act II" found in the Folio, but not in the Quarto, of *Titus Andronicus*—since Timon obviously would not leave the stage but would at most withdraw behind a pillar or into the inner stage, while the Poet and Painter, whose approach has already been announced, came on looking for him. (This particular Act division is therefore kept on one side as well as in square brackets, on the precedent of the New Arden edition of *Julius Cæsar*, IV. iii.) *Timon*, in fact, provides some of the best evidence we have for believing that Shakespeare did not compose in acts and scenes and that he would have been surprised at the awe with which his alleged five-act structure is regarded in some circles today.

The lineation and division of verse and prose have sometimes presented serious problems. One must always be on the look-out for a compositor's irresponsible re-lining and there are instances of the kind Hinman has warned us to expect, where lines are simply cut into two to fill a page neatly. But one must not alter the Folio recklessly in a play where, by hypothesis, the verse will not always be in regular pentameter; and I have been more conservative than previous editors in preserving Folio lineation and, in particular, in refusing to rearrange two good part-lines into one bad whole one of sometimes six or even more stresses.

Spelling is modernized; but in accordance with the practice of the New Arden edition, variant Elizabethan forms such as "vild", "burthen", "swound", "accompt" and "and" (meaning "if") are preserved. The collations of Folio 1 do not record mere differences of spelling except of proper names or when the word or form in question might easily be otherwise represented in a modernized text. Accordingly, I do note the Folio's "idlely" where I read "idly"; and while I silently replace the frequent "-t" of the past tense and past participle by " 'd", I record the Folio "-t" or " 'd" if, exceptionally, I read "-ed".[1]

Punctuation also is modernized (and again different Folio punctuation is not listed unless the meaning of a phrase or sentence is at issue). I am conscious of a dislike for over-exclamatory texts and have sometimes let a line stand as a question or rhetorical question or even as a comment in the indicative mood where other editors have replaced the Elizabethan mark of interrogation by the modern exclamation mark (to which it is often equivalent).

This is not a Variorum edition and the collations therefore do not pretend to be exhaustive. The later Folios, for example, are recorded only where their agreement with Folio 1 is presumptive evidence that a reading at least made sense then or where they are responsible for an emendation that is worthy of consideration. (On the same principles I have even mentioned in the notes once or twice a reading which Shadwell did or did not alter in his revision of the play.) Pope's emendations, since they are largely attempts to regularize the metre, are recorded rarely and only where they have some additional interest; and emendations of the eighteenth- and nineteenth- and earlier-twentieth-century editors are not listed unless they meet at least some of the requirements of modern bibliography or have a certain notoriety. Nor are the literal errors of Folio 1 considered worthy of mention.

One problem, fortunately, the editor of *Timon* may always be spared—that of different readings in different copies of the First Folio. Hinman has revealed that he found no variant readings in *Timon* (or *Coriolanus*) in the first twenty copies of the Folio which he collated. At least one page does in fact exist in two states—gg2^v (the first p. 82, the one wrongly so numbered). Here, apparently, the

---

1. Folio "-ed" is retained in many lines where other editors have preferred " 'd". This does not *necessarily* imply that the syllable is to be pronounced: often, of course, a line may be scanned correctly in either of two ways.

type was dropped and incorrectly replaced in three speech-prefixes, but the reading of the text is not affected in any way. Characteristically, too, an obvious misprint, of "fegin'd" for "feign'd", only a few lines lower, was not corrected; so that if in fact no variant readings exist, it was not because the proof-reading was thorough and because incorrect formes were rejected with unusual care, but more probably because there were no press-corrections at all. We shall not know for certain until Hinman has published the final result of his collation.

I have based my text on the splendid copy of the First Folio in the Public Library of New South Wales, collated with microfilms of Folios numbers 7 and 68 from the Folger Shakespeare Library and with the available facsimiles.

5. THE SOURCES

That Shakespeare's main source for the story of Timon was North's *Plutarch* is certain. Sir Thomas North's English translation of Amiot's French translation of Plutarch's Greek *Lives of the Noble Grecians and Romans*, published in 1579 and again with additions in 1595, provided also much of the material for *Julius Cæsar*, *Coriolanus* and *Antony and Cleopatra*; and from the section of the life of Mark Antony telling how, after the defeat in the battle of Actium, Antony dwelt for a time in "his solitary house he had built by the sea, which he called *Timoneon*" and followed the general example of Timon, Shakespeare learnt his basic facts. These were that Timon lived in solitude and hated mankind because he had been deceived by his friends and had suffered under their ingratitude; that the only men whose company he would tolerate were Alcibiades (and that because Timon predicted that one day Alcibiades would bring harm to the Athenians) and Apemantus (who was of similar disposition and could be the butt of Timon's insults); that he once invited the Athenians to hasten to hang themselves on his fig-tree before he cut it down; and that, in addition to an epitaph on him made by the poet Callimachus:

> Here lie I, Timon, who alive all living men did hate:
> Pass by and curse thy fill: but pass, and stay not here
>   thy gate [i.e. gait]

there was another written by Timon himself which was inscribed upon his tomb on the sea-shore:

> Here lies a wretched corse, of wretched soul bereft:
> Seek not my name: a plague consume you wicked
>   wretches left!

It was because he transcribed *both* these epitaphs, and apparently omitted to strike one of them out, that Shakespeare left a contradiction in his final scene.[1]

The often-repeated suggestion that Shakespeare could have derived the same material from another of his favourite source-books, William Painter's *Palace of Pleasure* (1566), may safely be rejected. Painter's twenty-eighth novella, "Of the straunge and beastlie nature of Timon of Athens, enemie to mankinde", traces back eventually to Plutarch, probably through intermediate versions of the story. But Painter omitted facts which Shakespeare knew from North. He omitted, for example, the explanation of Timon's misanthropy as the result of the ingratitude of his friends and merely presented Timon as a hater of mankind and a beast; he also had Timon living "in a little cabane in the fieldes"; and, most important, he gave only the one epitaph, Timon's own. One of the few reasons for believing that Shakespeare remembered Painter's version of the story is that in giving his translation of Timon's epitaph Painter used the word "caitiff":

> My wretched catife dayes, expired now and past:
> My carren corps intered here, is fast in grounde:
> In waltring waves of swelling Sea, by surges cast,
> My name if thou desire, The Gods thee doe confounde.

and Shakespeare has "wicked caitiffs left" where North has "wicked wretches". But even if it is maintained that this word betrays a knowledge of Painter's account of Timon, it will be clear that Painter would need to be regarded as a supplementary source and not as an alternative to North.[2]

One might well expect Shakespeare to have turned also in North to the Life of Alcibiades. He must have glanced through it at this or a later stage of his career, because Alcibiades is the general who, in the parallel lives, is compared with Coriolanus; but Shakespeare did not accept North's evaluation of the two men[3] and perhaps read the life of Alcibiades hastily and remembered only the main points and in particular the sentence in North's summary: "*Alcibiades* spite and malice did work great mischief and misery to his country: but when he saw they repented them of the injury they had done him, he came to himself and did withdraw his Army". In

1. The relevant section of North is printed as Appendix A.
2. Sir Richard Barckley's *Discourse on the Felicitie of Man* (1598) and John Alday's *Theatrum Mundi* (1566), a translation from the French of Boaistuau, also give versions of the story in the same tradition as Painter's, with no significant additions and with differences from Shakespeare's play that rule them out as sources.
3. H. J. Oliver, 'Coriolanus as Tragic Hero', *S.Q.*, x (1959), 53–60.

detail, Shakespeare could have remembered, from a somewhat formless and confusing account of the life of Alcibiades,[1] that he was a good-looking and ambitious young man, who was disliked by some of the Athenians because he may even have aimed at being King, but was loved by others (and in particular by Socrates, the only man of whom he stood in awe) because of his natural inclination to virtue. North stressed also his oratory (although he lisped), his love of women and fast living and, in spite of a certain unreliability as a man, his great qualities as a general. The Life then relates how Alcibiades left Athens in disgrace after he was condemned for mutilating images and profaning the mysteries of Ceres and Proserpina. His goods were confiscated and in revenge he aided Sparta against Athens, although he would not go to the extreme of destroying Athens by aiding yet another of her enemies, Tisaphernes. When he was recalled by the Athenian army, he wisely resisted the demand that he lead them against the tyranny of Athens, and instead led them to victory over her enemies. But again he was unjustly deposed—with the inevitable result that the Spartans under Lysander easily conquered Athens. Perhaps by Spartan orders, he was murdered in Phrygia; and the body was buried by "a Concubine of his called Timandra". Here, in essence, are all the facts used by Shakespeare in his portrait of Alcibiades. It may well be that more of them would have been worked in if the play had been further tightened up; in any case, it is worth noting that what many readers have felt to be an ambiguity in the character of Alcibiades is already in North and that there is ample warrant for Shakespeare's hesitation to admire unreservedly the man of action who can too easily take arms, particularly against his country.[2]

From various of North's *Lives*, Shakespeare would also seem to have remembered most of the Latin names which, somewhat incongruously, he gives to the Athenians in *Timon*. The names Ventidius, Flavius and Philotus (as Philotas) occur in the Life of Antony; Lucilius, Servilius and Hortensius in the Life of Brutus; Varro in the Life of Julius Caesar; and Lucullus, Flaminius, Sempronius and Caphis elsewhere in the volume.[3] Often, indeed, he seems to be

---

1. Specimen passages are given in Appendix B.

2. Dr Harold Brooks has pointed out to me that it was the ambiguity in the character of the historical Alcibiades that led Aristophanes (*Frogs*, 1009 and ff) to see him as a fitting subject for the varying interpretations of two great dramatists, Aeschylus and Euripides.

3. The point was first made by W. W. Skeat, *Shakespeare's Plutarch* (London, 1875), pp. xvii–xviii.

putting down the first name he thinks of; and as the notes will indicate, there was a great deal of tidying-up still to be done.

If, however, North's *Plutarch* gave Shakespeare what may be called his premises, it did not give him a plot of anything like the completeness of the plots he normally followed in his plays. This is why so many scholars have investigated other possible sources for *Timon*; in particular, Greek and Roman literature has been closely examined for a version of the Timon story that gives a fuller set of incidents appropriate for dramatic treatment than does Plutarch.[1] The name of Timon occurs frequently in classical literature, virtually as a symbol of misanthropy; but what was apparently the fullest treatment of his story, a comedy by Antiphanes, has not survived. Lucian's dialogue *Timon the Misanthrope*, however, *has* survived—and has often been suggested as the direct source of Shakespeare's tragedy.

Lucian begins with Timon in the days of his poverty and misanthropy calling on the great god Zeus, who has too long been slumbering, for some positive action against evil. Zeus, not without that fussiness which is characteristic of those who know that they have been long inactive, discusses the case with Hermes, whom he directs to visit Timon, taking Plutus (wealth) and Thesaurus (treasure) with him. Plutus is unwilling, because of the unceremonious way in which he has been treated by Timon in the days of the latter's prosperity: with some justification he points out that those who squander their wealth are as blameworthy as those who hoard it. But Zeus is determined; and to Timon Plutus and Hermes must go. They find him earning a pittance digging for hire; and Poverty resigns him to their care, though not before protesting that he has been happier without them. Timon threatens them with clods and stones, and himself repeats that he has been happier away from the parasites and flatterers who attended him in his days of luxury. But the will of the gods must be obeyed; he digs, and finds gold. His only satisfaction in it is that once the fact of his treasure is known to men generally, they will "all be fit to hang themselves over it"; and soon they do come running to seek him. Gnathonides, the flatterer, who has often been entertained by Timon but has offered him only a halter when appealed to for help, is the first; he is driven off with the spade. Next comes Philiades,

1. The main references are W. H. Clemons, 'The Sources of *Timon of Athens*', *Princeton University Bulletin*, xv (1903-4), 208-23; E. H. Wright, *The Authorship of "Timon of Athens"*; Willard Farnham, *Shakespeare's Tragic Frontier* (Cal., 1950); and Georges Bonnard, 'Note sur les sources de *Timon of Athens*', *Etudes Anglaises*, vii, i (1954), 59-69.

who, for praising a song sung by Timon, was once rewarded with a farm as a dowry for his daughter but who offered only blows when asked for assistance; he unctuously tenders money now that he knows Timon does not need it, and is also driven off with blows of the spade. The third is the lawyer Demeas, whom Timon redeemed from prison, to which he had been committed for defaulting in the payment of a fine; yet Demeas also scorned him when he was poor and so, although he has now composed in Timon's honour a special decree (made up of untruths and exaggeration, for instance on the subject of Timon's military service), he too is driven off. Finally comes Thrasycles, the hypocritical philosopher who wants nothing for himself but will make the sacrifice of distributing Timon's wealth to needy friends; instead of a few, he is given "a whole head-ful of clouts" to help him on his way. The dialogue ends as Timon prepares to pelt with stones the horde of other flatterers who come in search of his gold.[1]

Here, certainly, are many elements not in North's *Plutarch* which occur in the same or similar forms in the Shakespearian play: Timon's kindnesses to friends, including the release of one (like Ventidius) from imprisonment for debt and the aiding of another in the matter of a marriage dowry; the hypocritical offers of money to Timon only when he does not need it (again like Ventidius); the notion of flattering praise of Timon in specially composed words; Timon's refusal to be bluffed by the protestations of parasites after he digs up unwanted gold, and his driving them away; and, not least, the suggestion that a wiser man would have made more dis-criminating use of his wealth than did Timon in his earlier days of good fortune.[2]

Various attempts to "prove" Shakespeare's use of the dialogue by the citation of "echoes of Lucian's language"—as in Deighton's old Arden edition of the play (pp. xxviii–xxxi)—are, however, most unconvincing. It is indeed special pleading to quote the re-mark of Lucian's Zeus that it will be sufficient punishment for the parasites to see Timon now rich, then quote the jibe of one of Varro's servants that the Steward is "poor, and that's revenge enough" (III. iv. 62–3) and add "here the wealth and poverty are reversed, but the idea is the same"! Nor is the image used by Lucian's Timon (in reference, as Deighton has to admit, to Danae), that any girl will hold open the top of her clothing to receive a golden lover in her bosom, really like Timon's vicious "Hold up, you sluts, Your aprons mountant" (to Phrynia and Timandra, IV.

---

1. Selected passages are given, in translation, in Appendix C.
2. See also note on IV. iii. 94–6.

iii. 136–7).[1] And although Bonnard and Deighton, independently, derive Timon's "I am Misanthropos, and hate mankind" (iv. iii. 54) from Lucian's "let the name Misanthropos be most sweet to Timon and the distinguishing marks of the character unpleasantness and an aversion from everything human", the parallel loses all force when one remembers the marginal note in North that Antony followed the life and example of "Timon Misanthropos the Athenian". The only alleged parallel that does almost convince me of the borrowing is that cited by Deighton between Shakespeare's Poet's lines:

> even he drops down
> The knee before him, and returns in peace
> Most rich in Timon's nod   (i. i. 61–3)

and Lucian's Timon's:

οἱ τέως ὑποπτήσσοντες καὶ προσκυνοῦντες κἀκ τοῦ ἐμοῦ νεύματος ἀπηρτημένοι

("the men who once cringed and worshipped and hung upon my nod").[2] But the verdict must, I think, be "not proven", particularly as the tone of Lucian is, *pace* Clemons, different from Shakespeare's: Lucian may be cynical but behind the cynicism is a kind of joviality that neither Shakespeare nor any of his characters displays.

There was, so far as is known, no English translation of the dialogue available to Shakespeare.[3] He could, perhaps, have known, or known of, any one of three in Italian or one in French. And I think it has not been pointed out in studies of *Timon* that Lucian's Dialogues in Latin (just possibly in the translation by Erasmus) are known to have formed part of the curriculum of at least one grammar school in the sixteenth century.[4] If Shakespeare had somewhat vague memories of Lucian studied at school some twenty-five years before and only in a Latin translation, then I can well believe that his play would have exactly the kind of distant relationship with the original Greek that *Timon of Athens* has.

There is the further complication that the Greek dialogue was the source not only of at least two late fifteenth-century Italian

1. By a further irony, Bond and Bonnard saw in the same Lucian passage the original of Timon's apostrophe to his gold at iv. iii. 387–9.

2. T. M. Parrott, 'The Problem of *Timon of Athens*', *Shakespeare Association Papers*, x (1923), 6, also found this the only one of Deighton's verbal parallels "of real significance".

3. Thomas Heywood's dialogue *Misanthropos* was not published until 1637.

4. See M. B. Kennedy, *The Oration in Shakespeare* (N.C., 1942), pp. 200–1 and references cited there.

plays (neither likely to have been known to Shakespeare[1]) but also of one surviving Elizabethan drama, the so-called "old" *Timon* which was edited from the manuscript for the Shakespeare Society by Alexander Dyce in 1842.

The plot of this old play is certainly closer to Shakespeare's than is Lucian's. For a start, it devotes some attention to Timon in the days of his prosperity—although Wright's implication[2] that approximately the same proportion of the story is given to this as in the Shakespeare tragedy is misleading, since the farcical sub-plot in fact takes up most of the time. (One wonders, however, whether the unrelated scene of the Fool in *Timon of Athens* is a relic of an original attempt to have a similar sub-plot there.) This other Timon even helps one friend, Eutrapelus, with a gift of five talents:

> While I have gould,
> I will not see my ffreinds to stand in neede—

but generally he is a much more self-conscious spendthrift than Shakespeare's:

> It is to me a tryumph and a glorye,
> That people fynger poynt at me, and saye,
> This, this is he that his lardge wealth and store
> Scatters among the comons and the poore . . .

and altogether he is a less likeable person: in particular, he treats his faithful servant Laches as a mere slave, and dismisses him for sounding warnings about the improvidence. But Laches has at least one soliloquy:

> Soe are my master's goods consum'd: this way
> Will bring him to the house of poverty.
> O Jove, convert him, leaste hee feele to soone
> To much the rodde of desp'rate misery,
> Before his chests bee emptied, which hee
> Had lefte by his forefathers fill'd with golde!
> Well, howsoever fortune play her parte,
> Laches from Timon never shall departe   (III. iii. p. 48)

which reminds one of the Shakespearian Steward's soliloquies at I. ii. 155 and 189. Moreover, after Timon's false friends have rejected him, Laches is sent to invite them to a banquet (although Timon announces that he is giving this as his last entertainme with the last of his wealth); and from the mock-banquet flatterers are driven with stones which have been painted to lo͜o

---

1. R. W. Bond, 'Lucian and Boiardo in *Timon of Athens*', *M.L.R.*, xxvi (1931) 52–68, argued rather unconvincingly for Shakespeare's use of Boiardo.

2. *Op. cit.*, p. 14.

like artichokes. Laches then seeks out Timon in his solitude, comments aside on his changed appearance, and is at first rejected by him:

> *Laches:* What wickednesse doth make me soe abhor'd?
> *Timon:* Thou art a man, that's wickednesse enough
>
> (v. iii. p. 80)

—with which may be compared Timon's greeting of the Steward at iv. iii. 476–8:

> I have forgot all men.
> Then, if thou grant'st th'art a man,
> I have forgot thee

and iv. iii. 461 ff generally. Again, Timon's curses in the old drama have the same basic ideas as some of those in Shakespeare's play—invoking plagues on the earth, for instance; and his false fiancée's readiness to take the gold he finds, whatever the curses that go with it, is certainly like the attitude of Phrynia and Timandra. The procession of flatterers is, however, much as in Lucian, and the ending is similarly indefinite, except for an Epilogue in which Timon announces that he feels a sudden change of heart and, if the audience applauds the play, he will return to the city after all. (This completely detachable and conventional Epilogue, however, is certainly not reason for saying with Wright that the tone of the play proper is farcical and completely different from Lucian's.)

It was difficult enough to understand how Shakespeare could have known this play (which, judging from its erudite and pedantic references, was intended for an academic audience) even when, on the evidence of an allusion to Ben Jonson's *Every Man out of his Humour*, it was vaguely dated "1600". Now Bonnard, pointing to possible borrowings from *King Lear*, suggests that the old *Timon* play is more likely to have followed Shakespeare's *Timon* than to have preceded it[1]—and yet cannot have been based on it, since Shakespeare's play was not published until 1623 and was apparently never acted. The only solution seems to be a common source; and Bonnard, noting the coincidence that Shadwell, in his rewriting of Shakespeare's tragedy towards the end of the century, gave Timon a false mistress as did the author of the old *Timon* play[2]

1. Bond hinted at this possibility in his article in 1931, p. 66.

2. Perhaps not such a great coincidence if one remembers that no serious Restoration play could be without its love and honour and (preferably) two women! And where the old play has only a false fiancée, Callimela, Shadwell gave Timon both a false fiancée, Melissa (who turns from Alcibiades to Timon to Alcibiades and back to Timon again), and a true love, Evandra, who comes to him in his adversity and finally stabs herself over his dead body.

—and citing from the *Arabian Nights* a very interesting parallel to the full Timon story—asks whether one must not infer that the Timon legend, with Arabic or Byzantine accretions, assumed, probably in Italy,[1] a fuller form than that known in antiquity, a form known to Shakespeare, to the unknown author of the "old" *Timon*, and to Shadwell, and used by them independently in turn.

Perhaps some such source will one day be found. Meanwhile it is clear, from these various suggested sources and parallels, that the basic elements for Shakespeare's plot were ready to his hand, in North and in Lucian or whatever other version of the story analogous to Lucian's he may have known. Much more he would hardly have needed; and such theories as Deighton's half-hearted one that Shakespeare's Apemantus may have been based on the Diogenes of Lucian's dialogue, *The Sale of Creeds*, and Bond's that he may have been suggested by Lyly's Diogenes in *Campaspe*, look rather futile once it is remembered that Jaques in *As You Like It* is far more like Shakespeare's Apemantus than is either of the others.[2]

Elizabethan literature abounds in references to Timon's misanthropy and to Timonists; and allusions are found in Lyly, Greene, Nashe, Lodge, Dekker and Marston, to mention only the more prominent dramatists. But given the premise of Timon's hatred of mankind and the rough outlines of his story, Shakespeare was still faced with the basic problem of characterization: what *kind* of man would, in such circumstances, be eaten away by misanthropy when another might take arms against his sea of troubles and, by opposing, end them? It seems to have been a question which had a recurring interest for Shakespeare about the time of the composition of *Timon of Athens*.

6. THE DATE

That the composition of *Timon* can ever be assigned to an exact date seems unlikely. There is no reason to think that the play was ever acted in Shakespeare's lifetime and there is no contemporary mention of it. Nor does it contain a single allusion to any event or person such as generally forms the "external" evidence for dating Elizabethan work.

The freedom of the versification naturally suggests a late date

---

1. Chambers pointed out that the Folio's "Enter the Bandetti" "may indicate an Italian source" (*William Shakespeare*, I, 484).

2. There is, however, a good deal to be said for Farnham's suggestion (*op. cit.*, pp. 65–7) that Shakespeare could have taken a hint for the contrast between Timon and Apemantus from Montaigne's distinction between Timon's hatred of mankind and the attitude of a "professional cynic", Diogenes.

and one could say from the evidence of the more polished blank verse alone that the play in its present form would not have been written before 1604. In other passages, perhaps unrevised, the verse is "freer" than any found elsewhere in Shakespeare, even in the final "romances". (Significantly, the distinguished actor Michael Redgrave has classified *Timon* with the romances as plays in which "it becomes almost impossible except for someone with an exceptionally strong photographic memory to memorize the lines in the shape in which they were written".[1]) In spirit, however, *Timon* is naturally more akin to the late tragedies; and one's suggested dating is likely to depend on one's view of its affinity with some of those tragedies rather than others.

The parallel with *King Lear* has been most often mentioned. Like Lear, Timon takes at their face value protestations of love; just as Lear overlooks Cordelia's worth because of her plain bluntness, so Timon disregards the warnings of the unsociable Apemantus; and just as Kent is the one man true to Lear, so the Steward is true to Timon, and each has to hear his protests against his master's folly overruled. In a sense, the Steward, like Kent, accompanies his master into the wilderness when the heart breaks and the reason almost gives way at the shock of human unkindness; and the curses which the two tragic heroes hurl at mankind share not only their power but also, often, their details. Nor is it quite true to say, as some have said, that where Lear is redeemed by suffering, Timon goes unchanged to his grave. I think that Wilson Knight overstates his case on this question[2] but agree that Timon passes beyond worldly hate to a different state, a willingness for death. Certainly, as Hazlitt said, we esteem him more in the days of his tragedy than in his prosperity.

Yet *Timon* is not merely an inferior *King Lear*. It expresses many ideas which are not in the more famous tragedy; and at least one very important theme, that implied in the contrast between Alcibiades and Timon, is shared with *Coriolanus* and with *Antony and Cleopatra*.[3] The fact that Shakespeare found his basic material for *Timon* in the source for those two plays, North's *Plutarch*, would also suggest that these three tragedies were written about the same time, that is, in 1607–8. (Shakespeare had, of course, used North for *Julius Cæsar*; but for *Timon*, as we have seen, the Lives he used were those of Antony and of Alcibiades, whom Plutarch compared with Coriolanus.)[4]

1. 'Shakespeare and the Actors', in *Talking of Shakespeare*, ed. John Garrett (London, 1954), p. 143.
2. *The Wheel of Fire* (London, 1930, reprinted 1941), ch. XI.
3. See Section 7 of this Introduction, pp. xlvii–xlix.   4. See also III. iii. 34–5 n.

I think it unlikely, then, either that *Timon* was a "first attempt" at *King Lear* or that it was, quite in Clifford Leech's sense, "the doubtful harbinger of the romances".[1] But that it does at any rate belong with *Lear*, *Antony* and *Coriolanus* (rather than with *Othello* and *Macbeth*) and that in all three there was a certain shifting of emphasis which was carried further still in the romances is a conclusion with which most critics will probably agree. A theory that Shakespeare worked on *Timon* only spasmodically and perhaps over a period of years is also quite plausible but difficult to substantiate with evidence of any weight.

7. THE PLAY

Dedicating to the Duke of Buckingham his revision of *Timon of Athens*, Shadwell wrote: "it has the inimitable hand of *Shakespear* in it, which never made more masterly strokes than in this. Yet I can truly say, I have made it into a Play".[2] So extravagant a claim, one would have thought, was likely to be laughed at by twentieth-century readers: it has in fact often been quoted with approval. Although convinced that *Timon* is unfinished, I think that it is a far finer play than Shadwell imagined, and that Hazlitt was not so far wrong when, after making the rather odd remark that it is one of the few plays in which Shakespeare "seems to be in earnest throughout", he added, "He does not relax in his efforts, nor lose sight of the unity of his design".[3]

The "design" is announced most succinctly in the opening dialogue of Jeweller and Merchant, Poet and Painter. In a few brief lines, the atmosphere of hypocrisy is established (in, for example, the false modesty of the Poet's "A thing slipp'd idly from me"); and after a glimpse of the Senators who are paying court to Timon, the Poet describes his allegorical poem in which he has pictured one "of Lord Timon's frame" betrayed by false friends when misfortune overtakes him. Before the entrance of Timon himself, then, there is a clear announcement of what W. M. Merchant has called "the dual theme of the false appearance of friendship and the uncertainty of fortune".[4]

1. *Shakespeare's Tragedies and Other Studies in Seventeenth Century Drama* (London, 1950), ch. VI. (I cannot agree with Leech's distinction between the drama of private issues and the drama of statecraft which it allegedly replaced.)

2. *The History of Timon of Athens the Man-Hater*, 1678 (The Bankside-Restoration Shakespeare, ed. Willis Vickery, N.Y., 1907).

3. *Characters in Shakespeare's Plays* (first published in 1817).

4. '*Timon* and the Conceit of Art', *S.Q.*, VI, 3 (1955), 249–58.

The second premise is the noble generosity of Timon; and this too is established with remarkable economy of means in two brief interviews. The first (and it is all the more cogent in that it is also our first glimpse of Timon) is the conversation with the servant of Ventidius who comes asking Timon to send a letter of credit for a considerable sum to release his master from prison; and Timon's immediate answer shines out, like Portia's candle, as "shines a good deed in a naughty world":

> Noble Ventidius. Well,
> I am not of that feather to shake off
> My friend when he must need me. . .

The second is the discussion with the Old Athenian who for purely mercenary reasons (the background of corrupt Athens is being filled in all the time) objects to the marriage of his daughter to Timon's servant Lucilius. Here the brevity of Timon's comments is most telling: "What of him?—Well; what further?—The man is honest—Does she love him?—Love you the maid?" and then the immediate decision to endow Lucilius with an equal fortune. There is certainly in this nothing "ridiculous"[1]; there is nothing that is even open to criticism.

The first note of warning that there is nevertheless a lack of discrimination in Timon's choice of friends is sounded very gently indeed in his few words with the Poet, Painter and Jeweller; and then it is sounded loudly in the first "flyting" with Apemantus. It should be noted that Apemantus' cynical judgments of the Painter and Poet and then of the Athenian Lords are all later to be proved right and to be accepted by Timon himself: Timon later speaks of them in identical terms, agreeing that the Painter is fouler than any man he can paint and that the Poet's feigning is only lying. An audience which has absorbed anything at all from the opening section with the Poet and Painter will surely already sense which way the wind will blow. In an opening scene of under three hundred lines, then, bright with the exchange of wit and alive with the constant coming and going of characters on the stage, all the necessary data have been given.

Ventidius next offers to repay the money "from whose help I deriv'd liberty". I cannot see this as a false start. All Timon's alleged friends are prepared to give, when they know they will receive more in return. The audience cannot have forgotten from only four lines earlier (the modern scene division obscures the continuity) the Second Lord's

1. O. J. Campbell, *Shakespeare's Satire* (N.Y., 1943), p. 187.

> No meed but he repays
> Seven-fold above itself: no gift to him
> But breeds the giver a return exceeding
> All use of quittance

and the policy is later re-affirmed by a Senator:

> If I want gold, steal but a beggar's dog
> And give it Timon—why, the dog coins gold;
> If I would sell my horse and buy twenty moe
> Better than he—why, give my horse to Timon;
> Ask nothing, give it him, it foals me straight
> And able horses . . .

Even if Ventidius' offer is interpreted by an audience as meant in good faith, the play is to demonstrate that an offer of money to a man when he does not need it and the giving of money when he does are two different things. The alleged inconsistency is a figment of the critical imagination.

Indeed, it is interesting that as sensitive a critic as Hazlitt saw *no* inconsistencies in *Timon*: one wonders how many of its difficulties have been read into it by later commentators. In particular, I wonder whether those twentieth-century critics who have brought to the play their knowledge of the Elizabethan "background" have not sometimes been blinded by such knowledge—blinded to the facts of the play. Hardin Craig, for example, writes that "Timon's spending was set down as a mark of his nobility in the ancient world and was so understood in the Renaissance. Let us not intrude any bourgeois parsimony into the tale of *Timon of Athens*. It was noble to spend, and Timon was a spender".[1] J. W. Draper and E. C. Pettet carry the same reasoning further and see in *Timon* "a straightforward tract for the times",[2] an attack on usury; Draper even writes that "The play, indeed, is Shakespeare's *Gulliver*, a fierce and sweeping indictment of the ideals and social ethics of the age, an indictment largely consonant with popular opinion of the time. In *Lear*, Shakespeare depicts the social chaos consequent upon the abdication of royal authority; in *Timon of Athens*, upon the economic ruin of the nobility".[3] The argument is that usury was in Elizabethan eyes a sin; and that in the story of Timon, Shakespeare is dramatizing the fall of the feudal nobility who, borrowing to keep up their state, put themselves in the hands of usurers. Lending without interest, it is alleged, was the very symbol of the older feudal

1. *An Interpretation of Shakespeare*, p. 247.
2. Pettet, '*Timon of Athens*: the Disruption of Feudal Morality', *R.E.S.*, xxiii (1947), 321–36.
3. *M.L.R.*, xxix, 28.

morality, the passing of which Shakespeare was lamenting. I think it should be suggested that the economic history on which such views are based is itself none too sound: Wilson's *Discourse on Usury*, from which so much is quoted, was published in 1572 and deplored an already changing situation, so that Shakespeare's supposed lament of, say, 1608 would hardly have been topical.[1] The more important point, however, is that such theories as those of Draper and Pettet force their authors to see Timon as a symbol of an ideal, the feudal ideal. They have one advantage over those who speak of the play as an allegory of love and hate, in that they do see it as a dramatization of a particular situation; but they misrepresent the situation. In my judgment, they oversimplify. Could not Shakespeare hate usury and still not admire without qualification the kind of man who put himself into the hands of usurers? Timon is, in fact, not presented as an ideal, any more than are the other tragic heroes: indeed, ideal heroes probably do make tragedy impossible, and to this extent Draper and Pettet are at least being consistent in seeing the play as something less than tragedy. But perhaps the old-fashioned critics, for all their moral preoccupations, sometimes saw straighter; and it is illuminating to find Gervinus describing Timon as "refined in speech, brief, plain, select, but *never deep*".[2] That, surely, is the point—the point which Timon himself makes in his confession "Unwisely, not ignobly, have I given" (II. ii. 178).

We must stop short of saying, as J. C. Maxwell said, that Timon's regular giving is a form of presumption; but we must agree that there is a shallowness in his "complacently accepting" praise for his generosity as he does.[3] (Campbell similarly detected "self-satisfaction at the display of his own munificence".[4]) The crucial passages here are Timon's self-conscious speech to his guests (I. ii. 86–105) beginning "O no doubt, my good friends, but the gods themselves have provided that I shall have much help from you" and ending "O what a precious comfort 'tis to have so many like brothers commanding one another's fortunes. . . Mine eyes cannot hold out water, methinks. To forget their faults, I drink to you" and the later lines:

> Methinks I could deal kingdoms to my friends,
> And ne'er be weary (I. ii. 219–20)

Timon has not the wisdom to see that the people who say most

---

1. See, too, H. R. Trevor-Roper, *The Gentry, 1540–1640* (Camb., 1953). Nor was it only Christianity that objected to usury: Islam did so too.
2. *Shakespeare Commentaries*, trans. F. E. Bunnett (5th edition, 1892), p. 775.
3. J. C. Maxwell, '*Timon of Athens*', *Scrutiny*, xv (1948), 194–208.
4. *Op. cit.*, p. 186.

about their affection do not necessarily have the most (here the
parallel with *Lear* is perhaps closest). He is deaf to the unctuous
hypocrisy of the First Lord's

> Might we but have that happiness, my lord, that you would
> once use our hearts, whereby we might express some part of our
> zeals, we should think ourselves for ever perfect   (I. ii. 82–5)

and prefers this kind of company to that of Apemantus who, like
his Steward, tries to warn him of the truth. Apemantus is one whose
friendship cannot be won by giving:

> No, I'll nothing; for if I should be brib'd too, there would be none
> left to rail upon thee, and then thou wouldst sin the faster. Thou
> giv'st so long, Timon, I fear me thou wilt give away thyself
> in paper shortly. What needs these feasts, pomps, and vain-
> glories?   (I. ii. 240–4)

What need they indeed? Timon, who will not listen to Apemantus
now—and it is partly at least because Apemantus lacks the social
virtues and will not flatter—is to learn that even unattractive
cynics may be right. Apemantus, in his grace, prays that he may
never judge by appearances or even trust his friends if he should
need them; Timon, who scorns such cynicism now, is later to utter
a far more savage grace himself. The counterpointing of the two
graces should not be overlooked, nor should the ironical contrast of

> *Timon* Thou art proud, Apemantus.
> *Apem.* Of nothing so much as that I am not like Timon
> > (I. i. 189–90)

with the later:

> *Apem.*   Art thou proud yet?
> *Timon* Ay, that I am not thee   (IV. iii. 278–9)

—which perhaps establishes the further point that however low
a Timon may sink, he will always have reason for thinking himself
above an Apemantus. But it is essential that Apemantus should be
seen correctly as the Jaques of the play—that is, not as a fully likeable person (Alfred Harbage once remarked that whenever Shakespeare provides commentators, he seems always to make them in
some ways unlikeable, as if to prevent our fully identifying ourselves with them[1]) but as one who is often right and is at least a very
useful check on those who find sermons in stones and good in
everything. Fittingly, then, Apemantus closes the first act with the
lines

1. *As They Liked It* (N.Y., 1947), p. 110.

> O that men's ears should be
> To counsel deaf, but not to flattery.

Shakespeare must, I think, have started from the "fact" of Timon's misanthropy, a misanthropy for which he was proverbial and, incidentally, not admired[1]; and to the question "What might conceivably have reduced a man to this condition?" he offered the answer "the shock that betrayal might give to a noble but *not profound* mind". It would not do to have some arbitrary cause, such as the loss of Timon's ships; the shock must come from a situation for which Timon himself was partly responsible, in however worthy a way, namely the gradual dissipation of his estate. Act II, then, shows the tide flowing out. Creditors like the Senator of II. i—a perfect sketch of the purely mercenary mind—send for their money, and the Steward at last makes Timon understand the position. (The only break in the continuity comes from the interlude of Apemantus and the Fool.[2]) Timon, still not comprehending the situation as he should—although, ironically, he knows that "these old fellows have their ingratitude in them hereditary"— sends to his alleged friends for enormous sums of money, to stem the tide.

In the early scenes of Act III, the greasily confidential Lucullus, the heartily evasive Lucius and the hypocritically indignant Sempronius refuse Timon in turn. Of these scenes, particularly praised by Hazlitt also, Una Ellis-Fermor has justly commented: "The masterly skill of long experience lies behind the treatment of the parallel episodes of Lucullus, Lucius, Sempronius and Ventidius, so handled, in different ways, as to avoid repetition while building up the impression of accumulation, to reveal at once the individuality of characters and the monotony of their behaviour. No dramatic novice wrote this".[3] Nor is it certain that Shakespeare originally intended to dramatize the repudiation of Timon by Ventidius. There would have been something mechanical in a refusal by Ventidius as a climax; as it is, by letting us hear of Ventidius' refusal only casually, Shakespeare achieves a far finer effect: in the rising tide of ingratitude, even the baseness of a Ventidius becomes relatively insignificant. The bustle of the servants clamouring for their money (III. iv) and the scene of Alcibiades' pleading before the Senate then precede Timon's famous mock-banquet and his withdrawal from Athens. His tragedy, as Peter Alexander well says, "is not that he is reduced to poverty and

---

1. Farnham's analysis of earlier versions of the story makes this clear.
2. See note on II. ii. 50.   3. *Op. cit.* (p. xxv above), p. 277.

cast off, but that the godlike image of man in his heart is cast down, and his dreams of human fellowship destroyed".[1]

"To say that Timon took his trouble too much to heart", the same critic continues, "is just what the senators said of the soldier". This is true but, with respect, not quite the point. As Wilson Knight has said, "We are given no chance to sentimentalize Timon's hate. Its nobility derives solely from its utter reversal of love".[2] Shakespeare is not saying that Timon *ought* not to have taken his troubles so much to heart; he is saying that noble natures *do* take their troubles to heart and so their very virtues count against them because those virtues leave no place for such worldliness and practical efficiency as those of Alcibiades, worthy but less so than Timon.

The scene in which Alcibiades pleads before the Athenian senate is therefore perfectly placed to introduce this contrast between the ways in which two men of honour meet a given situation. The oration of Alcibiades is apparently of Shakespeare's own invention (as were many of the orations in his other plays)[3] and in its development of the theme of the necessity for mercy is comparable with the speeches of Portia in *The Merchant of Venice* ("The quality of mercy is not strained . . .") and of Isabella in *Measure for Measure* (". . . Why, all the souls that were, were forfeit once . . ."), and not far inferior to them. What has been found faulty here is the lack of "connection" with the Timon plot. Sir Walter Greg went so far as to say that "there is no clear link between the story of Timon and that of Alcibiades. . . They might almost belong to different plays"[4]; Shadwell and Cumberland in their versions of the play tried to link the two men through female characters, Cumberland by having Alcibiades love Timon's daughter Evanthe; and Una Ellis-Fermor suggested that Timon was perhaps the man for whom Alcibiades was pleading. I think that all these theories place insufficient emphasis on the dramatic principle on which *Timon of Athens* is constructed—that of counterpoint.

The play is indeed, as Miss Ellis-Fermor has herself implied, a most interesting experiment in dramatic technique; and the technique used is far in advance of its own day and is very like that of certain modern novels, those of which Aldous Huxley's *Point Counter Point* is the prototype. With an absolute minimum of chronological narrative, Shakespeare has set off against each other the reactions of one man to different situations, and the reactions of different men to the same situation. Timon's response to prosperity

1. *Shakespeare's Life and Art* (London, 1939), p. 184.
2. *The Wheel of Fire*, p. 253.
3. Kennedy, *op. cit.*   4. *The Shakespeare First Folio*, p. 409.

in one half of the play is counterpointed against his response to adversity in the other; the hypocritical flattery of Poet and Painter and the Athenian Lords is counterpointed against the unflattering cynicism of Apemantus. The third act sets against each other the refusals of the various creditors; and then in the unbroken second half ("Acts IV and V") the visits to Timon of Poet and Painter, Apemantus, Alcibiades and the Senators are counterpointed against each other and also against the visits which each of them paid to Timon in the first half of the play.

Any plot-link between Alcibiades and Timon, then, would have been gratuitous; it would have cut across the constructional principle of the play. Act III, Sc. v may be a trifle abrupt, as it stands; but what the dramatist needed to do, and what he has surely done, was to give each of the men justifiable reason for resentment against an ungrateful and corrupt state. In the remainder of the play their responses are set one against the other.

It would be easy to compile from the criticism of *Timon* an anthology of contradictory remarks about Alcibiades, and their very number is no doubt some indication that Shakespeare has not made his intention perfectly clear. Suffice it to say that to one school of thought Alcibiades is "young and fair",[1] "really noble" as against the "seemingly magnificent Timon" who "lacks greatheartedness"[2]; to the other he "is of much grosser grain than Timon and much inferior to him in spiritual worth, but nevertheless he has ability to meet and overcome hostile forces in the world whereas Timon can only let himself be crushed by them".[3] Can there be any real doubt that the second opinion is correct, even if it needs to be modified? The appearance of Alcibiades on the stage with retainers *and harlots*, while Timon digs for roots, itself makes the point clearly enough (and, incidentally, shows that the Alcibiades of *Timon* is not as far from Plutarch's as some critics would maintain). He *is* the Fortinbras who restores order only after the tragic hero is dead; still more, he is the Octavius, the Aufidius—the man who survives partly because he has a clearer view of things and is more efficient, but partly because (it is the thought that recurs most often in Shakespeare) efficiency has been bought at the price of a certain loss of sensitivity. Timon, like Hamlet, Coriolanus and Antony, has a greater *soul* than the man of action with whom he is contrasted.[4]

1. Henri Fluchère, *Shakespeare* (translated Hamilton, London, 1953), p. 256.
2. B. L. Joseph, *Elizabethan Acting* (Oxford, 1951), p. 110.
3. Willard Farnham, *op. cit.*, p. 74.
4. Wilson Knight has taken a similar view (*op. cit.*, p. 260), and so has A. S.

Timon's wrongs, then, have to be avenged by Alcibiades, while Timon, in a series of dialogues that are magnificently varied but still perhaps disappoint theatrically in that they give little sense of rising or falling action, hurls his incomparable invective against the hypocrites who come to see him, and against the world. I suspect, however, that the finest exchange in the last two acts is that between Timon and Apemantus. Even in his new-found misanthropy Timon feels superior to Apemantus, in not deriving from a refusal to love mankind a certain satisfaction or even enjoyment. But why Fluchère speaks of Apemantus' "fundamental villainy"[1] I do not understand. To the end, Apemantus has something on his side; he rightly tells Timon: "the middle of humanity thou never knewest, but the extremity of both ends". He has been right also about the Poet and Painter, of whom Timon now speaks in Apemantus' very words (v. i. 30–1); he has always been content with the roots which Timon truly appreciates only now (compare I. ii. 71 and 130–1 with IV. iii. 23 and 187–98). That he is also not without a certain regard for Timon is implied in the first act: "I *fear* me thou wilt give away thyself in paper shortly"; and the audience's knowledge of this must prevent it from accepting without modification Timon's charge that Apemantus comes to him later only to flatter misery. The philosopher might well have answered with Jaques "Out of these convertites / There is much matter to be heard and learn'd" (*AYL.*, v. iv. 190–1); and Apemantus and the Steward are, notably, the only characters in the second half of the play as in the first who cannot be bribed in any way with Timon's gold. The cynic's last interview with the misanthrope ought to be played with a certain half-amused tolerance: in the attitude of the philosopher (whose view that men cannot be trusted is at least based on a lifetime's disinterested observation) to the misanthrope (who is cursing all mankind simply because his own limited experience has found some men false) there is something of the contempt of the professional for the amateur.

The final impression of the play, however, is not determined by the attitude of Apemantus or even by Timon's misanthropy. "How fain would I have hated all mankind", Timon cries (IV. iii. 503)— but he cannot hate them all, for the Steward stands there to make such hatred impossible. The presence of the Steward among the characters, then, so far from being the puzzle or contradiction that Chambers found it, is essential to the meaning of the play and

---

Collins, '*Timon of Athens*: A Reconsideration', *R.E.S.*, XXII (1946), 107— although I cannot agree that Timon is "mad".

1. *Op. cit.*, p. 265.

expressly forbids us from identifying *our* judgment (or Shakespeare's) with Timon's. Ivor Brown's comment that "in *Timon of Athens* there is no affection left for man or woman, fair or dark"[1] is misguided. Timon's misanthropy, like everything else in Shakespeare's plays, is part of a dramatized situation and is in no sense a lyrical statement of the poet's own belief; and Timon's invective, for which the play has received most of such praise as has generally been given it, is all the more remarkable when one pauses to reflect that it states an attitude from which, through the presence of the Steward, Shakespeare has dissociated himself completely. The mood of *Timon*, it may be said, is akin both to that of *Lear*, in its portrayal of complete despair and yet its refusal to believe that suffering is all, and to that of the romances.

It remains to ask the question to which any answer is presumptuous: why then did Shakespeare leave the play unfinished? Unless my interpretation is very sadly astray, it was not, as Chambers and Brown believed, because the dramatist was "in a mood verging upon nervous breakdown"[2] nor, as G. B. Harrison insisted, because of "sheer boredom".[3] More probably Shakespeare was influenced by dramatic difficulties inherent in the subject. There are, it seems to me, two difficulties in particular. One is the problem of making a great tragic hero out of a man who by hypothesis lacks depth or profundity; and so it is not that Timon was "the wrong character to support his theme",[4] I suggest, but rather that he was the only right one—right for the given situation, that is to say, but not right for great tragedy. The other problem is similarly created by the fact that the story does not lend itself to treatment in *drama*. As Hardin Craig has said, "there is no drama in mere non-participation, where it arises from avoidance of the conflict or from definite refusal to participate".[5] In the second half of *Timon*, indeed, there is no true dramatic conflict; and neither the series of debates between Timon and those who seek him out in his solitude nor the contrast between Alcibiades and Timon can quite make up for this deficiency. This absence of conflict no doubt explains why so many critics have inferred wrongly that the play was *intended* as a parable or morality or something less than true drama, and why others have thought that Shakespeare was interested only in the lyrical possibilities and have assumed Timon to be only "a moral voice censuring humanity".[6] Could it have been because he felt a certain failure to overcome these weaknesses

1. *Shakespeare* (London, 1949), p. 214.   2. Brown, *op. cit.*, p. 211.
3. *Shakespeare's Tragedies* (London, 1951), p. 270.
4. Una Ellis-Fermor, *op. cit.*, p. 283.   5. *Op. cit.*, p. 246.
6. Hardin Craig, *op. cit.*, p. 249.

that Shakespeare turned from it, if he did, to not dissimilar themes which lent themselves more readily to treatment in drama, the themes of *Coriolanus* and *Antony and Cleopatra*?

But these weaknesses, if they are such, are so only by Shakespearian standards. One might still say of *Timon of Athens*, as Swinburne once said of another work, that whatever in it is not good is also less than important.

TIMON OF ATHENS

DRAMATIS PERSONÆ

TIMON *of Athens.*

LUCIUS ⎫
LUCULLUS ⎬ *flattering Lords.*
SEMPRONIUS ⎭

VENTIDIUS, *one of Timon's false Friends.*
ALCIBIADES, *an Athenian Captain.*
APEMANTUS, *a churlish Philosopher.*
STEWARD *to Timon.*

FLAMINIUS ⎫
LUCILIUS ⎬ *Servants to Timon.*
SERVILIUS ⎭

CAPHIS ⎫
PHILOTUS ⎬ *Several Servants to Usurers.*
TITUS ⎪
HORTENSIUS ⎭

Servants to Varro, Isidore and Lucius, usurers and Timon's creditors.
Poet, Painter, Jeweller, Merchant.
HOSTILIUS *and two other Strangers.*
An Old Athenian.
A Page.
A Fool.

PHRYNIA ⎫
TIMANDRA ⎬ *Mistresses to Alcibiades.*

Lords, Senators, Soldiers, Bandits, and Attendants.
Cupid and Amazons in the Masque.

SCENE: *Athens, and the woods nearby.*

DRAMATIS PERSONÆ] THE ACTORS NAMES F (*where the order of the names is different*). TIMON] TYMON *F.* SEMPRONIUS] *F lists him twice.* VENTIDIUS] *Ventigius F.* APEMANTUS] *Appemantus F.* STEWARD *to Timon*] *not in F.* LUCILIUS] *not in F.* PHILOTUS] *Philo. F.* HORTENSIUS] *Hortensis F.* *Servants . . . creditors*] *not in F (which lists "Varro" and "Lucius" among the "Seuerall Seruants to Vsurers"*). HOSTILIUS . . . *Strangers, An Old Athenian, A Page, A Fool,* PHRYNIA, TIMANDRA] *not in F.* *Lords . . . Masque*] *Certaine Senatours. Certaine Maskers. Certaine Theeues . . . Cupid . . . With diuers other Seruants, And Attendants. F.* SCENE . . . *nearby*] *not in F.*

2

TIMON OF ATHENS

ACT I

SCENE I

Enter Poet, Painter, Jeweller, Merchant at several doors

Poet. Good day, sir.
Pain.   I am glad y'are well.
Poet. I have not seen you long; how goes the world?
Pain. It wears, sir, as it grows.
Poet.   Ay, that's well known.
    But what particular rarity, what strange,
    Which manifold record not matches? See,   5
    Magic of bounty, all these spirits thy power

ACT I

Scene 1

TIMON OF ATHENS] THE LIFE OF TYMON OF ATHENS *F.*   ACT I
SCENE I] *Actus Primus. Scæna Prima. F.*   S.D. *Enter] F; A Hall in Timon's
House Enter/Rowe.   Merchant] Merchant, and Mercer, F.*

ACT I SCENE I] After its initial
Actus Primus, Scæna Prima (set up automatically by the compositor), the
Folio makes no division at all into
Acts and Scenes. Conventional divisions, deriving principally from
Capell, are here preserved in square
brackets, for the sake of easy reference
only.

S.D. Enter . . . Merchant] The
Folio *"and Mercer"* seems to refer to
a character originally intended to
appear in this scene but finally omitted, although the speech-prefix *"Mer."*
might conceivably stand for "Mercer"
as well as for "Merchant".

2. *I . . . long*] it is a long time since I
saw you. The adverbial use of "long"
survives in a phrase like "I have long
known him".

3. *It wears . . . grows*] A quibble: it
passes away as it goes on, and it
deteriorates . . .

4. *what strange*] i.e. what that is
strange, rather than "what strange
(rarity)" as Deighton suggested.

5. *manifold record*] i.e. records though
many and varied. "Record" is accent-
ed on the second syllable.

6. *Magic of bounty*] the power of
generosity equal to the magician's
power.

3

Hath conjur'd to attend! I know the merchant.
Pain. I know them both: th' other's a jeweller.
Mer. O, 'tis a worthy lord.
Jew.   Nay, that's most fix'd.
Mer. A most incomparable man, breath'd, as it were,   10
To an untirable and continuate goodness.
He passes.
Jew.   I have a jewel here—
Mer. O pray, let's see 't. For the Lord Timon, sir?
Jew. If he will touch the estimate. But for that—
Poet. [*Aside to Painter*] When we for recompense have
          prais'd the vild,   15
     It stains the glory in that happy verse
     Which aptly sings the good.
Mer. [*Looking at the jewel.*]   'Tis a good form.
Jew. And rich. Here is a water, look ye.
Pain. You are rapt, sir, in some work, some dedication
     To the great lord.

7.] *As Pope;* Hath . . . attend / . . . merchant / *F.*   12. here—] *Collier;* heere. *F.*
15. *Aside to Painter*] *not in F; Repeating to himself Hanmer, conj. Warburton; Reciting to
himself Camb. edd.*   17. *Looking at the jewel*] *As Pope; not in F.*   19–20. You . . .
lord] *As Pope; prose F.*

7. *conjur'd*] summoned as by a spell.
9. *'tis*] i.e. he is. A normal Shake-spearian use.
fix'd] certain.
10. *breath'd . . . to*] exercised or trained, and so "accustomed". The verb was normally used in Elizabethan times in reference to the brisk exercising of both humans and animals.
11. *continuate*] long-continued, or even habitual.
12. *passes*] surpasses, excels. Compare the frequent "passing", used adverbially, in the sense of "surpassingly".
14. *touch the estimate*] go as far as, or rise to, the price I expect for it.
15. *vild*] An obsolete alternative form of "vile".
15–17. *When . . . good*] Most editors regard these lines as part of a poem recited by the poet, and print them in italics. The Folio does not so distinguish them. In any case, the lines may

be taken as an aside, the poet commenting that, just as the fact that poetic praise can be bought lowers the value of praise in verse, so the jeweller's obviously mercenary interest in praising his own jewel must bring into question all his valuations. Compare the proverb "He praises who wishes to sell" (Tilley P 546).
16. *happy*] fortunate, in having an "apt" or appropriate, worth-while subject.
17. *a good form*] a well-cut shape or stone: or, possibly, a gem true to type.
18. *water*] transparency or lustre. The three highest grades of diamonds were formerly known as the *first*, *second* and *third water* (*O.E.D.*). Deighton compared *Per.*, III. ii. 98–103.
19. *rapt . . . in*] intent upon; the past participle of the verb "rap" meaning to carry off and so to transport with joy (*O.E.D.*).

Poet.   A thing slipp'd idly from me.   20
    Our poesy is as a gum which oozes
    From whence 'tis nourish'd; the fire i' th' flint
    Shows not till it be struck: our gentle flame
    Provokes itself, and like the current flies
    Each bound it chases. What have you there?   25
Pain. A picture, sir. When comes your book forth?
Poet. Upon the heels of my presentment, sir.
    Let's see your piece.
Pain.   'Tis a good piece.
Poet. So 'tis; this comes off well and excellent.
Pain. Indifferent.
Poet.   Admirable. How this grace   30
    Speaks his own standing! What a mental power

---

20. idly] idlely *F.*   21. gum] *Pope;* Gowne, *F1–2;* gown *F3–4.*   oozes]
Johnson; vses *F1–4;* issues *Pope.*   23. struck] *F3;* strooke *F1–2.*   24. flies] *as
F.;* flies; *conj. Mason.*   25. chases] *F;* chafes *Theobald.*

20. *idly*] F "idlely" may represent
the older form of the adverb; I read
"idly" for metrical reasons.

21. *gum which oozes*] This generally
accepted emendation seems probable,
the Folio "Gowne, which uses" being
explained as the compositor's misreading of "gumme" or "gomme" and
failure to understand "uses" or "oses".
The basic idea is of poetry, like gum,
flowing steadily.

23–4. *our gentle flame | Provokes itself*]
unlike the flint which has to be struck
to produce fire, poetic inspiration
needs no external stimulus.

25. *chases*] Editors prefer Theobald's
"chafes" and compare *Cæs.*, I. ii. 101,
"The troubled Tiber chafing with her
shores". But there is no "with"; and a
nine-syllable line might well seem
more probable than an eight-syllable
one. In either case the idea is of a
stream rebounding from the very bank
("bound") it had seemed to aim at:
apparently poetry, in a similar way,
avoids the subject that seems to be
natural for it and goes off in some unexpected direction of its own. Mason's
reading with a semi-colon after "flies"
and his explanation of "each bound it

chafes" as "every obstacle serves but
to increase its force" seem unlikely.

27. *Upon . . . presentment*] immediately
after my presenting it, to Timon, who
as patron will presumably sponsor the
publication.

29. *comes . . . excellent*] is well managed, succeeds admirably (almost in
the modern colloquial sense of
"comes off"). Compare Hamlet's
advice to the players "Now this over-
done, or come tardy off . . . cannot but
make the judicious grieve" (III. ii. 27–
9) or *Meas.*, II. i. 57. "Excellent" is a
regular Elizabethan adverbial form
(Abbott 397).

30–1. *How . . . standing*] how well the
grace (of the figure in your painting)
expresses or suggests the status of the
man portrayed (*O.E.D.* traces this
meaning of "standing" back to 1607).
It is not clear whether the painting is
a portrait of Timon, but Deighton
pointed out that when Timon accepts
it, he does not refer to its being one.
As Fletcher well said, the language of
all of these would-be artists is obscure
precisely because it is "pretentiously
affected" (p. 113); what is certain is
that each, after the fashion of bad

This eye shoots forth! How big imagination
Moves in this lip! To th' dumbness of the gesture
One might interpret.

Pain. It is a pretty mocking of the life.   35
Here is a touch: is't good?

Poet.   I will say of it,
It tutors nature; artificial strife
Lives in these touches, livelier than life.

Enter certain Senators, who go in to Timon.

Pain. How this lord is followed!
Poet. The senators of Athens, happy men.   40
Pain. Look, moe!
Poet. You see this confluence, this great flood of visitors.
I have in this rough work shap'd out a man,
Whom this beneath world doth embrace and hug
With amplest entertainment. My free drift   45

38. S.D. *who . . . Timon*] *nct in F; and pass over | Capell.*   40. men] *F;* man
Theobald.   41. Look, moe!] *As Rowe;* Looke moe. *F.*   44. beneath world] *F;*
beneath-world *Theobald (edn 2).*

artists, is hypocritical in his lavish
praise of the other's work.

32–3. *How big . . . lip*] How forcefully
the imagination (of the person portrayed) is suggested by this lip.

33. *To th'*] This spelling, characteristic of the Folio *Timon*, is preserved in
all such cases in this text. It is intended
to suggest the elision of "to the", the
two words being treated as one syllable. Sometimes in the Folio the
apostrophe is also used after the preposition, e.g. "by' th' ".

33–4. *To th' . . . interpret*] one might
easily supply words to accompany (or
explain) the gesture which cannot
speak itself. Malone believed the
allusion to be to the "interpreter", the
person who supplied the voice for a
puppet in a puppet-show; Maxwell
(the "New Shakespeare") suggests
reference to a dumb-show.

37. *strife*] Apparently in the rarer
sense of "striving", "effort", "action".
The poet asserts that action is sug-

gested by the "artificial" painting in a
way that outdoes nature. This notion
of art *at strife with* nature is common
enough but "artificial strife" can
hardly mean "the strife of art to emu-
late nature" (Fletcher) nor is it clear
how that strife could be "livelier than
life".

40. *happy men*] This Folio reading
makes good sense. The poet envies the
senators for their position and because
they are Timon's friends and equals.

41. *moe*] Used in its strict sense,
others of the kind specified. But "mo"
or "moe" came to be interchangeable
with "more".

44. *this beneath world*] Theobald's
hyphen, adopted by most editors,
makes the sense plain but obscures the
fact that this use of preposition as
adjective illustrates the popular Elizabethan rhetorical figure *anthimeria*
(Joseph, p. 62).

45–6. *My free . . . particularly*] my un-
impeded meaning does not stop to

Halts not particularly, but moves itself
In a wide sea of wax: no levell'd malice
Infects one comma in the course I hold,
But flies an eagle flight, bold, and forth on,
Leaving no tract behind.   50
Pain. How shall I understand you?
Poet. I will unbolt to you.
You see how all conditions, how all minds,
As well of glib and slipp'ry creatures as
Of grave and austere quality, tender down   55

47. of wax:] of wax, *F;* of verse *Collier (edn 2);* of tax *Staunton;* awax *conj. Dowden;* of wax— *Sisson.*   48. Infects] *F;* Inserts *conj. Deighton.*   hold,] *F;* hold— *Sisson.*

make particular or individual applications.

47. *wide sea of wax*] A notorious crux. That any emendation of "sea of wax" is misguided and unnecessary is best indicated by Armstrong's fascinating note in his *Shakespeare's Imagination*, pp. 37–8, in which he pointed out that "wax" and "eagle flight" occur "because in the background of the poet's thought is Icarus, who attached wings to his back with wax and for whom pride came before a fall. He also comes under the master idea Pride and is naturally linked with the image cluster in which the eagle appears". Moreover it should be noted that pride is mentioned in the two explicit Icarus passages in *1H6*, and that we have "sea of blood" in one of them and "sea" in the relevant context of *3H6*. Staunton's "tax" (=, presumably, taxation, criticism), although adopted by Alexander, may thus be dismissed both on this ground and because a misreading of "t" as "w" is improbable. Dowden, in manuscript annotations in a copy of the old Arden *Timon*, now in the Folger Shakespeare library, suggested "awax" (=in flood), acting on a hint from Ingleby (*The Still Lion*); "awax" could more easily have been misread (as "o' wax") but does not add much to the sense. The Folio text I take to mean that the poet's work does not pause to deal with individuals but moves freely as if in a whole sea, and a sea of wax at that; i.e. one which can be moulded at will and so, as it were, fit *any* case. The usual explanation refers to the practice of writing on tablets of wax and is perhaps most plausible in C. J. Sisson's paraphrase: "My movements are not restricted to the limits of a tablet of wax; I move freely in a wide sea of wax . . ." (*New Readings in Shakespeare*, II, 167).

levell'd] aimed as one aims a gun at one particular object. Compare *Ado*, IV. i. 239.

48. *comma*] Could mean a short part of a sentence, a mark of punctuation, or a minute interval of pitch (*O.E.D.*). Whichever meaning be adopted, the poet is affirming that malice against individuals plays not the smallest part in his work; and the clause is not parenthetic but parallel to "my free drift halts not particularly".

49. *But flies*] The subject to be understood is "my free drift".

50. *tract*] Had senses coinciding with both "trace" and "track" and could mean either here.

52. *unbolt*] explain, open out. The metaphor is not used elsewhere by Shakespeare.

53. *conditions*] Could mean either "ranks" (social levels) or "characters" (temperaments).

55. *quality*] Meant "rank" or "nobility" or "profession", as well as

Their services to Lord Timon: his large fortune,
Upon his good and gracious nature hanging,
Subdues and properties to his love and tendance
All sorts of hearts; yea, from the glass-fac'd flatterer
To Apemantus, that few things loves better   60
Than to abhor himself—even he drops down
The knee before him, and returns in peace
Most rich in Timon's nod.

Pain. I saw them speak together.

Poet.   Sir,
I have upon a high and pleasant hill   65
Feign'd Fortune to be thron'd. The base o' th' mount
Is rank'd with all deserts, all kind of natures
That labour on the bosom of this sphere
To propagate their states. Amongst them all,
Whose eyes are on this sovereign lady fix'd,   70
One do I personate of Lord Timon's frame,
Whom Fortune with her ivory hand wafts to her,
Whose present grace to present slaves and servants
Translates his rivals.

---

56. services] *F;* service *Pope.*   64–5. Sir, / . . . hill] *one line F.*   66.] *As Rowe;*
Feign'd . . . thron'd. / . . . Mount / *F.*

"character" or "temperament". Compare "sorts" in l. 59.

tender down] proffer, lay down as an offering (Latin *tendere*, to hold forth).

57. *Upon . . . hanging*] A subtle phrase. The poet says only that Timon's wealth in association with his good nature wins him many hearts; but he unconsciously implies the truth: that it is the wealth which attracts his friends, his "good nature" being of importance to them only in so far as it means lavish generosity.

58. *properties*] appropriates. But again perhaps there is unconscious irony in that Timon's pride in his friends has something of the pride of ownership.

his . . . tendance] loving and being in attendance on him.

59. *glass-fac'd*] So called because a flatterer reflects like a mirror the

moods and opinions of the person he flatters.

61. *abhor himself*] i.e., presumably, loathe himself, for being a man. Rolfe suggested "make himself abhorrent" but there is no authority for this.

63. *in Timon's nod*] for having been recognized by a nod from Timon.

67. *rank'd with all deserts*] lined in ranks by men of all degrees of worth.

68. *this sphere*] the globe or earth.

69. *propagate*] multiply (the original meaning).

states] possessions (*O.E.D.*).

71. *personate*] represent. A common sixteenth- and seventeenth-century use.

frame] disposition (*O.E.D.* compares "frame of mind") or physical build; probably both.

72. *ivory*] i.e. white. Deighton compared *Lucr.*, 464.

73–4. *Whose . . . rivals*] whose (For-

Pain.   'Tis conceiv'd to scope.
    This throne, this Fortune, and this hill, methinks,   75
    With one man beckon'd from the rest below,
    Bowing his head against the steepy mount
    To climb his happiness, would be well express'd
    In our condition.
Poet.   Nay, sir, but hear me on:—
    All those which were his fellows but of late,   80
    Some better than his value, on the moment
    Follow his strides, his lobbies fill with tendance,
    Rain sacrificial whisperings in his ear,
    Make sacred even his stirrup, and through him
    Drink the free air.
Pain.   Ay marry, what of these?   85
Poet. When Fortune in her shift and change of mood
    Spurns down her late beloved, all his dependants
    Which labour'd after him to the mountain's top
    Even on their knees and hands, let him sit down,

---

74. conceiv'd to scope.] *Johnson;* conceyu'd, to scope *F;* conceiv'd to th' scope.
Theobald.   89. hands] *F2–4;* hand *F1.*   sit] *Ff;* slip *Rowe;* sink *conj. Delius;*
fall *Sisson.*

tune's) present graciousness or generosity transforms his (Timon's) rivals
instantly into slaves and servants.
There is a quibble on "present" in the
senses of (1) being present and (2)
immediate. Compare "presently",
which always in Shakespeare means
"immediately".

74. *to scope*] to the purpose (*O.E.D.*).
Deighton, pointing out that "scope"
originally meant a target, paraphrased
"your conception has hit its aim".

77–8. *Bowing . . . happiness*] bending
forward, because of the steepness of
the climb, in his endeavour to attain
happiness.

78–9. *would . . . condition*] would find
a parallel in our status or profession (as
artists). Compare *Tp.*, III. i. 59.

81. *Some . . . value*] some even greater
than he was in value, or higher in
status.

82. *his lobbies . . . tendance*] fill the
halls of his house, dancing attendance

upon him. For "tendance" compare
l. 58.

83. *sacrificial whisperings*] whispers
offered as a sacrifice is offered or perhaps, as M. R. Ridley privately suggests to me, whispers which are like the
muted utterance of adoring priests at
a sacrifice.

84–5. *Make . . . free air*] treat even the
stirrup (which they hold to help him
mount his horse) as if it were sacred,
and act as if they were indebted to him
for breathing the free air. Maxwell
sees in the lines an "implication that
Timon's 'freeness' is oppressive to its
recipients" (p. 202) but I doubt it.

85. *marry*] to be sure (*O.E.D.*).
"Marry" is a mild oath or exclamation; originally "By Mary".

86. *shift and change*] I have the impression that such doublets are unusually frequent in *Timon*.

89. *sit down*] Most editors accept
Rowe's emendation "slip" (or substi-

Not one accompanying his declining foot.   90
Pain. 'Tis common.
          A thousand moral paintings I can show
          That shall demonstrate these quick blows of Fortune's
          More pregnantly than words. Yet you do well
          To show Lord Timon that mean eyes have seen   95
          The foot above the head.

Trumpets sound. Enter LORD TIMON, *addressing himself courteously
to every suitor; a Messenger from* VENTIDIUS, *talking with him;*
          LUCILIUS *and other Servants.*

Tim. Imprison'd is he, say you?
Mess. Ay, my good lord. Five talents is his debt;
          His means most short, his creditors most strait.
          Your honourable letter he desires   100
          To those have shut him up, which failing
          Periods his comfort.

93. Fortune's] *Malone;* Fortunes, *F1;* Fortune *F2–4.*   95. mean] meane *F;*
men's *Hanmer.*   96.] *Scene II Pope.*   96. S.D. *a Messenger . . . him] As Capell; not
in F.   Lucilius and other Servants] Camb. edd.; not in F.* .

tute a similar word, perhaps because
they find the Folio image undignified,
but the Folio "sit" could be right,
suggesting a sudden push that brings
the climber to a full stop. If "slip" is
accepted, one would have to postulate
not a misreading but an unconscious
substitution (not in itself unlikely) by
scribe or compositor.

     92. *moral paintings*] paintings point-
ing a moral. Shakespeare may be
thinking not only of single paintings
but also of strip paintings and of the
allegorical wall-hangings common in
his day (after the style of the famous
"cartoons" of Raffael and Mantegna).

     93. *demonstrate*] stressed on the
second syllable.

     quick] The common second mean-
ing, "pregnant", suggests "preg-
nantly" in the next line.

     95. *mean eyes*] i.e. even the eyes of
the lowly. Theobald's emendation
"men's" hardly seems necessary.

     96. *The foot above the head*] Not, prob-
ably, as Rolfe and Deighton believed,

"the highest and the lowest changing
places" but the foot poised above the
climber's head, ready to "spurn" or
force it down again.

     S.D. Enter . . . suitor] This reads
like an author's rather than a prompt-
book direction and is one of the most
specific in Shakespeare.

     98. *Five talents*] For a discussion of the
use of *talents* in the play, see the Introduction, Section 3. An Attic talent was
worth "more than half a hundred-
weight of silver"; it is generally calcu-
lated to be equivalent to £243 15s. 0d.
but would represent something between £500 and £1,000 today in purchasing power. Timon's offer to pay
five talents to release Ventidius is
therefore exceptionally generous. Interestingly, the word is not used to
specify sums of money in any other
Shakespeare play.

     99. *strait*] exacting, strict or severe
(M.E. *streit*).

     102. *Periods*] It is not clear whether
the verb is transitive ("the failure of

Tim.   Noble Ventidius. Well,
   I am not of that feather to shake off
   My friend when he must need me. I do know him
   A gentleman that well deserves a help,   105
   Which he shall have: I'll pay the debt, and free him.
Mess. Your lordship ever binds him.
Tim. Commend me to him; I will send his ransom;
   And being enfranchis'd, bid him come to me.
   'Tis not enough to help the feeble up,   110
   But to support him after. Fare you well.
Mess. All happiness to your honour!   [*Exit.*

Enter an Old Athenian.

Old Ath. Lord Timon, hear me speak.
Tim.   Freely, good father.
Old Ath. Thou hast a servant nam'd Lucilius.
Tim. I have so. What of him?   115
Old Ath. Most noble Timon, call the man before thee.
Tim. Attends he here or no? Lucilius!
Luc. Here, at your lordship's service.
Old Ath. This fellow here, Lord Timon, this thy creature,
   By night frequents my house. I am a man   120
   That from my first have been inclin'd to thrift,

102. Noble Ventidius. Well,] Noble *Ventidius,* well: *F;* Noble *Ventidius!* well—
Rowe.   104. must need] As *F1–2;* most needs *F3–4.*   109. enfranchis'd]
enfranchized *F.*   112. (*and throughout scene*) Old Ath.] Oldm *F* (*i.e.* Old Man).
117. Lucilius] *Lucillius F.*   119. Lord] *Rowe;* L. *F.*

which would put an end to his comfort") or intransitive ("and if this
fails, his comfort would end"). The
word as a verb is not common and is
not found elsewhere in Shakespeare's
plays. There may be an ellipsis, for the
common "to put a period to" or "make
a period".

 103. *feather*] type, disposition. Compare "in fine feather" and "a bird of
another feather".

 108. *Commend me to him*] greet him
from me, "remember me to him".

 109. *enfranchis'd*] liberated, set free.
The grammatical construction "being
enfranchis'd, bid him", i.e. "bid him,

being enfranchis'd", is a normal Elizabethan one (Abbott 376 and ff).

 111. *But . . . after*] An ellipsis: "but it
is also necessary to support him after-
wards" (Abbott 385).

 113. *father*] Frequently so used as a
respectful term of address to an older
man.

 119. *creature*] Like "fellow" in the
same line, a term of contempt.
Originally "anything created", it
came to mean one who owed his being
or his position to another, a mere
puppet or even hanger-on.

 121. *my first*] the first or earliest part
of my life.

And my estate deserves an heir more rais'd
Than one which holds a trencher.
Tim.   Well; what further?
Old Ath. One only daughter have I, no kin else,
On whom I may confer what I have got.   125
The maid is fair, o' th' youngest for a bride,
And I have bred her at my dearest cost
In qualities of the best. This man of thine
Attempts her love. I prithee, noble lord,
Join with me to forbid him her resort;   130
Myself have spoke in vain.
Tim.   The man is honest.
Old Ath. Therefore he will be, Timon.
His honesty rewards him in itself;
It must not bear my daughter.
Tim. Does she love him?
Old Ath.   She is young and apt: 135
Our own precedent passions do instruct us
What levity's in youth.
Tim. [*To Lucilius.*]   Love you the maid?
Luc. Ay, my good lord, and she accepts of it.
Old Ath. If in her marriage my consent be missing,
I call the gods to witness, I will choose   140
Mine heir from forth the beggars of the world,

---

126. o'] *Rowe;* a' *F.*   132–5.] *As F;* Therefore ... honesty / ... bear / ... apt /
Deighton.   132. be, Timon.] *F4;* be *Timon, F1;* be, *Pope.*   137. levity's]
F3–4; leuities *F1–2.*   *To Lucilius*] *As Johnson; not in F.*

---

123. *one ... trencher*] i.e. a domestic
servant. A trencher is a wooden plate
or shallow dish on which meat is
served.

126. *o' th' youngest ... bride*] Seems to
mean "young but just old enough to be
married", among the youngest who
are of marriageable age. I can find
no obvious parallel, but interestingly
Shadwell preserved the phrase without alteration.

127. *bred*] educated, brought up.

130. *her resort*] resort or access to
her.

132. *Therefore ... Timon*] Many
emendations have been proposed, un-

necessarily. The meaning is clearly:
"and simply because he is honourable
('honest') he will act as an honourable
man (and not pursue my daughter
against my will)". The sentiment is
like that of the proverb "Honesty
is its own reward".

134. *bear*] win possession of. Deighton compared *Err.,* v. i. 8, "His word
might bear my wealth at any time".

135. *apt*] susceptible.

136. *precedent*] former, earlier. Compare *Ham.,* III. iv. 98, "A slave that is
not twentieth part the tithe / Of your
precedent lord". The word is stressed
on the second syllable.

  And dispossess her all.

Tim.   How shall she be endow'd
  If she be mated with an equal husband?

Old Ath. Three talents on the present; in future, all.

Tim. This gentleman of mine hath serv'd me long. 145
  To build his fortune I will strain a little,
  For 'tis a bond in men. Give him thy daughter;
  What you bestow, in him I'll counterpoise,
  And make him weigh with her.

Old Ath.   Most noble lord,
  Pawn me to this your honour, she is his. 150

Tim. My hand to thee; mine honour on my promise.

Luc. Humbly I thank your lordship. Never may
  That state or fortune fall into my keeping
  Which is not owed to you.   *[Exit.*

Poet. Vouchsafe my labour, and long live your lordship! 155

Tim. I thank you; you shall hear from me anon.
  Go not away. What have you there, my friend?

Pain. A piece of painting, which I do beseech
  Your lordship to accept.

Tim.   Painting is welcome.
  The painting is almost the natural man: 160

---

142. endow'd] *Capell;* endowed *F.* 145.] *As Rowe;* This ... mine / ... long: / *F.*
151.] *As Pope;* My ... thee, / ... promise. / *F.* 154. owed] *F;* own'd *Hanmer.*
155.] *As Pope;* Vouchsafe ... Labour, / ... Lordship. / *F.*

---

142. *all*] Used as an adverb: wholly, completely (Abbott 28).

142–3. *How shall ... husband*] what dowry shall she have if she is married to a husband who is her equal (in the sense either of one who is her social equal or, possibly, of one who can match her wealth)?

144. *on the present*] immediately.

146. *strain*] It will be clear from what has been said about the value of the talent (see l. 98 above) that Timon's offer might well involve a "strain".

147. *bond*] tie or obligation.

148. *counterpoise*] counterbalance, balance exactly.

150. *Pawn ... honour*] i.e. if you will pawn me your honour to do this,

or towards this end. (Abbott 186.)

153. *state or fortune*] For "state", compare l. 69 above. The words therefore constitute another doublet.

154. *owed to you*] acknowledged as being due to you. The same word as "own", as in the modern "own up". Johnson read "owed" in the other sense and paraphrased: "let me never henceforth consider any thing that I possess, but as *owed* or *due* to you; held for your service, and at your disposal"; and Malone aptly compared *Mac.,* I. vi. 25–8.

155. *Vouchsafe*] deign to accept (a meaning which has not survived, *O.E.D.* 3).

160. *the natural man*] man as he really is, not the man whom dishonesty

For since dishonour traffics with man's nature,
He is but out-side; these pencill'd figures are
Even such as they give out. I like your work,
And you shall find I like it. Wait attendance
Till you hear further from me.

Pain.   The gods preserve ye! 165

Tim. Well fare you, gentleman. Give me your hand;
We must needs dine together. Sir, your jewel
Hath suffer'd under praise.

Jew.   What, my lord, dispraise?

Tim. A mere satiety of commendations.
If I should pay you for 't as 'tis extoll'd,   170
It would unclew me quite.

Jew.   My lord, 'tis rated
As those which sell would give; but you well know,
Things of like value, differing in the owners,
Are prized by their masters. Believe 't, dear lord,
You mend the jewel by the wearing it.

Tim.   Well mock'd. 175

Enter APEMANTUS.

168. suffer'd] *Pope;* suffered *F.*   169. satiety] *F4;* society *F1–3.*   175. S.D.]
Enter Apermantus F; at 178, Pope.

makes pretend to be better than he is. Here again an important theme of the play is announced, ironically by Timon himself.

161. *traffics with*] In the pejorative sense: has improper dealings with.

162. *pencill'd*] painted with the artist's brush (the original meaning of "pencil").

163. *Even . . . out*] exactly what they claim or seem to be.

168. *Hath . . . praise*] Apparently means "has suffered in so far as your chances of selling it are concerned, because it has been rated so highly by those who praise it". Perhaps the Jeweller misunderstands Timon to say "suffer'd underpraise", i.e. been underrated.

171. *unclew*] undo, and so, figuratively, ruin. The metaphor is from the unwinding of a ball of wool.

171–2. *'tis rated . . . give*] its price is determined by what those who sell it would themselves be prepared to pay for it.

174. *Are . . . masters*] have different values put upon them in accordance with the status or reputation of their owners (and so this jewel will be more valuable if Timon wears it). Compare I. ii. 165–6 later, where Timon suggests that the value of a jewel will be enhanced if the First Lord wears it.

175. *mock'd*] Perhaps in the sense of "acted" or "counterfeited". Timon is congratulating the Jeweller on the skill with which he has played his cards, and the Merchant replies that the Jeweller's compliment to Timon is no more than everybody else would pay.

S.D. Enter Apemantus] The Folio entrances and exits are marked with

Mer. No, my good lord; he speaks the common tongue,
       Which all men speak with him.
Tim. Look who comes here: will you be chid?
Jew. We'll bear, with your lordship.
Mer.   He'll spare none.
Tim. Good morrow to thee, gentle Apemantus.   180
Apem. Till I be gentle, stay thou for thy good morrow,
       When thou art Timon's dog, and these knaves honest.
Tim. Why dost thou call them knaves, thou know'st them
       not?
Apem. Are they not Athenians?
Tim. Yes.   185
Apem. Then I repent not.
Jew. You know me, Apemantus?
Apem. Thou know'st I do, I call'd thee by thy name.
Tim. Thou art proud, Apemantus.
Apem. Of nothing so much as that I am not like Timon.   190
Tim. Whither art going?
Apem. To knock out an honest Athenian's brains.
Tim. That's a deed thou'lt die for.
Apem. Right, if doing nothing be death by th' law.
Tim. How lik'st thou this picture, Apemantus?   195
Apem. The best, for the innocence.
Tim. Wrought he not well that painted it?
Apem. He wrought better that made the painter, and yet
       he's but a filthy piece of work.
Pain. Y'are a dog.   200

178.] *Scene III Pope.*   179. We'll bear, with] *Camb. edd.;* Wee'l beare with *F;*
We'll bear it with *Pope.*   180.] *As Rowe;* Good . . . thee, / . . . *Apermantus.* / *F.*
191. Whither] *F4;* Whether *F1–3.*   193. thou'lt] *F4;* thou't *F1–3.*

an excellent understanding of stage
practice, and are therefore preserved
wherever possible in this edition. Most
editors transfer this one to after l. 178
but characters are not necessarily seen
by the others on stage immediately
they appear.

  179. *We'll . . . lordship*] we can stand
it, if your lordship can.

  181–2. *Till . . . honest*] i.e. you will
get no greeting from me until I am
really gentle, Timon is transformed

into his dog, and these knaves into
honest men—that is to say, never.

  188. *I call'd . . . name*] When he
addressed them all as "knaves".

  196. *innocence*] Perhaps, freedom
from evil intent (unlike the man who
painted it) or possibly guilelessness,
lack of sophisticated artistry, or even
simple folly (an "innocent" is a fool).

  200. *dog*] Apemantus is a cynic
philosopher; and "cynic" is derived
from the Greek word for "dog". This

Apem. Thy mother's of my generation. What's she, if I be
    a dog?

Tim. Wilt dine with me, Apemantus?

Apem. No; I eat not lords.

Tim. And thou shouldst, thou'dst anger ladies.   205

Apem. O they eat lords; so they come by great bellies.

Tim. That's a lascivious apprehension.

Apem. So thou apprehend'st it; take it for thy labour.

Tim. How dost thou like this jewel, Apemantus?

Apem. Not so well as plain-dealing, which will not cast a   210
    man a doit.

Tim. What dost thou think 'tis worth?

Apem. Not worth my thinking. How now Poet?

Poet. How now Philosopher?

Apem. Thou liest.   215

Poet. Art not one?

206.] *As Pope;* O . . . Lords; / . . . bellies. / *F.*   208.] *As Pope;* So, . . . it, /
. . . labour. / *F.*   So] *F3;* So, *F1.*   210. cast] *F1;* cost *F3.*   213.] *As
Pope;* Not . . . thinking. / . . . Poet? / *F.*

may be the idea behind the Painter's
taunt.

201. *generation*] Generally taken in
the sense of "species", "breed", but
probably there is a quibble on this
sense and that of persons born at
approximately the same time.

203. *Wilt*] wilt thou. "Thou" is often
omitted thus after the second person
singular inflection in questions (Abbott
241).

204. *No . . . lords*] Apemantus is
asserting that the people who dine
with Timon virtually dine *on* him, since
they eat up all he has. See note on
I. ii. 40.

205. *And*] an, if. So also at I. ii. 158,
I. ii. 245 and IV. iii. 310.

207. *apprehension*] A quibble on the
mental and physical senses of the
word: (1) perception or interpretation; and (2) seizure (of the men by
the women or vice versa). Similarly in
l. 208.

208. *So . . . labour*] Most editors pass
over this line in silence, but I find it
difficult. Deighton, who printed "So

thou apprehendest it, take it for thy
labour", explained "since you put that
interpretation on my words, you are
welcome to it for your pains". But "so"
can hardly mean "since"; it would
more normally mean "provided that"
(and perhaps does, with stress on
"thou" and "thy"). I take the line to
mean (as I have printed it): "It's
your interpretation, not mine; you
may have it for your pains", perhaps
with a further pun on "labour".
"To have one's labour for one's
pains" was, of course, proverbial
(Tilley L 1).

210. *Not . . . plain-dealing*] Steevens
(1778) first saw the reference to the
proverb "Plain-dealing is a jewel, but
they that use it die beggars" (Tilley
P 381–2).

211. *doit*] A small Dutch coin, less
than the value of a farthing.

213. *Not . . . thinking*] Apemantus'
reply is an example of the figure *anti-
metabole*—reversing the order of words
or turning them round (Joseph,
pp. 81–2).

Apem. Yes.

Poet. Then I lie not.

Apem. Art not a poet?

Poet. Yes.   220

Apem. Then thou liest. Look in thy last work, where thou
　　hast feign'd him a worthy fellow.

Poet. That's not feign'd, he is so.

Apem. Yes, he is worthy of thee, and to pay thee for thy
　　labour. He that loves to be flattered is worthy o' th'   225
　　flatterer. Heavens, that I were a lord!

Tim. What wouldst do then, Apemantus?

Apem. E'en as Apemantus does now: hate a lord with my
　　heart.

Tim. What, thyself?   230

Apem. Ay.

Tim. Wherefore?

Apem. That I had no angry wit to be a lord. Art not thou a
　　merchant?

Mer. Ay, Apemantus.   235

Apem. Traffic confound thee, if the gods will not!

Mer. If traffic do it, the gods do it.

Apem. Traffic's thy god, and thy god confound thee!

Trumpet sounds. Enter a Messenger.

Tim. What trumpet's that?

Mess. 'Tis Alcibiades, and some twenty horse,   240
　　All of companionship.

221-2.] *As Pope;* Then . . . lyest / . . . Fellow. / *F.*   222. feign'd] *F2;* fegin'd *F*
(*both states*).   233-4.] *As Theobald;* That . . . Lord. / . . . Merchant? / *F.*
233. no angry wit] *F;* so hungry a wit *Theobald (Warburton).*

221. *Then . . . liest*] A possible reference to the proverb "Painters and
poets have leave to lie" (Tilley P 28).
　222. *him*] i.e. Timon.
　233. *That . . . lord*] This contentious
Folio reading can perhaps be retained
and explained, as Delius virtually
explained it when he put a comma
after ' wit": "that I had no more
sense in my anger than to wish to be a
lord". "Angry" is the difficulty,
although Malone interestingly quoted

the common expression "he has wit
in his anger", which may well have
been in Shakespeare's mind. None of
the recorded emendations is very
convincing.
　236. *Traffic*] In its original meaning,
i.e. trade.
　241. *All of companionship*] forming a
party, all of one body. Steevens, however, explained as "all such as Alcibiades honours with his acquaintance,
and sets on a level with himself".

Tim. Pray entertain them, give them guide to us.

[*Exeunt some Attendants.*

You must needs dine with me. Go not you hence
Till I have thank'd you. When dinner's done
Show me this piece. I am joyful of your sights.   245

Enter ALCIBIADES, *and Attendants.*

Most welcome, sir!

Apem.   So, so, there!
Aches contract and starve your supple joints!
That there should be small love amongst these sweet
    knaves,
And all this courtesy! The strain of man's bred out
Into baboon and monkey.   250

Alcib. Sir, you have sav'd my longing, and I feed
Most hungerly on your sight.

Tim.   Right welcome, sir.
Ere we depart, we'll share a bounteous time
In different pleasures. Pray you, let us in.

[*Exeunt. Manet Apemantus.*

Enter two Lords.

242. S.D.] *Capell; not in F.*   245. S.D.] *As Capell; Enter Alcibiades with the rest F.*
246–50. So . . . monkey] *As Capell; prose F.*   246–7. so, there! Aches] *Capell;* so;
their Aches *F.*   248. amongst] amongest *F.*   254.] *As Rowe;* In . . . pleasures./
. . . in. / *F.*   254. S.D. Manet Apemantus] *Rowe; not in F.*   254. S.D. Enter] *F;*
Scene IV. / Enter / *Pope.*   two Lords] *F; Lucius and Lucullus / Rowe.*

245. *of your sights*] in seeing you, at
sight of you. A common construction.

245. S.D. Enter . . . Attendants]
The Folio direction cited in the collations is another good instance of an
author's indefiniteness: "the rest"
would hardly be left in a prompt-book.

246. *So, so, there!*] well, well! This is
Apemantus' first comment on the
bowing and saluting that takes place
as Alcibiades and his friends greet
Timon.

247. *Aches*] Pronounced as two syllables, "aitches".

starve] In its original and more
general sense as a transitive verb,
"destroy" or "kill".

249. *courtesy*] courtliness, outward
form of politeness. Compare *All's W.*,
v. iii. 324.

249–50. *bred out | Into*] evolved or
degenerated into.

251. *sav'd my longing*] *O.E.D.* records
uses of the phrase meaning to anticipate and so prevent a woman's longing, but the phrase seems to be affected
here, as is the following clause.

252. *hungerly*] hungrily. Used also in
Oth., iii. iv. 105.

253. *depart*] take leave of one another. Compare *3H6*, ii. vi. 43.

254. *different*] various.

254. S.D. Enter two Lords] Here
and elsewhere in the play producers

First Lord. What time o' day is't, Apemantus?   255

Apem. Time to be honest.

First Lord. That time serves still.

Apem. The most accursed thou that still omitt'st it.

Second Lord. Thou art going to Lord Timon's feast?

Apem. Ay, to see meat fill knaves and wine heat fools.   260

Second Lord. Fare thee well, fare thee well.

Apem. Thou art a fool to bid me farewell twice.

Second Lord. Why, Apemantus?

Apem. Shouldst have kept one to thyself, for I mean to
    give thee none.   265

First Lord. Hang thyself!

Apem. No, I will do nothing at thy bidding. Make thy
    requests to thy friend.

Second Lord. Away, unpeaceable dog, or I'll spurn thee
    hence!   270

Apem. I will fly, like a dog, the heels o' th' ass.   [*Exit.*

First Lord. He's opposite to humanity. Come, shall we in
    And taste Lord Timon's bounty? He out-goes
    The very heart of kindness.

Second Lord. He pours it out. Plutus the god of gold   275

---

258. most] *F;* more *Hanmer.*   267-8.] *As Pope;* No . . . bidding: / . . . Friend. / *F.*
269-70.] *As Pope;* Away . . . Dogge, / . . . hence. / *F.*   271. o'] *Rowe;* a' *F.*
Exit] *As Hanmer; not in F.*   272-4.] *As Capell;* Hee's . . . humanity. / Comes . . .
in, / . . . outgoes / . . . kindnesse. / *F;* He's . . . humanity. / . . . bounty. / . . . kindness. / *Pope.*

and readers may wish to equate unnamed Lords, Senators, and Creditors
with named characters. Rowe identified the First and Second Lords here
with Lucius and Lucullus. It could
equally be the other way round.
Compare II. i and III. vi and notes.
(Folio seems to distinguish First and
Second Lord from Lucius and Lucullus by giving to "*Luc.*" l. 126, alone, in
I. ii: see also I. ii. 179–89.) "Third
Lord", elsewhere, has been equated
with Sempronius by some editors.

258. *The most . . . it*] The construction seems to be a combination of two:
the self-contained "the most accursed
art thou" and the comparative "the
more accursed art thou for constantly

failing to take the opportunity provided". "Omit" in the sense of "fail to
profit by" is frequent in Shakespeare
and is used, for example, in a famous
passage in *Cæs.*, IV. iii. 220. "Still"
means "always".

269. *unpeaceable*] quarrelsome, refusing to remain peaceful. This is
the only time Shakespeare uses the
word.

272. *opposite to*] Probably means
both "the reverse of" and "antagonis-
tic to".

273. *out-goes*] goes beyond, tran-
scends.

275. *pours it out*] The construction,
preserved in modern colloquial English, is frequent in Shakespeare. "It"

Is but his steward. No meed but he repays
Seven-fold above itself: no gift to him
But breeds the giver a return exceeding
All use of quittance.
First Lord.   The noblest mind he carries
That ever govern'd man.   280
Second Lord. Long may he live in fortunes. Shall we in?
I'll keep you company.   [*Exeunt.*

[SCENE II]

*Hautboys playing loud music. A great banquet serv'd in; and then
enter* LORD TIMON, *Athenian Lords and Senators;* VENTIDIUS *which
Timon redeem'd from prison;* LUCULLUS *and* ALCIBIADES. *Steward
and others in attendance. Then comes, dropping after all,* APEMANTUS,
discontentedly, like himself.

Ven. Most honoured Timon,

282. I'll . . . company] As F; Rowe and edd. give to First Lord (Lucius).

Scene II

SCENE II] *Capell; not in F; Scene V Pope.*   S.D. *Athenian Lords and Senators*] the
States, the Athenian Lords F.   *Ventidius*] Ventigius F.   *Lucullus and Alcibiades*] not
in F.

has no specific reference (and does not
stand for "heart", for example). Compare *Lr.*, IV. i. 54 and Abbott 226.
  275–6. *Plutus . . . steward*] This is
quoted by Fleay and others as part of
their "proof" that Shakespeare knew
Lucian's dialogue; but references to
Plutus are not uncommon.
  276. *No . . . repays*] there is no form
of merit which he fails to reward. For
"repay" in this sense, compare Folio
R3, IV. iv. 123: "repayes he my deep
service / With such contempt?" (*Qq*
"rewards he").
  279. *All use of quittance*] A somewhat
elliptical phrase for "all customary
rates of repayment with interest".
("Use" often means "interest"; "quittance" is "repayment", "recompense".)
  carries] bears, or has (with no motion

or effort implied). See examples cited
by Schmidt, "Carry", sense 10.
  282. *I'll . . . company*] The line may
safely be left to the Second Lord as in
the Folio. He now finally accepts the
suggestion of ll. 272–3 that they go in
together.

Scene II

S.D. Hautboys] High-pitched
wooden wind-instruments, character-
ized by the use of the double reed as
against the single reed of the clarinet;
the modern oboe.
  Ventidius . . . prison; Then comes
. . . himself] Excellent examples of the
"descriptive" stage directions which
show that the author's draft (or a
transcript of it) was "copy" for the
printed text. See Greg, *First Folio*,
pp. 124–5.

It hath pleas'd the gods to remember my father's
   age,
And call him to long peace.
He is gone happy, and has left me rich.
Then as in grateful virtue I am bound   5
To your free heart, I do return those talents,
Doubled with thanks and service, from whose help
I deriv'd liberty.

Tim.   O by no means,
Honest Ventidius. You mistake my love;
I gave it freely ever, and there's none   10
Can truly say he gives, if he receives.
If our betters play at that game, we must not dare
To imitate them; faults that are rich are fair.

Ven. A noble spirit!

Tim. Nay, my lords, ceremony was but devis'd at first   15
To set a gloss on faint deeds, hollow welcomes,
Recanting goodness, sorry ere 'tis shown;
But where there is true friendship, there needs none.
Pray, sit; more welcome are ye to my fortunes
Than my fortunes to me.   20

First Lord. My lord, we always have confess'd it.

Apem. Ho, ho, confess'd it? Hang'd it, have you not?

---

9. Ventidius] *F4; Ventigius F1–3.*   21. *First Lord] As F; Luc[ius] Rowe.*   22.
Hang'd] *F2;* Handg'd *F1.*

Lucullus] l. 126 is attributed to
"*Luc.*" who could be either Lucullus or
Lucius (or just possibly Lucilius!).
Shakespeare obviously had not tidied
up the minor characters.

6. *free*] generous.

7. *service*] Used, as in "my duty and
most humble service", as a term of
mere courtesy, almost equivalent to
"homage".

12. *our betters*] One would hardly
think the line worthy of comment if
E. C. Pettet had not written "There is
a slight difficulty here. Shakespeare
himself must be commenting in these
lines since Timon has no 'betters' "!
(*op. cit.*, p. 325, n. 4). The reference is
surely to the senators. Cf. *Luke*, vi. 34.

13. *faults . . . fair*] Compare the old
proverb "Rich men have no faults"
(listed by Fuller, *Adagies and Proverbs*,
1732). "The faults which in rich men
are not criticized might well be criticized in us".

15. *ceremony*] ceremonious or formal
modes of conduct and address in the
presence of superiors. Compare *Ant.*,
III. xiii. 38, and the proverb "Full of
courtesy, full of craft" (Tilley C 732).

16. *faint deeds*] faint-hearted or
trivial deeds, perhaps with a quibble
on "faint" in the sense of "not vivid",
lacking the "gloss" that "ceremony"
adds.

22. *confess'd . . . not?*] Malone pointed out that Apemantus is referring

Tim. O Apemantus, you are welcome.

Apem. No, you shall not make me welcome:
    I come to have thee thrust me out of doors.   25

Tim. Fie, th'art a churl, y'have got a humour there
    Does not become a man; 'tis much to blame.
    They say, my lords, *Ira furor brevis est,*
    But yond man is very angry.
    Go, let him have a table by himself,   30
    For he does neither affect company,
    Nor is he fit for't, indeed.

Apem. Let me stay at thine apperil, Timon;
    I come to observe: I give thee warning on't.

Tim. I take no heed of thee; th'art an Athenian, there- 35
fore welcome. I myself would have no power; prithee
let my meat make thee silent.

Apem. I scorn thy meat; 'twould choke me, for I should
ne'er flatter thee. O you gods! What a number of
men eats Timon, and he sees 'em not! It grieves me 40

---

23. Apemantus] *F3; Apermantus F1–2.*   26. y'have] ye' haue *F.*   28–32.] *As F; prose Camb. edd.*   29. very] *As F;* ever *Rowe.*   38–42.] *As F;* I . . . should / . . . number / . . . not / . . . meat / . . . is / . . . too / *Capell; prose to* see, then . . . blood / . . . too / *Pope.*   40. eats] *F;* eat *Rowe.*

---

to the proverbial "Confess and be hanged", also quoted in *Oth.,* IV. i. 37–9; but the point of the joke is none too clear.

26. *humour*] In the strict old sense: a twist of temperament (coming about from an imbalance of the four "humours" or elements in the human body).

28. Ira furor brevis est] i.e. anger is a brief fury or madness (Horace, *Epistles,* I. ii. 62).

29. *very*] Most editors accept Rowe's emendation "ever", and explain: "They generally say great anger is brief, yet Apemantus is *always* angry". But the Folio's "very" also makes good sense: "They say fierce anger is always brief; yet Apemantus is fiercely angry —and his anger is obviously not brief!"

31. *affect*] Means both "to like" and "to aim at" or "seek".

33. *apperil*] peril. A comparatively

rare alternative form, used also by both Middleton and Jonson and last found in the first half of the seventeenth century.

36–7. *no power* . . .] i.e. to keep you quiet myself (but I hope my meat will do it).

38–9. *'twould . . . thee*] Variously explained, but the basic idea is that Timon's meat is intended for flatterers and paid for by flattery; Apemantus will not so pay for it and would therefore choke over food to which he had no right.

40. *eats*] Most editors alter to "eat" but the singular verb is common after "number" in Elizabethan as in modern usage. W. H. Clemen pointed out that this metaphor of the eating of Timon himself by those who eat his food recurs effectively two or three times. See, for example, III. ii. 79 and III. iv. 91–5, and I. i. 204 above.

to see so many dip their meat in one man's blood;
and all the madness is, he cheers them up too.
I wonder men dare trust themselves with men.
Methinks they should invite them without knives:
Good for their meat, and safer for their lives.   45
There's much example for't; the fellow that sits next
him, now parts bread with him, pledges the breath
of him in a divided draught, is the readiest man to
kill him. 'T'as been proved. If I were a huge man, I
should fear to drink at meals,   50
Lest they should spy my windpipe's dangerous notes,
Great men should drink with harness on their throats.

Tim. My lord, in heart; and let the health go round.
Second Lord. Let it flow this way, my good lord.
Apem. Flow this way? A brave fellow. He keeps his tides   55
well. Those healths will make thee and thy state look
ill, Timon.
Here's that which is too weak to be a sinner,

---

49. proved. If] *Rowe;* proued, if *F.*   51–2.] *As Rowe (edn 3); prose F.*   54.
Second Lord] *Lucul[lus] / Rowe.*   58–9.] *As F; prose Pope.*

---

41. *blood*] Carrying on the idea that
the guests are eating Timon; here the
dish in which the food is dipped is
thought of as containing his life-blood;
and the miracle is that the victim is
encouraging his enemies to drink it.
There may be, as Evans suggested, a
submerged metaphor, of a pack of
hounds being rewarded with the blood
of the animal they have killed.

42. *and all the madness is*] i.e. the real
madness, the summit of his mad-
ness.

44. *without knives*] Guests in Shakespeare's day normally brought their
own knives.

46. *There's . . . for 't*] there are many
instances of it. Apemantus is obviously
thinking of Judas among others.

48. *a divided draught*] a drink that is
shared, from a cup that is passed
round.

49. *huge*] great (with no implication
of physical size).

51. *Lest . . . notes*] A somewhat difficult line. It is clear *both* that there is a

quibble on "pipe", in that the windpipe produces "notes", like a bagpipe,
and that drinking in the company of
men equipped with knives is thought
of as dangerous (perhaps because the
head is tilted back in drinking deep
and the throat fully exposed). Shadwell apparently aimed at making this
second point clear when he altered it
to "dangerous places".

52. *harness*] armour, as often in
Shakespeare.

53. *in heart*] in all sincerity and good
fellowship. Spoken as a toast, with the
request that the cup now circulate.

55. *tides*] Apemantus speaks of the
"tides" instead of the "times" (and
"tide" can mean "time" as in "Whit-
suntide") because the Second Lord has
used "flow" instead of "come", i.e. it
is a scornful comment on the flatterer's
knowledge of the tactful thing to say.

56–7. *Those . . . ill*] A variation on
the proverb "To drink Health(s) is to
drink sickness" (Tilley H 292).

58. *sinner*] No emendation is needed,

Honest water, which ne'er left man i' th' mire.
This and my food are equals, there's no odds;   60
Feasts are too proud to give thanks to the gods.

Apemantus' Grace.

Immortal gods, I crave no pelf;
I pray for no man but myself.
Grant I may never prove so fond,
To trust man on his oath or bond;   65
Or a harlot for her weeping,
Or a dog that seems a-sleeping,
Or a keeper with my freedom,
Or my friends, if I should need 'em.
Amen. So fall to't: 70
Rich men sin, and I eat root.   [*Eats and drinks.*

Much good dich thy good heart, Apemantus.
Tim. Captain Alcibiades, your heart's in the field now.
Alcib. My heart is ever at your service, my lord.
Tim. You had rather be at a breakfast of enemies than a   75
dinner of friends.
Alcib. So they were bleeding new, my lord, there's no

---

61. S.D. *Apemantus'*] *Apermantus* F.   71. *Eats and drinks*] *Johnson; not in* F.
73. Captain Alcibiades] *As Hanmer;* Captain, / *Alcibiades* F.

---

for, as the following line makes clear, water is sinless or innocent in that it does not lead the drinker into trouble. ("To leave in the mire" was also a common saying: Tilley M 989.)

60. *there's no odds*] The older equivalent of our "there's nothing to choose between them". "Odds" is the regular word for the amount by which one quantity differs from another. Compare "it makes no odds".

61. *Feasts . . . gods*] There is possibly a quibble on "proud" in the two senses of "lavish" and "arrogant". "Lavish feasts are given by men who are too arrogant to give thanks to the gods"; but Apemantus will give thanks for his plain food and water.

62. pelf] In the more general sense of "booty" or "recompense" rather than merely "money".

64. fond] foolish.

65. To] as to.

68. keeper] gaoler, warder.

72. *dich*] Not satisfactorily explained but generally taken as a corruption of "do it" (do it ye—dit ye—dich ye). The phrase "much good do it your good heart!" was certainly proverbial and is used in *Wiv.* i. i. 83. Shadwell altered it to "Much good may't do thee"; already by his time, then, Shakespeare's phrase would presumably not have been clear to a London audience.

74. *your service*] "Your" is to be stressed; Alcibiades gallantly replies that to be at Timon's service is more important than to be "serving" as a soldier.

75. *of enemies*] i.e. *upon* enemies, as against a meal *with* friends.

77. *So*] provided that, if only.

meat like 'em; I could wish my best friend at such a
feast.

Apem. Would all those flatterers were thine enemies then,   80
that then thou mightst kill 'em—and bid me to 'em.

First Lord. Might we but have that happiness, my lord,
that you would once use our hearts, whereby we
might express some part of our zeals, we should think
ourselves for ever perfect.   85

Tim. O no doubt, my good friends, but the gods themselves have provided that I shall have much help
from you: how had you been my friends else? Why
have you that charitable title from thousands, did
not you chiefly belong to my heart? I have told more   90
of you to myself than you can with modesty speak in
your own behalf; and thus far I confirm you. O you
gods, think I, what need we have any friends, if we
should ne'er have need of 'em? They were the most
needless creatures living should we ne'er have use for   95
'em, and would most resemble sweet instruments
hung up in cases, that keeps their sounds to themselves. Why, I have often wish'd myself poorer that I
might come nearer to you. We are born to do benefits; and what better or properer can we call our own   100

99. born] *F3;* borne *F1–2.*

81. *bid*] invite.

82–5. *Might . . . perfect*] This speech
is affected and gives a remarkable
impression of unctuous hypocrisy.

83. *use our hearts*] make some request
that would try our affection for you.

85. *for ever perfect*] i.e. completely
happy, in being privileged to demonstrate their affection for Timon.

87. *help*] Presumably Timon means
here "psychological help", friendship
itself. But of course the words are an
example of the bitterest dramatic
irony.

89. *charitable*] loving, kindly (an
obsolete sense).

from thousands] i.e. from among
thousands, you alone of all the thousands I know; this rather than "given
by thousands (of others)".

92. *confirm you*] corroborate or ratify
your claims to be worthy friends. But
there may be—as so often in this play
—a religious overtone; Timon's position is all the more ironical if even
momentarily he is pictured, or pic-
tures himself, as conveying to these
flatterers that special grace which
makes the person confirmed a truer
Christian.

97. *keeps*] The relative often in this
way takes a singular verb, even
though the antecedent is plural
(Abbott 247).

98–9. *that . . . you*] by asking for your
help, become more closely tied to your
hearts; or perhaps simply "come
closer to your status", "not be re-
moved from you by my superior
wealth".

than the riches of our friends? O what a precious
comfort 'tis to have so many like brothers command-
ing one another's fortunes. O joy's e'en made away
ere't can be born! Mine eyes cannot hold out water,
methinks. To forget their faults, I drink to you.   105
Apem. Thou weep'st to make them drink, Timon.
Second Lord. Joy had the like conception in our eyes,
    And at that instant like a babe sprung up.
Apem. Ho, ho: I laugh to think that babe a bastard.
Third Lord. I promise you, my lord, you mov'd me much. 110
Apem. Much.   [*Tucket sounded.*
Tim.   What means that trump? How now?

Enter Servant.

Serv. Please you, my lord, there are certain ladies most
    desirous of admittance.
Tim. Ladies? What are their wills?
Serv. There comes with them a forerunner, my lord, 115
    which bears that office to signify their pleasures.
Tim. I pray let them be admitted.

Enter CUPID.

Cup. Hail to thee, worthy Timon, and to all that of his

103. joy's] ioyes, F; Joy *Rowe.*   104. born!] *As Rowe;* borne: F.   105. methinks. To] *As Rowe;* me thinks: to F (*some copies*); me thinks. to F (*other copies*).
faults, I] *As Rowe;* Faults. I F.   111. *Tucket sounded*] Sound Tucket. Enter the
Maskers of Amazons, with Lutes in their hands, dauncing and playing F.   112. most]
Pope; Most F (*as if verse*).   117. S.D. Enter] F; Scene VI. | Enter | Pope.   117.
S.D. Enter Cupid] Capell; Enter Cupid with the Maske of Ladies F.   118–21.] *As F;*
Hail ... all / ... senses / ... freely / ... th'ear | *Rann;* Hail ... all / ... taste /
... freely / ... bosom | *Pope.*

103–4. *e'en . . . born*] Apparently,
"that expresses itself in tears and so
seems to turn to sorrow before the joy
itself can be truly said to exist".
Deighton compared *Ado,* I. i. 21–9.

105. *To forget their faults*] to cover up
my weakness in weeping.

106. *Thou . . . Timon*] Probably
means: the main result of your weeping is not that you drink but that they
do.

107. *Joy . . . eyes*] joy was born in
our eyes in the same way—i.e. accom-

panied by tears (referring back to
Timon's statement in ll. 104–5).

108. *like a babe*] Tilley (B 8) compared the proverbial phrase "to look
babies in another's eyes", i.e. to see the
small images of oneself reflected in
another's eyes. The Second Lord is
thus saying that Timon's joy was
immediately reflected in the eyes of his
friends.

116. *which . . . pleasures*] whose func-
tion it is to indicate what they propose.

118–21.] Even granting that the

bounties taste! The five best senses acknowledge thee
their patron, and come freely to gratulate thy plen- 120
teous bosom.
There, taste, touch, all, pleas'd from thy table
    rise;
They only now come but to feast thine eyes.
Tim. They're welcome all; let 'em have kind admittance.
    Music, make their welcome!   [*Exit Cupid.* 125
Lucullus. You see, my lord, how ample y'are belov'd.

122. There] *F;* Th'ear *Theobald* (*Warburton*).   touch, all] touch all *F;* Touch,
smell *Theobald* (*Warburton*); touch, smell, all *Steevens* (*1793*); touch and smell
Rann.   123. They] *F;* These *Theobald.*   124–5.] *verse F3; prose F1–2.*
125. *Exit Cupid*] *Capell; not in* F.   126. *Lucullus*] Luc. *F; 1* Lord *Capell.*

verse spoken in Shakespearian
masques is generally different in kind,
and apparently made so to give
it an archaic or formal sound, the
attempts of the various editors to
rearrange into verse ll. 118–21, printed
in the Folio as prose, are not fully convincing and therefore there is a certain
presumption against emendations
which give the alleged verse form
as their justification for transferring
"there" or "th'ear" from l. 122 to the
previous line. Nor is there need for the
transfer, since even if "th'ear" is
adopted (on the supposition that
Shakespeare wrote "th'ere") it should
be read as one syllable. If Warburton's
ingenious emendation "Th'ear, taste,
touch, smell . . ." is accepted, Cupid is
saying that four senses have already
been gratified at the banquet, and the
masquers have come to gratify the
fifth, i.e. sight. But the Folio reading is
not necessarily wrong. Cupid points to
the table and says that there taste and
touch and in fact *all* the senses have
been gratified (through Timon's
generosity) whereas the masquers
modestly aim at pleasing only one
sense, that of sight. (And the eye may
just as reasonably be said to have been
already satisfied at the banquet as the
ear has been by the accompanying
music of the hautboys.)
There are signs that there was some

dislocation here during the printing
of the Folio. The exceptionally light
mark after "tast" is not a normal
printing of the comma; the letters of
"tast" are out of alignment; in the
earlier part of the speech the spacing is
wrong, the "a" of "acknowledge" being separated from the rest of the word
and attached to "sences"; and in the
first line of the following speech the
letter "l" is missing from "welcome".
Apparently the type was dropped and
not properly reset; and if this is so,
the full rearrangement suggested by
Sisson, combining Steevens' emendation with Rann's lineation, would be
even more attractive.
    There is further difficulty in l. 120,
which is generally passed over in
silence. "Gratulate" elsewhere in
Shakespeare means "congratulate",
"greet"; it could also mean "gratify",
"satisfy". Perhaps it has both meanings here, where the presenter of the
masque is using the stylized language
of compliment.
    Similar masques appear in other
Elizabethan and Jacobean plays, and
notably in *H8*, I. iv. The masque
was a popular form of Court entertainment, particularly in the reigns of
the early Stuarts; its appearance in
ancient Athens is a typical Shakespearian anachronism.
    126. *ample*] amply (Abbott 1).

Music. Re-enter CUPID, *with a masque of Ladies as Amazons, with lutes in their hands, dancing and playing.*

Apem. Hoy-day!
    What a sweep of vanity comes this way.
    They dance? They are madwomen.
    Like madness is the glory of this life,   130
    As this pomp shows to a little oil and root.
    We make ourselves fools, to disport ourselves,
    And spend our flatteries to drink those men
    Upon whose age we void it up again
    With poisonous spite and envy.   135
    Who lives that's not depraved or depraves?
    Who dies that bears not one spurn to their graves
    Of their friends' gift?
    I should fear those that dance before me now
    Would one day stamp upon me. 'T'as been done.   140
    Men shut their doors against a setting sun.

---

126. S.D.] *As Capell; not in* F (*see 117. S.D.*).   127–8.] *As* F; *one line Pope.*   129. dance?] *As* F; Dance, *Rowe;* dance! *Steevens.*   135–8.] *As* F; With . . . that's not / . . . bears / . . . gift? / *Hanmer.*   138. friends' gift?] *As* F4; Friends guift: F1.

127–8. *Hoy-day! . . . way*] "Hoy-day", variously spelt, is a common exclamation. The editors' printing of this as one line obscures the intended rhyme.

128. *sweep of vanity*] The meaning is obviously derived from the sweeping movement of the dancers (= "What a parade of frivolity!"). "Sweep" as a noun is not elsewhere used by Shakespeare.

130–1. *Like madness . . . root*] "Like" is perhaps an adjective, as often in Shakespeare (compare particularly "upon the like devotion as yourselves", *R3*, iv. i. 9). The lines may be paraphrased: "The vainglory of this life is the same form of madness as that of these women—and so is the ostentation (of this banquet) when compared to the little oil and a root (which are all that is necessary for sustenance)".

132. *disport ourselves*] amuse our-

selves, keep ourselves occupied.

133. *drink*] The modern equivalent might be "swallow whole", although Sisson (*New Readings,* p. 168) explains as "drink the health of".

134–5. *Upon . . . envy*] upon whom, when they (and we) are old, we regurgitate our knowledge of them, but now mingled with spite and envy. "It" is the characteristic indefinite pronoun: what we have swallowed.

136. *not depraved or depraves*] neither the object of slander nor a slanderer. Compare *Ado,* v. i. 95, "lie and cog and flout, deprave and slander".

137. *spurn*] hurt, insult, or rejection.

138. *gift*] giving. It will be noticed that this line and others in the speech are not full pentameters: it reads indeed like a mere draft.

141. *Men . . . sun*] Tilley (S 979) records a proverb "The rising, not the setting, sun is worshipped by most men".

The Lords rise from table, with much adoring of TIMON, *and to show*
their loves each single out an Amazon, and all dance, men with women,
a lofty strain or two to the hautboys, and cease.

Tim. You have done our pleasures much grace, fair ladies,
    Set a fair fashion on our entertainment,
    Which was not half so beautiful and kind;
    You have added worth unto 't and lustre,   145
    And entertain'd me with mine own device.
    I am to thank you for 't.
First Lady. My lord, you take us even at the best.
Apem. Faith, for the worst is filthy; and would not hold
    taking, I doubt me.   150
Tim. Ladies, there is an idle banquet attends you;
    Please you to dispose yourselves.

142.] *As Pope;* You . . . pleasures / . . . Ladies / *F.*   148. *First Lady*] *Steevens;*
1 Lord F.   even] *F;* ever *Collier (edn 2) (conj. Tyrwhitt).*

S.D. adoring of] paying of homage
to (Latin *adorare*).

  142. *done . . . grace*] added grace to
our enjoyments (a common Elizabethan meaning of "pleasures").

  143. *Set . . . fashion on*] given an attractive appearance to, lent glamour to.

  144. *kind*] gracious; exactly the
sense in which Pericles uses it to
Marina "Thy name, my most kind
virgin?" (v. i. 141) and probably the
sense in which it is used in the famous
song "Is she kind as she is fair?" *Gent.*,
IV. ii. 44. There may be a secondary
meaning "true to its kind", "what its
kind ought to be".

  146. *mine own device*] This has been
taken to mean that Timon had suggested the masque and possibly
written the prologue; he thanks the
masquers for entertaining him as well
as his guests, by the way they have
performed. But Cupid's prologue is
not the kind of address a man would
compose to himself. Timon probably
means "You have taken my own
'device' (the feast) as an occasion
for entertaining me also." For "device" (meaning "invention", "contri-

vance", "something fancifully de-
vised") compare *LLL.*, V. i. 144.

  147. *am to thank*] ought to, and do,.
thank.

  148. *you take . . . best*] you rate us as
highly as we can possibly be rated,
give us our full due. For "at the best"
compare III. vi. 27 later. Steevens gave
the line to "First Lady" instead of
"First Lord" (on Johnson's hint that it
was probably marked only "L" in the
"copy") and Malone pointed out that
Apemantus' reply "puts the matter
beyond a doubt".

  149–50. *hold taking*] bear "taking"
or handling—because it is rotten. The
innuendo no doubt refers to carnal
possession and sexual disease. (Par-
tridge, pp. 112, 200.)

  150. *doubt me*] suspect, or fear.

  151. *idle*] trifling or, perhaps, unpre-
tentious: spoken in self-depreciation.
Steevens (1793) compared *Rom.*, I. v.
124 where Capulet in a similar tone
refers to his own entertainment: "We
have a trifling foolish banquet towards".

  152. *dispose yourselves*] take your
places.

All Ladies. Most thankfully, my lord.

                              [*Exeunt Cupid and Ladies.*

Tim.   Flavius!

Steward. My lord?

Tim.   The little casket bring me hither.

Stew. Yes, my lord. [*Aside.*] More jewels yet!   155
    There is no crossing him in's humour,
    Else I should tell him well, i' faith, I should,
    When all's spent, he'd be cross'd then, and he
        could.
    'Tis pity bounty had not eyes behind,
    That man might ne'er be wretched for his mind.   [*Exit.*

First Lord. Where be our men?   161

Serv. Here, my lord, in readiness.

Second Lord. Our horses!

Re-enter Steward, with the casket.

Tim.   O my friends, I have one word
    To say to you: look you, my good lord,
    I must entreat you honour me so much   165

---

153. S.D.] *Capell; Exeunt F.*   154, 155. *Steward*] *Fla. F.*   155. *Aside*] *Johnson; not in F.*   157. *him well*] *F; him—well Rowe.*   163. S.D.] *not in F (see 172. S.D.).*   163–4. O . . . lord] O . . . Friends: / . . . good L. / F.

153. *Flavius*] This is the only scene in the play in which the name "Flavius" is given (apparently) to the character elsewhere designated only as "Steward". At II. ii. 189 the name is also given by the Folio to a servant, perhaps the one elsewhere called "Flaminius". The name in I. ii seems to have been either a first thought, not proceeded with, or an after-thought, put in when the particular scene was revised (if it ever was, which I doubt). I have thought it better to preserve the speech-prefix elsewhere used in the Folio text, *Stew(ard)*.

156. *crossing . . . humour*] thwarting him in his (unbalanced) disposition. For "humour" see note on I. ii. 26 above.

157. *tell him well*] The Folio text is surely right: tell him firmly.

158. *he'd be cross'd . . . could*] he'd like to be free of debt then, if only he could—and he won't be able to! The Steward is playing on "crossed" (1) in the sense in which it is used in l. 156 and (2) in its other common sense, crossed off a list of debts when the debt is paid. Deighton, who was able to cite parallels from Jonson, Marston, Shirley and Day for this second meaning of the word (also, of course, recorded in *O.E.D.*), perhaps wrongly rejected the theory of Theobald and most earlier editors who saw a further quibble on crossing the palm with money (many coins bore a cross); they interpreted it to mean "he'll then seek in vain for people to provide him with money".

160. *for his mind*] for (the generous conduct prompted by) his mind and heart.

As to advance this jewel; accept it and wear it,
Kind my lord.
First Lord. I am so far already in your gifts—
All. So are we all.

Enter a Servant.

Serv. My lord, there are certain nobles of the senate newly 170
alighted, and come to visit you.
Tim. They are fairly welcome.   [*Exit Servant.*
Stew. I beseech your honour, vouchsafe me a word; it
does concern you near.
Tim. Near? Why, then, another time I'll hear thee. I 175
prithee, let's be provided to show them entertainment.
Stew. [*Aside.*] I scarce know how.

Enter another Servant.

Second Serv. May it please your honour, Lord Lucius,
Out of his free love, hath presented to you   180
Four milk-white horses, trapp'd in silver.
Tim. I shall accept them fairly. Let the presents
Be worthily entertain'd.   [*Exit Servant.*

166. accept it] *F1*; accept *F2–4*.   168. gifts—] *Pope*; guifts. *F*.   170.] *Scene VII Pope*.   170–1.] *As F*; My . . . senate / . . . you / *Capell*.   172. S.D. *Exit Servant*] *This ed.; Enter Flauius. F*.   173. Stew.] *Fla. F*.   173–4.] *As F*; I . . . Honour / . . . near / *Capell*.   178. Stew. [*Aside*]] *Fla. F*.   179. Second Serv.] *Rowe; Ser. F*.   179–81.] *As F; prose Pope*.   183. *Exit Servant*] *This ed.; not in F*.

166. *advance*] enhance in value (perhaps with a quibble: "place, or wear,
in a prominent position"). The sentiment is identical with that expressed
by the Jeweller at I. i. 173–4.
    167. *Kind my lord*] A regular trans-
position (Abbott 13).
    168. *so far . . . gifts*] so far in your
debt already, for your gifts.
    172. *fairly*] kindly; compare l. 182
later. It will be noticed that the senators do not in fact appear, and this has
been thought a further sign of hasty
composition or textual corruption.
But Shakespeare may well have been
satisfied to give the impression of an
indefinite number of wealthy influ-

ential men flooding Timon's house.
    175. *Near . . . thee*] Deighton and
Maxwell compare Caesar's "What
touches us ourself shall be last serv'd",
Cæs., III. i. 8, although Maxwell's
additional comment "a proper attitude in a ruler but presumption in a
private person" seems to me un-
necessarily critical of Timon.
    181. *trapp'd in silver*] with silver (or
silver-mounted) trappings or harness
ornaments. Strictly the trapping is the
covering spread over the saddle or
harness.
    183. *worthily entertain'd*] fittingly
received, given the attention that such
gifts deserve.

Enter a third Servant.

                  How now? What news?

Third Serv. Please you, my lord, that honourable gentleman Lord Lucullus entreats your company to- 185
morrow, to hunt with him, and has sent your honour
two brace of greyhounds.

Tim. I'll hunt with him; and let them be receiv'd,
Not without fair reward.

Stew. [*Aside.*]   What will this come to?
He commands us to provide, and give great gifts, 190
And all out of an empty coffer;
Nor will he know his purse, or yield me this,
To show him what a beggar his heart is,
Being of no power to make his wishes good.
His promises fly so beyond his state   195
That what he speaks is all in debt; he owes for ev'ry word:
He is so kind that he now pays interest for 't;
His land's put to their books. Well, would I were
Gently put out of office before I were forc'd out!
Happier is he that has no friend to feed   200
Than such that do e'en enemies exceed.
I bleed inwardly for my lord.   [*Exit.*

Tim. You do yourselves much wrong,

188–9.] *As Hanmer;* Ile . . . him, / . . . Reward. / F; *prose Pope.*   189. *Stew.*
[*Aside*]] *Fla. F.* 190–1.] *As Steevens; prose F.* 196–9.] *As F;* That . . . owes /
. . . now / . . . books / . . . office / . . . out *Capell.* 203–4.] *As F; prose Pope;* You
. . . yourselves / . . . merits / *Malone.*

189. *fair*] generous, fitting.

192. *yield me this*] grant me this
privilege, namely . . .

194. *Being*] There is perhaps no one
antecedent for this. Deighton took it
as "his heart being"; the sense rather
demands "he" or even "I" (the
Steward) being . . .

195. *state*] estate or means.

196–9.] The lineation is in dispute,
again because the speech is little more
than a draft, not given its final verse
form. Passages like this suggest that
Shakespeare did not always compose
fluently in perfect iambic pentameters. One is in fact reminded of Ben

Jonson's practice of writing his verses
first in prose, "for so his master Cam-
den had learn'd him". In cases of such
doubt, it seems better to preserve
the Folio lineation, particularly if
rearrangement into shorter lines
tends to obscure the marked speech
rhythm.

197. *for 't*] for being so kind.

198. *put . . . books*] entered up in
their books as part of their assets, not
Timon's, since it is all mortgaged to
them.

201. *exceed*] i.e. in the harm they do
him, in the demands they make upon
him.

You bate too much of your own merits.
Here, my lord, a trifle of our love.   205
Second Lord. With more than common thanks I will receive it.
Third Lord. O he's the very soul of bounty.
Tim. And now I remember, my lord, you gave good
words the other day of a bay courser I rode on. 'Tis
yours, because you lik'd it.   210
Third Lord. O I beseech you pardon me, my lord, in that.
Tim. You may take my word, my lord, I know no man
Can justly praise but what he does affect.
I weigh my friend's affection with mine own,
I'll tell you true. I'll call to you.   215
All Lords. O none so welcome.
Tim. I take all and your several visitations
So kind to heart, 'tis not enough to give:
Methinks I could deal kingdoms to my friends,
And ne'er be weary. Alcibiades,   220
Thou art a soldier, therefore seldom rich;
It comes in charity to thee: for all thy living
Is 'mongst the dead, and all the lands thou hast
Lie in a pitch'd field.
Alcib. Ay, defil'd land, my lord.   225

206.] *As Pope;* With . . . thankes / . . . it / *F.*   211. *Third Lord*] *conj. Capell;*
1. L. F; 2 *Lord* / *Pope.*   212–15.] *As Steevens; prose F.*   225. Ay, defil'd] Ay,
defiled *As Reed (Malone);* I, defil'd *F1;* I defie *F2–4.*

204. *bate*] An aphetic form of
"abate", reduce, remit, undervalue.
209. *of*] concerning, about (Abbott
174).
   courser] stallion (*O.E.D.* sense 2),
rather than "racehorse".
211. *pardon . . . that*] allow me to
decline your gift, rather than "excuse
me for having praised it aloud".
213. *affect*] desire, like.
214. *weigh . . . own*] consider my
friend's desires to be equivalent to my
own.
215. *I'll . . . true*] I assure you. Compare *John*, v. vi. 39.
   call to you] The modern idiom is
"call *on*" a person or "*at*" a dwell-
ing.

217. *all*] of you; or, possibly, all your
gifts and assurances.
218. *kind*] kindly, affectionately.
219. *deal*] give out, distribute.
222. *It . . . thee*] whatever you receive
represents true charity (since you can
have no property of your own).
   living] With a quibble on the senses
of (1) property, (2) being alive, and,
possibly, (3) means of earning a living,
livelihood.
224. *pitch'd field*] field in which
troops have been arranged for battle;
but Alcibiades replies with a quibble
deriving from the Apocrypha: "He
that toucheth pitch shall be defiled"
Ecclesiasticus, xiii. 1. Compare *1H4*, II.
iv. 454–6.

First Lord. We are so virtuously bound—
Tim. And so am I to you.
Second Lord. So infinitely endear'd—
Tim. All to you. Lights, more lights!
First Lord. The best of happiness, honour and fortunes,   230
    Keep with you, Lord Timon!
Tim. Ready for his friends. [*Exeunt; manent Timon, Apemantus.*
Apem.   What a coil's here,
    Serving of becks and jutting-out of bums!
    I doubt whether their legs be worth the sums
    That are given for 'em. Friendship's full of dregs;   235
    Methinks false hearts should never have sound legs.
    Thus honest fools lay out their wealth on curtsies.
Tim. Now Apemantus, if thou wert not sullen,
    I would be good to thee.
Apem. No, I'll nothing; for if I should be brib'd too, there   240
    would be none left to rail upon thee, and then thou
    wouldst sin the faster. Thou giv'st so long, Timon, I

---

226. bound—] *Pope;* bound. *F.*   227.] *As F;* so / *Am Steevens (1793).*   228.
endear'd—] *Rowe;* endeer'd. *F.*   230–1.] *As F;* The...happiness /...Timon! /
Steevens; prose Camb. edd.   232. S.D.] *Exeunt Lords F.*   232.] *Scene VIII Pope.*
232–5. What... 'em] *As Rowe; prose F.*   233. Serving] *F;* serring *Warburton.*
238. Apemantus] *Apermantus F.*

---

228. *endear'd*] obliged or indebted. The word, not common in Shakespeare, is used thus by Middleton (and is one of Sykes's reasons for attributing to him a share in the play). It is used again at III. ii. 30.

229. *All to you*] i.e. all the indebtedness is on my part, to you.

232. *Ready . . . friends*] sc. that he may be . . .

232–5. *What . . . 'em*] Rowe's rearrangement of the lines as verse has been accepted, after hesitation; but it will be noticed how often the dramatist seems to have given to Apemantus, in particular, speeches which as they stand in the Folio begin as prose and end with a rhyming couplet (e.g. the final speech in this scene).

232. *coil*] confusion, turmoil, fuss: the regular Elizabethan meaning,

notably in Hamlet's "When we have shuffled off this mortal coil" (i.e. this turmoil that is life), III. i. 67.

233. *Serving of becks*] The phrase has aroused controversy, but seems to mean serving-up or parading of becks (nods or curtsies. Compare "to be at his beck and call"). Warburton read "serring", and explained it as joining close together (French *serrer*) and as a metaphor from the billing of pigeons.

234. *legs*] With a pun: (1) bows (compare "to make a leg"), (2) the limbs themselves.

236. *sound legs*] i.e. sound enough to deceive people by their obeisances.

237. *curtsies*] With a further pun (1) bows, obeisances, (2) acts of courtesy.

fear me thou wilt give away thyself in paper shortly.
What needs these feasts, pomps, and vain-glories?

Tim. Nay, and you begin to rail on society once, I am   245
sworn not to give regard to you. Farewell, and come
with better music.   [*Exit.*

Apem. So. Thou wilt not hear me now; thou shalt not
then. I'll lock thy heaven from thee.
O that men's ears should be   250
To counsel deaf, but not to flattery.   [*Exit.*

---

243. paper] *F;* proper *Warburton;* person *Hudson.*

243. *in paper*] i.e., presumably, in the form of promissory notes, since you will have no money left. The various emendations are mostly unacceptable as possible misreadings of Elizabethan script.

244. *What needs*] what is the necessity for.

245. *and . . . once*] if once you begin. Abbott, however, wanted to put the comma before "once" and interpret the word as "then above all" (57).

247. *with better music*] with more pleasant sounds (than your present harsh criticism).

248–9. *thou shalt not then*] you will not have the opportunity later.

249. *thy heaven*] i.e. the advice which might have kept you "in heaven", happy.

[ACT II

SCENE I]

Enter a Senator.

Sen. And late, five thousand; to Varro and to Isidore
He owes nine thousand, besides my former sum,
Which makes it five and twenty. Still in motion
Of raging waste? It cannot hold, it will not.
If I want gold, steal but a beggar's dog   5
And give it Timon—why, the dog coins gold;
If I would sell my horse and buy twenty moe
Better than he—why, give my horse to Timon;
Ask nothing, give it him, it foals me straight
And able horses. No porter at his gate,   10
But rather one that smiles and still invites
All that pass by. It cannot hold; no reason

ACT II

Scene 1

ACT II SCENE I] *As Rowe; not in F.*   S.D. *Enter*] *F1 ; A publick Place in the City.*
Enter | Rowe; Athens. A Room in a Senator's House. | Enter | Capell.

S.D. Enter a Senator] I preserve the Folio S.D. but, as Sisson suggests (*New Readings*, p. 169), the scene would probably be set on the inner stage and the Senator "discovered" there, going through his accounts.

1. *late*] lately, recently.

3–4. *Still . . . waste?*] always involved in this process of ceaseless extravagance? Here again the Folio question-mark could indicate either a rhetorical question or an exclamation.

4. *hold*] last.

5. *steal*] I need only steal.

beggar's dog] The practice of training dogs to lead blind beggars, particu-larly, was known in the seventeenth century.

9–10. *straight | And able horses*] Probably, strong horses, immediately; but "straight" might mean "upstanding". All these examples are, of course, to make the point that Timon recipro-cates by giving presents that are worth several times the price of the original gift. The sentiment is exactly that of i. i. 276–9.

10. *porter*] The porter or gatekeeper is thought of here, as in *Err.*, II. ii. 211–13, as one who keeps unwanted people out.

11. *still*] always.

36

Can sound his state in safety. Caphis, ho!
Caphis, I say!

Enter CAPHIS.

Caph.   Here, sir, what is your pleasure?
Sen. Get on your cloak, and haste you to Lord Timon;   15
Importune him for my moneys; be not ceas'd
With slight denial, nor then silenc'd when
"Commend me to your master" and the cap
Plays in the right hand, thus—but tell him,
My uses cry to me; I must serve my turn   20
Out of mine own; his days and times are past,
And my reliances on his fracted dates
Have smit my credit. I love and honour him,
But must not break my back to heal his finger.
Immediate are my needs, and my relief   25
Must not be toss'd and turn'd to me in words,
But find supply immediate. Get you gone;
Put on a most importunate aspect,
A visage of demand: for I do fear,
When every feather sticks in his own wing,   30
Lord Timon will be left a naked gull,

---

13. sound] *Ff;* found *Hanmer.*   17. when] *F1;* then *F2.*   18. "Commend] *As Pope;* Commend *F1.*   master"] *As Pope;* Master, *F.*

---

13. *sound*] The Folio reading, although cryptic, is probably correct, as against Hanmer's "found". The metaphor is from sounding or testing the depth of water or the nature of the bottom (with a plummet); and the meaning is that no person of any reason could possibly test Timon's estate and think that it was safe.

16. *ceas'd*] stopped, caused to cease. The verb is thus used transitively often in Shakespeare.

19. *Pla s . . . thus*] i.e. with elaborate courtesy.

20. *uses*] necessities. Compare III. ii. 34 later.

20–1. *serve . . . own*] meet my own requirement with my own money.

21. *his . . . times*] i.e. the days and times specified in his promises to re-

pay money borrowed, the due dates.

22. *fracted*] broken (compare *H5*, II. i. 130).

23. *smit*]An alternative form of the past participle: "smitten", or "injured".

26. *Must . . . words*] will not be found in words that are tossed back to me. The metaphor is from tennis.

29. *visage of demand*] a demanding visage. A common Elizabethan construction.

30. *When . . . wing*] i.e. when all property is in the hands of its rightful owner. "His", of course, was regularly used for "its". The saying was proverbial (Tilley B 375).

31. *gull*] With a quibble: (1) any unfledged bird, especially a gosling, and (2) a credulous fool.

Which flashes now a phœnix. Get you gone.
Caph. I go, sir.
Sen. Ay, go sir! Take the bonds along with you,
    And have the dates in. Come.
Caph.   I will, sir.
Sen.   Go. [*Exeunt.* 35

[SCENE II]

Enter Steward, with many bills in his hand.

Stew. No care, no stop; so senseless of expense,
    That he will neither know how to maintain it,
    Nor cease his flow of riot. Takes no accompt
    How things go from him, nor resumes no care

34. Ay, go sir! Take] *As Pope;* I go sir? / Take *F;* Take *Dyce.*   35. in. Come] *F;*
in compt *Theobald.*

Scene II
SCENE II] *Scene II. Timon's Hall. Rowe; not in F.*   4. resumes] *Rowe;* resume *Ff.*

32. *Which*] who.
34. *Ay, go sir!*] This interpretation of the Folio reading, first suggested by Mason, may seem more acceptable if it is compared with Lucullus' similar ironic echoing of a servant's words at III. i. 12. Most editors either omit, on the theory that the compositor unconsciously repeated the words, or print "I go, sir?" on the assumption that the Senator is absent-mindedly repeating Caphis' question.
35. *And . . . in*] Theobald's emendation "in compt" was made (and has been frequently accepted) on the reasoning that the dates were already in the bonds and (presumably) that "come" is odd when the next direction is "go"; and Steevens (1778), supporting Theobald, referred to *Mac.*, I. vi. 25–6: "Your servants ever / Have theirs, themselves and what is theirs, in compt / To make their audit at your highness' pleasure". Is it not possible, *pace* Theobald, that the dates were *not* in the bonds but only the *periods* ("six

months" etc.) and that the Senator is urging Caphis to specify the actual date so that it will be quite clear that the bonds are overdue?

Scene II
SCENE II] Most editors have the S.D. "A Hall in Timon's House", which creates insoluble difficulties when Apemantus says to the Fool at ll. 91–2: "I will go with you to Lord Timon's"; and so, having created the "inconsistency" by their own unwarranted S.D., commentators must argue that the dialogue of Apemantus, the Fool and the Page was an interpolation and meant for some other position in the play! Actually the "scene" is unlocalized.
2. *know*] trouble to find out.
3. *riot*] irresponsible revelling (one of the two normal Elizabethan meanings).
accompt] An alternative form of "account".
4–5. *nor . . . of*] and takes no interest

Of what is to continue. Never mind　　　　　5
Was to be so unwise, to be so kind.
What shall be done? He will not hear, till feel.
I must be round with him, now he comes from
　　hunting.
Fie, fie, fie, fie!

Enter CAPHIS, *and the Servants of* ISIDORE *and* VARRO.

Caph. Good even, Varro; what, you come for money?　　10
Var. Serv. Is't not your business too?
Caph. It is; and yours too, Isidore?
Isid. Serv. It is so.
Caph. Would we were all discharg'd!
Var. Serv. I fear it.　　　　　　　　　　　　　15
Caph. Here comes the lord.

Enter TIMON *and his Train, and* ALCIBIADES.

6. Was to be] *F;* Was, to be *Hanmer.*　　9. S.D.] *As Johnson; Enter Caphis, Isidore,
and Varro F.*　11. *Var. Serv.*] *Malone; Var. F (throughout scene).*　13. *Isid. Serv.*]
Malone; Isid. F (throughout scene).　16. S.D.] *Enter Timon, and his Traine F.*

in or responsibility for. There is no
parallel to this use of "resumes" in
Shakespeare, unless the Steward
implies that Timon once took the
responsibility of his own affairs but is
unwilling to *re*sume it. The double
negative is normal Elizabethan usage.

5. *what . . . continue*] what there is to
be to continue with.

6. *Was . . . kind*] was destined to be
so unwise as to be so generous. "To"
is regularly used in the sense of "as
to".

7. *hear, till feel*] listen, until he feels,
in person, the results of his folly. *Feel* is
subjunctive, and there is ellipsis of the
subject "he".

8. *round*] plain-spoken, uncom-
promising or severe. The word was
used as late as the eighteenth century
of a severe blow or whipping, and survives in the cliché "a good round
oath".

him, now] All editors print thus; but
the Folio comma can be a heavy stop,

and perhaps a modern text should
have a semi-colon or even a full-stop
after "him".

9. S.D.] The Folio's "Isidore, and
Varro" is apparently Shakespeare's
own shorthand for "The Servants of
Isidore and Varro" (see ll. 30–1) although Caphis does seem to be the
name of the servant and not of his
master the Senator in II. i. There is
similar confusion later in III. iv.

10. *Good even*] This form of salutation
was used any time after noon. Compare *Rom.,* II. iv. 114–18.

14. *Would . . . discharg'd*] Shakespeare uses "discharge" both of paying
the debt and of paying the creditor.
Hence either "I wish we were all
paid" or "I wish all debts owing to us
(or our masters) were paid".

15. *I fear it*] "It" is indefinite, and
the preposition "for" may be understood: so, "I have my fears in the
matter". The modern idiom would no
doubt be: "I fear the worst".

Tim. So soon as dinner's done, we'll forth again,
　　My Alcibiades. [*To Caphis.*] With me? What is your will?
Caph. My lord, here is a note of certain dues.
Tim. Dues? Whence are you?
Caph.　　　　　　　Of Athens here, my lord.　　20
Tim. Go to my steward.
Caph. Please it your lordship, he hath put me off
　　To the succession of new days this month.
　　My master is awak'd by great occasion
　　To call upon his own, and humbly prays you　　25
　　That with your other noble parts you'll suit,
　　In giving him his right.
Tim.　　　　　　　Mine honest friend,
　　I prithee but repair to me next morning.
Caph. Nay, good my lord—
Tim.　　　　　　　Contain thyself, good friend.
Var. Serv. One Varro's servant, my good lord—　　30
Isid. Serv. From Isidore; he humbly prays your speedy
　　payment.
Caph. If you did know, my lord, my master's wants—
Var. Serv. 'Twas due on forfeiture, my lord, six weeks and
　　past.　　35
Isid. Serv. Your steward puts me off, my lord, and I am
　　sent expressly to your lordship.
Tim. Give me breath.
　　I do beseech you, good my lords, keep on;
　　I'll wait upon you instantly.　　40
　　　　　　　[*Exeunt Alcibiades and Lords.*

18. *To Caphis*] *not in* F.　　29. lord—] *As Rowe;* Lord. F.　　33. wants—] *Rowe;*
wants. F.　　36-7.] *This ed.;* Your . . . I / Am *F;* Your . . . lord; / And I am
Malone.　　40. *Exeunt . . . Lords*] *As Rowe; not in* F.　　40-1. I'll . . . Pray you] *one
line* F.

17. *forth again*] Presumably, to their
hunting.
23. *To the . . . days*] i.e. from one day
to the next.
24. *awak'd*] aroused.
occasion] need, necessity.
25. *call upon his own*] make a call
upon, or realize, his own assets. It
might also mean "call in or request the
return of his own money".

26. *with . . . suit*] you will act consistently with your other noble qualities.
28. *repair*] return. Often simply
means "go" or "come".
29. *Contain thyself*] be calm.
34. *on forfeiture*] under penalty of
forfeit if it were not paid.
39. *keep on*] go ahead (without
me).

[*To Steward.*] Come hither. Pray you,
How goes the world, that I am thus encounter'd
With clamorous demands of debt, broken bonds,
And the detention of long since due debts
Against my honour?

Stew. [*To Caphis and other servants.*] Please you, gentlemen, 45
The time is unagreeable to this business.
Your importunacy cease till after dinner,
That I may make his lordship understand
Wherefore you are not paid.

Tim.   Do so, my friends.
See them well entertain'd.   [*Exit.*
Stew.   Pray draw near. [*Exit.* 50

Enter APEMANTUS *and Fool.*

Caph. Stay, stay; here comes the fool with Apemantus:
let's ha' some sport with 'em.
Var. Serv. Hang him, he'll abuse us!
Isid. Serv. A plague upon him, dog!
Var. Serv. How dost, fool?   55
Apem. Dost dialogue with thy shadow?
Var. Serv. I speak not to thee.
Apem. No, 'tis to thyself. [*To the Fool.*] Come away.

---

41. *To Steward*] *As Johnson; not in F.*   42. encounter'd] encountred *F.*   43.
debt, broken] *F;* date-broken *Malone.*   45. *To . . . servants*] *not in F.*   49–50.]
As Malone; Wherefore . . . paid / . . . entertain'd / . . . neere. / *F.*   50. *Exit*
[*Timon*]] *Pope; not in F.*   51.] *Scene III Pope.*   58. *To the Fool*] *Steevens; not
in F.*

42. *How . . . world*] i.e. what is happening . . .

44. *detention*] failure to pay.

45. *Against my honour*] with the result that my honour is called into question.

50. *draw near*] come this way (for the refreshment he offers them).

S.D. Enter Apemantus and Fool] The following dialogue (to l. 127) has often been thought un-Shakespearian but not on grounds of style so much as of irrelevance. The Fool does not appear elsewhere; at l. 128 Timon and

the Steward resume their conversation practically at the point at which it was broken at l. 50. At the same time, the scene has important dramatic functions: to leave the Steward time to explain details of Timon's finances to him, to provide comic relief and also to build up the impression of the general corruption of Athens. See Introduction, Section 3.

57. *I . . . thee*] Possibly intended as an insult to Apemantus: I wasn't speaking to you and therefore I wasn't speaking to a shadow.

Isid. Serv. [*To Varro's Servant.*] There's the fool hangs on
    your back already.   60
Apem. No, thou stand'st single; th'art not on him yet.
Caph. Where's the fool now?
Apem. He last ask'd the question. Poor rogues, and
    usurers' men, bawds between gold and want!
All Serv. What are we, Apemantus?   65
Apem. Asses.
All Serv. Why?
Apem. That you ask me what you are, and do not know
    yourselves. Speak to 'em, fool.
Fool. How do you, gentlemen?   70
All Serv. Gramercies, good fool. How does your mistress?
Fool. She's e'en setting on water to scald such chickens
    as you are. Would we could see you at Corinth!
Apem. Good! Gramercy.

Enter Page.

Fool. Look you, here comes my master's page.   75

59. *To Varro's Servant*] As Malone; not in F.   65. *All Serv.*] *Al. F.*   67, 71. *All
Serv.*] *All. F* (throughout scene).   71. fool. How] As Pope; Foole: / How F.
75. master's] *As Ff;* mistress's *Theobald.*

59. To Varro's Servant] Malone's
S.D. is generally adopted and certainly helps to make sense of the
passage.
59–60. *There's . . . already*] i.e. you
have already been associated with the
Fool, because of Apemantus' rejoinder
that you spoke to yourself when you
said "How dost, fool?"
62. *Where's . . . now*] i.e. you
(Isidore's servant) are the fool now,
not Varro's servant as you alleged.
63. *He last*] i.e. he who last. Compare
the proverbial "A fool asks much".
64. *bawds*] i.e. go-betweens, who
bring needy men to the usurers.
71. *Gramercies*] Derived from OF
grant (i.e. *grand*) *merci* (God reward you
greatly): thanks or many thanks. More
often used in the singular, as in l. 74,
the word did not survive the eighteenth
century.
72. *scald*] (1) Because scalding is a

method of removing feathers from
poultry (the alternative to plucking)
and (2) because "scalding" or sweat-
ing in a heated tub (the "powdering
tub") was a recognized treatment for
venereal disease.
73. *Corinth*] Ancient Corinth was
notorious for its luxury and licentiousness, and the name is apparently
applied here to the section of a city
where courtesans dwell. Compare
"Corinthian" in the sense of "profli-
gate", and *1H4*, II. iv. 13. Tilley
(M 202) sees a reference also to the
proverb "It is not given to every man
to go to Corinth".
75. *master's*] Theobald's emendation
"mistress's", accepted by nearly all
editors, may, of course, be right (the
manuscript may have read "M.");
but I see no reason for supposing that
the Fool's mistress could not have had
a "master" who employed a page or

Page. [*To the Fool.*] Why, how now, captain? What do
　　you in this wise company? How dost thou, Apeman-
　　tus?

Apem. Would I had a rod in my mouth, that I might
　　answer thee profitably.　　　　　　　　　　　　　80

Page. Prithee, Apemantus, read me the superscription of
　　these letters: I know not which is which.

Apem. Canst not read?

Page. No.

Apem. There will little learning die then that day thou　85
　　art hang'd. This is to Lord Timon; this to Alcibiades.
　　Go, thou wast born a bastard, and thou'lt die a
　　bawd.

Page. Thou wast whelp'd a dog, and thou shalt famish a
　　dog's death. Answer not; I am gone.　　　　[*Exit.*　90

Apem. E'en so thou outrun'st grace. Fool, I will go with
　　you to Lord Timon's.

Fool. Will you leave me there?

Apem. If Timon stay at home. You three serve three
　　usurers?　　　　　　　　　　　　　　　　95

All Serv. Ay; would they serv'd us.

Apem. So would I—as good a trick as ever hangman
　　serv'd thief.

Fool. Are you three usurers' men?

All Serv. Ay, fool.　　　　　　　　　　　　　　100

76. *To the Fool*] Johnson; *not in* F.　　77. company? How] *As Pope;* Company. /
How F.　　77–8. Apemantus] *Apermantus* F.　　81. *Page*] *F4; Boy F1–3.*
90. death. Answer] *As Pope;* death. / Answer F.　　91. grace. Fool] *As Capell;*
grace, / Foole F.　　94. home. You] *As Capell;* home. / You F.　　96. Ay; would]
Capell; I would *Ff.*　　97. I—as] *As Pope;* I : / As F; I— / As *Rowe.*

shared her page as well as her house.
Compare l. 104.

79–80. *that . . . profitably*] i.e. by
chastising you. Noble pointed out the
allusion to *Prov.*, xxvi. 3–4.

89–90. *famish . . . death*] by famish-
ing suffer a death appropriate to a dog.

91. *E'en so . . . grace*] i.e. grace can
never catch up with you; you will
never receive it. Fletcher explained:
"run away from my instruction,
which would help you to salvation".

92. *to Lord Timon's*] See notes on

original setting of this scene and on
l. 50.

94. *If . . . home*] Either so long as
Timon is at home there will be a
fool there *or* I shall leave you there
if Timon be there to provide fitting
company for you.

96. *Ay*] Capell's modernization perhaps makes the joke clearer. Apemantus deliberately misunderstands
the servants' reply. (The Folio regularly uses "I" for both "I" and
"ay".)

Fool. I think no usurer but has a fool to his servant; my
    mistress is one, and I am her fool. When men come
    to borrow of your masters, they approach sadly,
    and go away merry; but they enter my master's
    house merrily, and go away sadly. The reason of   105
    this?

Var. Serv. I could render one.

Apem. Do it then, that we may account thee a whore-
    master and a knave; which notwithstanding, thou
    shalt be no less esteemed.   110

Var. Serv. What is a whoremaster, fool?

Fool. A fool in good clothes, and something like thee.
    'Tis a spirit; sometime 't appears like a lord, some-
    time like a lawyer, sometime like a philosopher,
    with two stones moe than's artificial one. He is very 115
    often like a knight; and generally in all shapes that
    man goes up and down in, from fourscore to thir-
    teen, this spirit walks in.

Var. Serv. Thou art not altogether a fool.

Fool. Nor thou altogether a wise man. As much foolery 120
    as I have, so much wit thou lack'st.

Apem. That answer might have become Apemantus.

All Serv. Aside, aside; here comes Lord Timon.

Re-enter TIMON *and Steward.*

Apem. Come with me, fool, come.

Fool. I do not always follow lover, elder brother and   125
    woman; sometime the philosopher.

104. master's] *As Ff;* mistress's *Theobald.*   108. *Apem.*] *Ff; Fool Hanmer.*
120. man. As] *As Pope;* man, / *As F.*   123. S.D. *Re-enter*] *Capell; Enter F.*

101. *I think . . . servant*] I believe
there is no usurer who has not a fool for
his servant (no doubt with the implication that only a fool would serve a
usurer).

104. *master's*] See note on l. 75.

107. *one*] Obviously, that they have
lost money and gained only disease.

109–10. *which . . . esteemed*] i.e. because in Athens these professions are
regarded just as highly as any others.

115. *than's artificial one*] than his arti-

ficial stone, his philosopher's stone
which would turn base metal into
gold.

116–18. *in . . . in*] The preposition is
often so repeated, particularly, but not
only, in constructions involving long
phrases (Abbott 407).

122. *become*] been fitting for.

125–6. *lover . . . woman*] Who, in different ways and for different reasons,
might be generous (the elder brother
because he inherits the family wealth).

Stew. Pray you, walk near: I'll speak with you anon.

> [*Exeunt Apemantus, Fool and Servants.*

Tim. You make me marvel wherefore ere this time
    Had you not fully laid my state before me,
    That I might so have rated my expense   130
    As I had leave of means.

Stew.   You would not hear me.
    At many leisures I propos'd—

Tim.   Go to.
    Perchance some single vantages you took,
    When my indisposition put you back,
    And that unaptness made your minister   135
    Thus to excuse yourself.

Stew.   O my good lord,
    At many times I brought in my accompts,
    Laid them before you; you would throw them off,
    And say you found them in mine honesty.

127.] *As Pope;* Pray . . . neere / Ile *F.*   S.D.] *Exeunt F.*   128.] *Scene IV Pope.*
marvel wherefore] *As F;* marvel; wherefore *Theobald.*   131. me.] me: *Ff;* me,
Capell.   132. propos'd] *F2–4;* propose *F1.*   135. your] *F1;* you *F2–4.*
139. found] *F2;* sound *F1.*

126. *sometime*] The word is now rare or obsolete in this sense, in which it is equivalent to "sometimes", "occasionally".

127. *walk near*] remain nearby but leave us for a minute.

129. *state*] general financial position.

130. *rated*] reckoned or estimated (a once common sense of the verb, now rare).

131. *As . . . means*] in accordance with what my means or resources would allow.

132. *At . . . propos'd*] many a time when you were free and at leisure I attempted (to tell you). But the verb "propose" also had an intransitive use in Shakespeare's day, meaning to carry on a discussion or to discourse, and is possibly used in this sense here; if so, there is no need to punctuate as if Timon interrupts.

Go to.] A normal exclamation, of impatience.

133. *single vantages*] particular opportunities. (Both words are used in regular Elizabethan meanings.)

134. *When . . . back*] when, because of my temporary unwillingness, I put you off or told you to come another time.

135–6. *And . . . yourself*] and used my disinclination to listen to you (on these particular occasions) as your method of, or justification for, excusing yourself (for not trying again). "Minister" is used here in an unusual way. I take it to be the noun from the verb "to minister" used in the sense of "to prompt" or "suggest" (compare *Meas.*, IV. v. 6); but it could perhaps be "minister" in the fairly common sense of "servant" ("you made my unwillingness virtually your servant, to serve you as an excuse").

139. *you . . . honesty*] i.e. that my honesty was your real system of accounts and you needed to know nothing further.

When for some trifling present you have bid me   140
Return so much, I have shook my head and wept:
Yea, 'gainst th' authority of manners, pray'd you
To hold your hand more close. I did endure
Not seldom, nor no slight checks, when I have
Prompted you in the ebb of your estate   145
And your great flow of debts. My lov'd lord,
Though you hear now, too late, yet now's a time:
The greatest of your having lacks a half
To pay your present debts.

Tim.   Let all my land be sold.

Stew. 'Tis all engag'd, some forfeited and gone,   150
And what remains will hardly stop the mouth
Of present dues. The future comes apace.
What shall defend the interim, and at length

147.] Though you heare now (too late) yet nowes a time, *F;* Though you hear now, yet now's too late a time *Hanmer.*

142. *'gainst . . . manners*] in contradiction to what good manners dic-
tated.

143. *To . . . close*] to be less generous,
more economical. Compare the same
metaphor in the modern "close-
fisted".

144. *Not . . . checks*] rebukes that were
neither rare nor slight. "Seldom" is
used elsewhere by Shakespeare as an
adjective. The denying of a contrary
("not seldom" and "no slight") is the
common figure *litotes*; and the double
negative "nor no" is common Elizabethan usage, particularly, as here, for
emphasis.

145. *Prompted you in*] spoken like a
prompter in the theatre, and so told
you what you have to say or do about.

ebb] the flowing out (of the tide).
Here and in the following line, the
Steward is elaborating on the usual
metaphor "ebb and flow".

147. *Though . . . time*] I suspect a
reference here to an old proverb "Now
is a time"—i.e. the present moment is
just as much a moment of time as any
other; and so I understand the Steward
to mean (as Ritson virtually suggested): "Though it is now too late (for

you to do anything about it), yet even
now I must still tell you". Malone,
preserving the comma after "time",
explained: "Though now at last you
listen to my remonstrances, yet now
your affairs are in such a state that
(the whole of your remaining fortune
will scarce pay half your debts). You
are therefore wise too late".

148–9. *The . . . debts*] what you have
(your property), even if valued at the
highest possible figure, still is only half
of what is necessary to pay your immediate debts.

150. *engag'd*] mortgaged (the original meaning).

152. *present dues*] immediate debts.
apace] Literally, at a pace; hence,
swiftly.

153–4. *What . . . reck'ning?*] The
interim, or intervening time (compare
Cæs., II. i. 62–4), is metaphorically
spoken of as a position to be defended
against the attacks of debts about to
fall due and so approaching like an
attacking army. An "interim" could
also be a provisional arrangement, and
the word might conceivably be used
here in this sense, of mortgages, promissory notes, etc. For "at length"

How goes our reck'ning?

Tim. To Lacedæmon did my land extend. 155

Stew. O my good lord, the world is but a word:
Were it all yours, to give it in a breath,
How quickly were it gone!

Tim. You tell me true.

Stew. If you suspect my husbandry or falsehood,
Call me before th' exactest auditors, 160
And set me on the proof. So the gods bless me,
When all our offices have been oppress'd
With riotous feeders, when our vaults have wept
With drunken spilth of wine, when every room
Hath blaz'd with lights and bray'd with minstrelsy, 165
I have retir'd me to a wasteful cock

---

156. word] *F1*; world *F2–4*. 159. or] *F*; of *various conj.* 165. bray'd] *Pope*;
braid *F*. 166. me ... cock] me to a wastefull cocke *F*; me from a wasteful cock
conj. Knight; me, like a wasteful cock *conj. Mitford*; (me too a wasteful cock) *conj.*
Staunton; me to a wakeful cot *Daniel*; me to a wakeful couch *Deighton*; etc.

Deighton compared *Mer.V.*, II. ii. 84–
5: "at the length truth will out".
"What steps can be taken to meet the
immediate situation and how is our
problem to be solved in the long run?"

155. *Lacedæmon*] Sparta.

156–8. *the world . . . gone*] even the
world is, in one sense, only a word; and
if it were all yours, and could be given
away in one breath, it would quickly
disappear.

159. *suspect . . . falsehood*] i.e. if you
suspect me of falsehood in my management. "Husbandry", originally meaning management of a household, also
came to mean economy or thrift (i.e.
good husbandry).

161. *on the proof*] The common expression would be "to the proof". But
compare *Oth.*, III. iii. 191.

So . . . me] Compare "So help me
God". "May the gods not bless me if
what I say is not true".

162. *offices*] all those rooms of a house
devoted to "service" or household
duties, including, for example, the
pantry and the kitchen.

162–3. *have . . . feeders*] have had to
cope with the "oppression" or extra
weight of people regaling themselves
at your expense and without restraint.
"Feeder" is used both of one who
supplies food and of one who takes it
(particularly one who takes it parasi-
tically); from the latter use, it also
came to mean "servant", as witness
Ant., III. xiii. 109.

164. *spilth*] spilling. The wine spilt is
represented as the tears wept by the
wine-cellars.

165. *minstrelsy*] playing and singing,
as of minstrels. But that the word
"minstrel" had come to have a bad
connotation is suggested by Mercutio's
use of it, *Rom.*, III. i. 48–50.

166. *I . . . cock*] The emendations
listed in the textual apparatus will
suggest the general dissatisfaction with
the line; and Shadwell apparently did
not know what it meant, since in a passage where he otherwise preserved
Shakespeare word for word (although
he transferred it to Apemantus), he
substituted: "I have retir'd / To my
poor homely Cell, and set my eyes / At
flow for thee". But those who prefer,

And set mine eyes at flow.

Tim.   Prithee no more.

Stew. Heavens, have I said, the bounty of this lord!
How many prodigal bits have slaves and peasants
This night englutted! Who is not Timon's?   170
What heart, head, sword, force, means, but is Lord
    Timon's,
Great Timon, noble, worthy, royal Timon?
Ah, when the means are gone that buy this praise,
The breath is gone whereof this praise is made.
Feast-won, fast-lost; one cloud of winter show'rs,   175
These flies are couch'd.

Tim.   Come, sermon me no further.
No villainous bounty yet hath pass'd my heart;
Unwisely, not ignobly, have I given.
Why dost thou weep? Canst thou the conscience lack,

171. Lord] *Rowe; L. F.*   175. Feast-won] *Pope;* Feast won *F;* Fast won *conj.*
Becket.   fast-lost] *Theobald;* fast lost *F.*

for example, "wakeful cot" find it difficult to explain how the other reading
got into the text; and Caroline Spurgeon's proof (p. 193) that vaults–eyes–
tears was a common chain of association for Shakespeare must also be
remembered. The best explanation is
probably that of Clarke, Ridley, and
Sisson (*New Readings*, p. 170), who see
an extension of the metaphor in the
previous lines and take the Steward to
mean that he has gone below to a wine
barrel whose tap is running and added
his tears to the general flow.

169. *prodigal bits*] "Prodigal" or
wasteful is transferred from the person
who lavishly supplies the food, to the
food itself. For "bits", meaning morsels of ood, compare *LLL.*, I. i. 26–7.
The word survives in "tit-bits".

170. *englutted*] swallowed, gulped
down.

Who . . . Timon's?] who does not
claim to be devoted to or specially
favoured by Timon?

172. *Great . . . Timon?*] The Steward
ironically echoes the words of the
flatterers.

175. *Feast-won, fast-lost*] what is won
only by providing a feast is quickly
lost; but there is a quibble on "fast" in
the sense of "fasting", the direct opposite of "feasting", and so a secondary
meaning: "would be lost if fasting
were necessary instead of feasting".
The vowels in "feast" and "fast" were
then closer to each other than they
are in modern English pronunciation.
(See, for example, Kökeritz, p. 167.)

175–6. *one cloud . . . couch'd*] if there
is even one cloud bringing winter
showers, these flies go to shelter.

177. *No . . . heart*] at least my heart
has never yet given approval to any
expenditure that involved dishonesty.

178. *Unwisely . . . given*] A finer
judgment on Timon's situation than
has been given by many commentators.

179–80. *Canst . . . friends?*] "Conscience" had a wider meaning in
Shakespeare's day: "knowledge" or
"conviction", not necessarily involving judgment of good and evil. Hence,
"can you really doubt that I shall have
friends?"

To think I shall lack friends? Secure thy heart.   180
If I would broach the vessels of my love,
And try the arguments of hearts by borrowing,
Men and men's fortunes could I frankly use
As I can bid thee speak.

Stew.   Assurance bless your thoughts.

Tim. And in some sort these wants of mine are
          crown'd,   185
That I account them blessings; for by these
Shall I try friends. You shall perceive how you
Mistake my fortunes; I am wealthy in my friends.
Within there! Flaminius! Servilius!

Enter FLAMINIUS, SERVILIUS, *and another Servant.*

Servants. My lord, my lord.   190

Tim. I will dispatch you severally: [*to Servilius*] you to
Lord Lucius; [*to Flaminius*] to Lord Lucullus you (I
hunted with his honour to-day); [*to Third Servant*]
you, to Sempronius. Commend me to their loves;

187–8.] *As Capell (Pope); Shall , . . perceiue / . . . Fortunes: / . . . Friends F.*
189. Flaminius!] *As Rowe; Flauius, F.*   190.] *Scene V Pope.*   S.D.] *Enter three*
Seruants F.   191. severally: you] *seuerally. / You F.*   *to Servilius] not in F.*
192. *to Flaminius] not in F.*   193. *to Third Servant] not in F.*

---

180. *Secure*] to make free from care
or apprehension (Latin *securus*).

181. *would ... love*] wanted to tap the
containers in which people's love for
me is stored.

182. *try the arguments*] test the protestations. I agree with Deighton in
querying the interpretation of "argument" here as a synopsis, the summary
of the subject-matter of a book, and of
"try" as "sample".

183. *frankly*] as frankly (freely,
without concealment or deceit).

184. *Assurance ... thoughts*] may your
thoughts have the blessing of being
proved right.

185. *in some sort*] in one way.

crown'd] given a special added dignity or significance. Deighton compared *Ant.*, I. ii. 174, "this grief is
crown'd with consolation".

186. *That*] so that, or, possibly, *in*

that, inasmuch as.

189. *Flaminius!*] This, Rowe's emendation for the Folio "Flavius," is
generally accepted; but as Wright
insisted (though he drew strange conclusions) "Flavius" makes a better
metrical line. "Flavius" is therefore
more likely to have been the author's
slip (if slip it was) than the scribe's
or compositor's. Perhaps, however,
Shakespeare was still thinking of
"Flavius" as a possible name for the
servant later called "Flaminius" or
conceivably was using it here as the
name for the third servant, the one
who goes to Sempronius. All this is
further reason for not always calling
the Steward "Flavius" because of
I. ii. 153. See Introduction, Sections
1B and 4.

191. *severally*] separately, on various
missions.

and I am proud, say, that my occasions have found   195
time to use 'em toward a supply of money. Let the
request be fifty talents.

Flam. As you have said, my lord.   [*Exeunt Servants.*

Stew. [*Aside.*] Lord Lucius and Lucullus? Humh!

Tim. [*To Steward.*] Go you, sir, to the senators,   200
    Of whom, even to the state's best health, I have
    Deserv'd this hearing: bid 'em send o' th' instant
    A thousand talents to me.

Stew.   I have been bold,
    For that I knew it the most general way,
    To them to use your signet and your name;   205
    But they do shake their heads, and I am here
    No richer in return.

Tim.   Is 't true? can 't be?

Stew. They answer in a joint and corporate voice
    That now they are at fall, want treasure, cannot
    Do what they would, are sorry; you are honourable,   210
    But yet they could have wish'd—they know not;
    Something hath been amiss—a noble nature

---

198. S.D.] *not in F.*   199. *Aside*] *Capell; not in F.*   200. *To Steward*] *As Rowe; not in F; To another Serv. Malone.*   201. health,] *F3–4;* health; *F1;* health? *F2.* 209. treasure] *F2;* treature *F1.*

195. *occasions*] needs (as before).

196. *time*] the occasion or opportunity.

197. *fifty talents*] A preposterous sum if it be remembered that a talent was worth, in terms of modern money, something between £500 and £1,000. Shakespeare has forgotten what a talent is worth (see note on I. i. 98)— unless one argues that it is Timon who has no notion whatever of the value of money. (But the Steward comments on the proposal to address the request to Lucius and Lucullus, not on the amount itself.) And by l. 203 Timon is asking for a *thousand* talents (though he asks it of the senators as a group).

201. *even . . . health*] to the utmost limits of, but without imperilling, the prosperity of the State. Wright surprisingly took it to mean "because of the service I, Timon, have given to

preserve the 'health' of the state" (p. 73). Shadwell did not alter the phrase in his version.

204. *general*] usual. Johnson explained it as "compendious" (comprehensive), "the way to try many at a time".

205. *signet*] The signet ring was often sent with a messenger as a guarantee that he was duly authorized to act. So Richard III apparently gives his to Tyrrel, when he commissions Tyrrel to murder the princes in the Tower (IV. ii. 80).

208. *corporate*] The old past participle, "united in one body".

209. *at fall*] at a low ebb; but "fall" meant also a loss of value, depreciation, and so perhaps "at fall" means "in a period when their money was losing its purchasing power".

want] lack, need.

May catch a wrench—would all were well—'tis pity—
And so, intending other serious matters,
After distasteful looks, and these hard fractions,   215
With certain half-caps, and cold-moving nods,
They froze me into silence.

Tim.   You gods reward them!
Prithee, man, look cheerly. These old fellows
Have their ingratitude in them hereditary;
Their blood is cak'd, 'tis cold, it seldom flows;   220
'Tis lack of kindly warmth they are not kind;
And nature, as it grows again toward earth,
Is fashion'd for the journey, dull and heavy.
Go to Ventidius. Prithee, be not sad,
Thou art true and honest; ingeniously I speak,   225
No blame belongs to thee. Ventidius lately
Buried his father, by whose death he's stepp'd
Into a great estate. When he was poor,
Imprison'd, and in scarcity of friends,
I clear'd him with five talents. Greet him from me,   230

---

216. cold-moving] *Theobald;* cold moving *Ff.*   224.] *As F;* Go . . . Ventidius
[*To a Serv.*] 'Pr'ythee [*To Flavius.*] . . . sad, *Malone.*   224, 226. Ventidius]
Ventiddius F.

213. *catch a wrench*] accidentally be twisted awry (so that it acts in a different way).

214. *intending*] *Either* pretending (as elsewhere in Shakespeare) *or* occupying themselves with. For the second sense, now recorded by *O.E.D.*, Steevens cited an apt parallel in *The Spanish Curate.*

215. *distasteful looks*] *Not* looks distasteful to the Steward or unpleasant, *but* looks indicating that they found the matter distasteful.

hard fractions] harsh fragments of sentences. For "fraction" in this sense, compare *Troil.*, v. ii. 158, "The fractions of her faith, orts of her love"; but in the same play, II. iii. 107, the word means "discord" and it is perhaps that sense which makes easier the adjective "hard".

216. *half-caps*] salutations only half given.

cold-moving] coldly-moving, indicating only coldness (as well as producing it).

217. *You . . . them!*] Spoken, one imagines, more in sorrow than in anger.

218. *cheerly*] cheerful (or cheerily). Compare *Tp.*, I. i. 6.

219. *hereditary*] as a natural inheritance coming to them with their years.

221. *kindly*] With a quibble: (1) generous, (2) natural. Similarly in "kind". Compare *Ham.*, I. ii. 65: "A little more than kin and less than kind".

222. *as . . . earth*] i.e. as it approaches the grave (and will again become earth, or dust).

225. *ingeniously*] candidly, in all sincerity. "Ingenious" was then almost interchangeable with "ingenuous", originally meaning "of noble birth" and so "noble" generally.

Bid him suppose some good necessity
Touches his friend, which craves to be remember'd
With those five talents. That had, give 't these fellows
To whom 'tis instant due. Ne'er speak or think
That Timon's fortunes 'mong his friends can sink.   235
Stew. I would I could not think it.
That thought is bounty's foe;
Being free itself, it thinks all others so.   [*Exeunt.*

236–7.] *As F; one line Capell.*

231. *good necessity*] genuine need. "Good" may be only intensive, but Steevens (1793) compared III. ii. 39: "If his occasion were not virtuous".

232–3. *which . . . talents*] which calls out for the return of those five talents as proof that he remembers my earlier action.

233. *That had*] when it is in your possession. (Timon never doubts that Ventidius will repay his debt.)

234. *instant*] instantly, now.

235. *'mong his friends*] in the midst of friends.

237. *That . . . foe*] Commentators pass over this in silence but I am not sure that I understand it. Perhaps "That belief (that one's friends will not desert) is the enemy to a truly generous person—*because* it means that he gives his money away to those who will not reciprocate"; perhaps "That knowledge (that friends can desert) is fatal to generosity such as Timon's".

238. *free*] generous, open-handed.

[ACT III

SCENE I]

FLAMINIUS *waiting to speak with Lucullus from his Master.*
Enter a Servant to him.

Serv. I have told my lord of you; he is coming down to you.
Flam. I thank you, sir.

Enter LUCULLUS.

Serv. Here's my lord.
Lucul. [*Aside.*] One of Lord Timon's men? A gift, I war-
    rant. Why, this hits right: I dreamt of a silver basin   5
    and ewer to-night.—Flaminius, honest Flaminius,
    you are very respectively welcome, sir. Fill me some
    wine. [*Exit Servant.*] And how does that honourable,
    complete, free-hearted gentleman of Athens, thy
    very bountiful good lord and master?   10
Flam. His health is well, sir.
Lucul. I am right glad that his health is well, sir. And

ACT III
Scene I

ACT III SCENE I] *As Rowe; not in F.*   S.D. *Flaminius*] *F; The City. | Flami-
nius | Rowe; Lucullus's House in Athens. | Flaminius | Theobald.*   *Lucullus*] *Rowe;
a Lord F.*   *Master. Enter*] *Rowe; Master, enters F.*   4. *Aside*] *Johnson; not in F.*
8. S.D.] *Capell; not in F.*

S.D. Lucullus . . . him] Another
"descriptive" S.D. that must come
from author's manuscript or direct
transcript.

5. *hits right*] fits in perfectly, is
appropriate.

5-6. *silver . . . ewer*] Malone, noting
that basins and ewers were highly
prized possessions in Shakespeare's
day, aptly quoted from Gremio's bid
for Bianca: "First, as you know, my

house within the city / Is richly fur-
nished with plate and gold; / Basins
and ewers to lave her dainty hands"
(*Shr.*, II. i. 348–50).

7. *respectively*] respectfully, with becoming respect (as often).

9. *complete*] The Elizabethan and
Jacobean ideal was "the *complete*
gentleman", that being the title of
Peacham's famous manual of conduct.

what hast thou there under thy cloak, pretty Flaminius?

Flam. Faith, nothing but an empty box, sir, which, in   15
my lord's behalf, I come to entreat your honour to
supply; who, having great and instant occasion to
use fifty talents, hath sent to your lordship to furnish
him, nothing doubting your present assistance there-
in.   20

Lucul. La, la, la, la: "nothing doubting", says he? Alas,
good lord; a noble gentleman 'tis, if he would not
keep so good a house. Many a time and often I ha'
din'd with him, and told him on 't, and come again
to supper to him of purpose to have him spend less;   25
and yet he would embrace no counsel, take no warning by my coming. Every man has his fault, and
honesty is his. I ha' told him on 't, but I could ne'er
get him from 't.

Re-enter Servant, with wine.

Serv. Please your lordship, here is the wine.   30
Lucul. Flaminius, I have noted thee always wise. Here's
to thee.
Flam. Your lordship speaks your pleasure.
Lucul. I have observed thee always for a towardly prompt
spirit, give thee thy due, and one that knows what   35

29. *Re-enter*] Capell; *Enter* F.

13. *pretty*] In its more general
meaning, expressing admiration not
only of appearance but also of manner
and worth. But Lucullus is probably
meant to sound condescending.

17. *supply*] fill. Compare "supply a
vacancy".

18. *fifty talents*] See II. ii. 197 and n.
furnish] supply (with what is necessary).

19. *present*] immediate.

23. *so good a house*] one in which hospitality is so lavish.

24–5. *come again to supper*] have returned for supper; or, on still other
occasions have come to supper.

25. *have him*] i.e. persuade him to.
26. *embrace*] accept.
27. *by*] from. The phrase is, of
course, unintentionally ironical.

27. *Every . . . fault*] The proverb
comes glibly to Lucullus' lips.

28. *honesty*] Probably, as Mason suggested, in the obsolete sense of
liberality (*O.E.D.* 3 c). Liberality to a
Lucullus *is* over-generosity.

33. *Your . . . pleasure*] you are pleased
to say so, i.e. it is good of you to say so
(when I am so undeserving). Flaminius is now on his guard.

34. *towardly*] friendly.
prompt] well-disposed.

belongs to reason; and canst use the time well, if the
time use thee well. Good parts in thee. [*To the Ser-*
vant.] Get you gone, sirrah. [*Exit Servant.*] Draw
nearer, honest Flaminius. Thy lord's a bountiful
gentleman: but thou art wise, and thou know'st well   40
enough, although thou com'st to me, that this is no
time to lend money, especially upon bare friendship,
without security. Here's three solidares for thee;
good boy, wink at me, and say thou saw'st me not.
Fare thee well.   45

Flam. Is't possible the world should so much differ,
　　And we alive that lived? Fly, damned baseness,
　　To him that worships thee!
　　　　　　　　　　　[*Throwing the money back at Lucullus.*
Lucul. Ha? Now I see thou art a fool, and fit for thy
　　master.   [*Exit.*   50
Flam. May these add to the number that may scald thee!
　　Let molten coin be thy damnation,
　　Thou disease of a friend, and not himself!

37, 38. S.D.] *not in F.*　　48. S.D.] *As Capell; not in F.*

36–7. *if . . . well*] i.e. if you have
reasonable opportunity, if luck is your
way.

37. *parts*] qualities, attainments.
Compare "a man of parts".

42. *especially . . . friendship*] Shakespeare's ironical portrait of Lucullus
is nowhere finer than in these four
words.

43. *solidares*] The coin is not known,
but there was a Roman coin the
solidus (pl. *solidi*) and an Italian coin,
the *solido*, mentioned by Florio. Perhaps Shakespeare uses "solidares" as a
plural for one of these. A solidus was
worth 25 denarii, roughly a pound,
but the name was applied in England
to a shilling (and is now used of the
shilling-mark, the sloping line that se-
parates shillings and pence, as in 3/6).

44. *wink at me*] We might say "shut
your eyes". Compare *Mac.*, I. iv. 52.

46. *differ*] change.

47. *And . . . lived?*] and yet the same
people still be alive? Flaminius may be

expressing surprise either that the
change could have come about in one
lifetime or that anybody could have
seen it and lived.

51. *May . . . thee!*] The following line
makes the meaning clearer. *Either*
scalding with one's own coin, melted,
is thought of as part of the damnation
of the covetous in Hell (and Steevens,
1778, quoted a possible parallel) *or*, as
Mason suggested, there is reference to
the story of the Parthians pouring molten gold down the throat of the dead
Marcus Crassus in mockery of his
great avarice. It will be noted,
however, that classical allusion is
astonishingly rare in *Timon*: perhaps
because Shakespeare was not working
continuously from a detailed literary
source which suggested it?

53. *disease*] The stress is on the first
syllable or equally on the two.
Lucullus is said to bear the same relation to a true friend ("himself") as a
disease bears to a healthy body. Com-

Has friendship such a faint and milky heart
It turns in less than two nights? O you gods!   55
I feel my master's passion. This slave unto his honour
Has my lord's meat in him:
Why should it thrive and turn to nutriment
When he is turn'd to poison?
O may diseases only work upon 't,   60
And when he's sick to death, let not that part of nature
Which my lord paid for, be of any power
To expel sickness, but prolong his hour!   [*Exit.*

[SCENE II]

Enter LUCIUS, *with* HOSTILIUS *and two other Strangers.*

Luc. Who, the Lord Timon? He is my very good friend
      and an honourable gentleman.
First Stran. We know him for no less, though we are but
      strangers to him. But I can tell you one thing, my
      lord, and which I hear from common rumours: now   5

56–7.] *As F; slave,* / Unto his honour, . . . him / *Steevens (1778).*

Scene ii

SCENE II] *Pope; not in F.*   S.D. *Enter] F; A publick Place. | Enter | Capell; A
publick Street | Enter | Theobald.   Hostilius . . . strangers] Sisson; three strangers F.*
3. *First Stran.] As Rowe; 1 F.*

pare l. 59 below. There may, secon-
darily, be something of the old literal
meaning of dis-ease, i.e. discomfort
or cause of discomfort (*O.E.D.* 1).
      55. *turns*] curdles (carrying on the
notion of "milky" in the previous line).
      56. *my master's passion*] the violent
suffering my master himself would feel
or is feeling. Here and in the following
sentence there are clearly religious
overtones.
      This . . . honour] A bitterly ironical
description of Lucullus as the devoted
slave of his sense of honour. Steevens
suggested commas after "slave" and
"honour", interpreting "This slave,
much to his honour, still has . . ." But
in that case why "slave"?

61–2. *that . . . for*] i.e. that part of his
body developed by Timon's food.
      63. *his hour*] i.e. of suffering before
death.

Scene ii

SCENE II.] Another excellent example of the "unlocalized scene",
common in Elizabethan drama. The
"setting" was *any* place where Lucius
and three strangers might conceivably
meet; the dramatist himself had no
special location in mind but thought in
terms of his bare stage.
      3. *know . . . less*] know him by repute
as being all that you say (and possibly
more).
      5. *and which*] Abbott does not discuss

Lord Timon's happy hours are done and past, and
his estate shrinks from him.

Luc. Fie, no, do not believe it; he cannot want for money.

Host. But believe you this, my lord, that not long ago, one
of his men was with the Lord Lucullus, to borrow   10
so many talents, nay, urg'd extremely for 't, and
showed what necessity belong'd to 't, and yet was
denied.

Luc. How?

Host. I tell you, denied, my lord.   15

Luc. What a strange case was that! Now before the gods,
I am asham'd on 't. Denied that honourable man?
There was very little honour show'd in 't. For my
own part, I must needs confess I have received some
small kindnesses from him, as money, plate, jewels,   20
and such like trifles—nothing comparing to his; yet
had he mistook him, and sent to me, I should ne'er
have denied his occasion so many talents.

Enter SERVILIUS.

Ser. See, by good hap, yonder's my lord; I have sweat to
see his honour. My honour'd lord!   25

8. *Luc.*] *Lucius F.*   9, 15. *Hostilius*] *As Sisson; 2 F.*   13. denied] deny'de
F.   14, 16, 30, 43. *Luc.*] *Luci. F.*   22. mistook] *As F;* not mistook *conj.*
Johnson.

this use of the relative. "And one
which".

  11. *so many*] an indefinite number of.
Apparently Shakespeare intended to
put in the exact figure on revision. So
in l. 23 and l. 35. See Introduction,
Section 3.
  urg'd] pressed or importuned.
  21. *his*] i.e. Lucullus'.
  22. *mistook him*] Various emendations have been made, either because
the reflexive construction with "mistake" has no parallel in Shakespeare or
because the meaning has not seemed
clear. But the verb "mistake", particularly in something like its literal
meaning (mis+take), so often has as
object a person, and particularly a
pronoun, that the reading need not be

questioned. I take it that Lucius is
being humorously ironical: "had
Timon made a slip and sent to *me*
(the right person) . . ." Such an interpretation adds to the irony of the following conversation with Sempronius.
Steevens (1778) took it to mean "made
a mistake" in the sense of overlook-
ing Lucullus' greater indebtedness to
him; Onions and Deighton explained
it as "misdoubted".
  23. *denied his occasion*] i.e. denied him
in his need.
  24. *by good hap*] by good luck.
  sweat] i.e. made myself perspire in
my anxiety. The word does not
necessarily suggest violent *physical*
movement but may be used metaphorically of eagerness.

Luc. Servilius? You are kindly met, sir. Fare thee well;
commend me to thy honourable virtuous lord, my
very exquisite friend.

Ser. May it please your honour, my lord hath sent—

Luc. Ha? What has he sent? I am so much endeared to   30
that lord; he's ever sending. How shall I thank him,
think'st thou? And what has he sent now?

Ser. H'as only sent his present occasion now, my lord:
requesting your lordship to supply his instant use
with so many talents.   35

Luc. I know his lordship is but merry with me,
He cannot want fifty — five hundred talents.

Ser. But in the meantime he wants less, my lord.
If his occasion were not virtuous,
I should not urge it half so faithfully.   40

Luc. Dost thou speak seriously, Servilius?

Ser. Upon my soul, 'tis true, sir.

Luc. What a wicked beast was I to disfurnish myself
against such a good time, when I might ha' shown
myself honourable! How unluckily it happen'd, that   45
I should purchase the day before for a little part, and
undo a great deal of honour! Servilius, now before

26, 36. *Luc.*] *Lucil. F.*   33. H'as] *F4*; Has *F1–3*.   37. fifty—five] fifty fiue *F*;
fifty-five *Capell*.   46–7. for . . . undo] *As F*; for a little dirt, and undo *Theobald*;
for a little profit and undo *conj. Heath*; and for a little part undo *conj. Jackson*.

30. *endeared*] obliged (as before, in
I. ii. 228).

34. *supply . . . use*] make good his
financial position by providing him
for immediate use with . . . ("Use" was
the regular word for the employment
of borrowed money; it also, of course,
meant "interest".)

37. *fifty—five hundred*] It has been
suggested that Shakespeare wrote 50
and 500 (probably in figures) as alter-
natives, intending to strike out one of
them, and that both should therefore
not be in the text. In any case, Lucius
is intended to mention a huge sum—or
two ("fifty or even five hundred")—
and say that Timon is already so rich
that no sum, however large, could add
significantly to his wealth. Servilius

dryly disregards the exaggeration and
tries to keep Lucius to the facts.

39. *virtuous*] incurred in honesty, not
the result of waste, for example.

43–4. *disfurnish myself against*] leave
myself inadequately prepared for.
"Against" has the full meaning of "to
meet the eventuality of", as when we
insure *against* accident or death.

46–7. *for . . . honour*] Emendations are
unnecessary. "Part", I think, means
roughly "business" but the word is
chosen because it *is* vague: Lucius,
who is lying, cannot afford to be too
specific, and says that unfortunately he
invested his money in a small financial
transaction and so lost the opportunity
of doing something very honourable,
lending money to Timon.

the gods, I am not able to do (the more beast, I say!)
—I was sending to use Lord Timon myself, these
gentlemen can witness; but I would not, for the   50
wealth of Athens, I had done 't now. Commend me
bountifully to his good lordship; and I hope his
honour will conceive the fairest of me, because I have
no power to be kind. And tell him this from me: I
count it one of my greatest afflictions, say, that I can-   55
not pleasure such an honourable gentleman. Good
Servilius, will you befriend me so far as to use mine
own words to him?

Ser. Yes, sir, I shall.   [*Exit.*

Luc. [*Calling out after him.*] I'll look you out a good turn,   60
Servilius.

[*To the others.*] True, as you said, Timon is shrunk
    indeed;

And he that's once denied will hardly speed.   [*Exit.*

First Stran. Do you observe this, Hostilius?

Host. Ay, too well.

First Stran.   Why, this is the world's soul,   65
    And just of the same piece

Is every flatterer's sport. Who can call him his friend

---

48. beast, I say] *As Reed;* beast I say *F;* beast I, say *Hanmer;* beast I, I say *Collier*
(*edn 2*).   59. S.D.] *As F; after 61 Johnson.*   60. *Calling . . . him*] *not in F.*
62. S.D.] *not in F.*   63. denied] deny'de, *F.*   64, 65, 78. *First Stran.*] *1 F.*
65. *Hostilius*] *2 F.*   65–8.] *As F;* Why . . . piece / . . . him / . . . in / *Capell;*
Why . . . soul / . . . sport / . . . friend / . . . knowing / *Pope.*   67. sport] *F;* spirit
Theobald.

49. *use*] make use of, i.e. borrow
from.

53. *conceive the fairest*] think the best.

55. *say*] It is evidence of a certain
limitation in Pope as a critic that he
wanted to omit "say", which helps
to establish the colloquial but hypocritical tone of the speech. Sykes found
it and also the use of "pleasure" as
meaning "accommodate with a loan"
a mannerism of Middleton and therefore attributed to him a share in this
part of the play, quite implausibly.

60. *look . . . turn*] think it up a good turn
to do for you ("one good turn deserves
another"). The phrase has more point
if it is called out after Servilius, who

has turned on his heel and left—i.e. i
the Folio "Exit" is left in its position
and not transferred to the end of l. 61.
Fitzroy Pyle also made this point, in
N. & Q., cxcvii, 3 (Feb. 1952), 48–9.

62. *shrunk*] i.e. diminished in estate.

63. *speed*] flourish (as often).

65. *the world's soul*] the principle on
which the world works. The Stranger
is contrasting this with the principle of
spiritual harmony on which the uni-
verse was commonly believed to be
constructed.

66. *just . . . piece*] exactly of the same
kind.

67. *sport*] plaything or diversion.
Emendation seems unnecessary.

That dips in the same dish? For in my knowing
Timon has been this lord's father,
And kept his credit with his purse;   70
Supported his estate; nay, Timon's money
Has paid his men their wages. He ne'er drinks
But Timon's silver treads upon his lip;
And yet—O see the monstrousness of man,
When he looks out in an ungrateful shape!—   75
He does deny him, in respect of his,
What charitable men afford to beggars.

Second Stran. Religion groans at it.

First Stran.   For mine own part,
I never tasted Timon in my life, .
Nor came any of his bounties over me,   80
To mark me for his friend. Yet I protest,
For his right noble mind, illustrious virtue,
And honourable carriage,
Had his necessity made use of me,
I would have put my wealth into donation,   85

---

78. *Second Stran.*] *3 F.*   78-9. For . . . life] *As Rowe; one line F.*   85. donation]
F; location conj. Deighton.

68. *That . . . dish*] Steevens (1793) noted that the phrase is again biblical: *Matt.*, xxvi. 23, referring, of course, to Judas.

69. *been . . . father*] i.e. has acted as a father to him.

70. *kept . . . purse*] kept up, sustained his (Lucius') credit with his (Timon's) money.

72. *his*] i.e. Lucius'.

73. *treads upon*] presses upon. There is no close parallel in Shakespeare to this figurative use.

75. *When . . . shape*] *Either* when it (the monstrousness, personified) appears, or shows itself, in the form of ingratitude *or* when man shows the ungrateful side of his nature.

76-7. *He . . . beggars*] he (Lucius) refuses to Timon help which, in relation to what Lucius possesses, represents no greater assistance than charitable men give to any beggar. For "in respect of" in the sense of "in relation

to", compare *Ado*, III. iv. 16-19: "the Duchess of Milan's gown that they praise so . . .'s but a night-gown in respect of yours", and *LLL.*, v. ii. 639-40.

79. *tasted*] tested, had experience of. Compare *Troil.*, III. ii. 99: "praise us as we are tasted, allow us as we prove".

80. *Nor . . . me*] nor did any of his bounty descend unasked upon me.

83. *carriage*] conduct.

85-6. *I . . . him*] These lines present a difficulty, in that there is no exact contemporary parallel to "donation". But the word seems to be used in the legal sense defined by *O.E.D.* as "the legal process of transferring the ownership of a thing from oneself to another". Deighton suggested "location" in the legal sense of "letting out for hire", and "donation" is certainly a possible misreading of it; but the emendation hardly makes better sense. "Return'd" is probably also used as a technical term, implying the

And the best half should have return'd to him,
So much I love his heart. But I perceive
Men must learn now with pity to dispense,
For policy sits above conscience.　　　　　　　[*Exeunt.*

[SCENE III]

Enter Timon's Third Servant with SEMPRONIUS, *another of
Timon's friends.*

Sem. Must he needs trouble me in 't? Humh!
　　'Bove all others?
　　He might have tried Lord Lucius, or Lucullus;
　　And now Ventidius is wealthy too,
　　Whom he redeem'd from prison. All these　　　　5
　　Owes their estates unto him.
Serv.　　　　　　　　　　　　　My lord,
　　They have all been touch'd and found base metal,
　　For they have all denied him.
Sem. How? Have they denied him?
　　Has Ventidius and Lucullus denied him?　　　　10

Scene III

SCENE III] *Pope; not in F.*　　　S.D. *Enter*] *F; Sempronius's House. | Enter | Steevens
(1778).　　Timon's Third Servant*] a third seruant F.*　　1–2.] *As F; one line Pope.*
4, 10. Ventidius] *Ventidgius F.*　　7–8.] *As F; They . . . for / They . . . him.
Capell.*　　9, 10. denied] *deny'de F.*

return from an investment, and here, I
assume, "return" from the legal transfer. An interpretation of the lines originally suggested by Steevens (1778),
and accepted by Mason and others, is:
"I would have treated my wealth as a
present originally received from him,
and on this occasion have returned to
him the half of that whole for which I
supposed myself to be indebted to his
bounty". This makes excellent sense
but is hard to derive from the text as it
stands.

89. *policy*] The word has a connotation of evil ("Machiavellian policy"):
working towards a desired end without
caring about the means used.

Scene III

S.D. another of Timon's friends]
Another characteristic "descriptive"
direction. Since this scene has often
been thought un-Shakespearian, the
similarity of this S.D. to others in the
play should be noticed.

6. *Owes*] For this form of the third
person plural in "s", see Abbott 333.

7. *all*] The rejection by Ventidius
has not, of course, been shown. See
Introduction, Sections 1B and 7.

touch'd] tested (by being rubbed
upon the touchstone).

10. *Has*] For the singular verb preceding such a plural subject, see
Abbott 335.

And does he send to me? Three? Humh?
It shows but little love or judgment in him.
Must I be his last refuge? His friends, like physicians,
Thrive, give him over; must I take th' cure upon me?
H'as much disgrac'd me in 't; I'm angry at him   15
That might have known my place. I see no sense for 't
But his occasions might have wooed me first:
For, in my conscience, I was the first man
That e'er received gift from him.
And does he think so backwardly of me now,   20
That I'll requite it last? No:
So it may prove an argument of laughter
To th' rest, and 'mongst lords I be thought a fool.
I'd rather than the worth of thrice the sum,
H'ad sent to me first, but for my mind's sake;   25
I'd such a courage to do him good. But now return,
And with their faint reply this answer join:
Who bates mine honour shall not know my coin.   [*Exit.*

---

14. Thrive] *F;* That thriv'd *F2–4;* Thrice *Knight, conj. Johnson.*   15. H'as]
Rowe; Has *F.*   23. I] *F2–4; not in F1.*   25. H'ad] *F4;* Had *F1–3.*

Ventidius and Lucullus] It seems too
mechanical altogether for editors to
insist that the name of Lucius ought to
be included too.
  14. *Thrive, give him over*] Emendation
has not improved the line, and
attempted explanation (such as that
"thrive" equals "who thrive") has not
helped. Steevens (1778) pointed out
that there is a similar thought in Webster's *Duchess of Malfi,* III. v. 11–13:
"physitians thus, / With their hands
full of money, use to give ore / Their
Patients" (Lucas, II. 85); and Shakespeare's line apparently means "thrive
(on his money) and then give him up".
  15. *much disgrac'd*] put a severe slight
upon.
  16. *That . . . place*] who (Timon)
ought to have known that my place in
his list of friends was not *after* Lucius,
Lucullus and Ventidius.
  16–17. *I see . . . first*] I see no logical
reason why in his necessity he should
not have sought my help first.

20–21. *does . . . last?*] does he think
both so late (or slowly) and so poorly
of me as to believe that I shall be the
last to repay him (and therefore ask
me last)? There is a quibble on "backwardly" and "last".
  22. *argument*] occasion, justification.
  23. *I*] The reading of F2 here avoids
what would be an extreme but not
unprecedented ellipsis if F1 is right;
and "I" seems to be demanded by the
metre.
  25. *but . . . sake*] simply because of
my good feeling towards him.
  26. *courage*] disposition or inclination. The word traces back to the
Latin *cor,* heart, and had this more
general meaning as well as that of
"bravery' until the later seventeenth
century.
  27. *faint*] weak, not offering support; or, possibly, inducing faint-
ness.
  28. *bates*] abates, undervalues. Compare note on I. ii. 204.

Serv. Excellent: your lordship's a goodly villain. The
 devil knew not what he did when he made man 30
 politic; he crossed himself by 't: and I cannot think
 but in the end the villainies of man will set him clear.
 How fairly this lord strives to appear foul! Takes
 virtuous copies to be wicked, like those that under
 hot ardent zeal would set whole realms on fire: of 35
 such a nature is his politic love.
 This was my lord's best hope; now all are fled
 Save only the gods. Now his friends are dead,
 Doors that were ne'er acquainted with their wards
 Many a bounteous year, must be employ'd 40
 Now to guard sure their master.
 And this is all a liberal course allows:
 Who cannot keep his wealth must keep his house. [*Exit.*

29–36.] *As F;* Excellent . . . lordship's / . . . what / . . . politick / . . . think / . . .
man / . . . strives / . . . copies to / . . . hot / . . . fire / . . . love. *Capell.* 35–6. of
. . . love] *As F; verse Johnson.* 38. Save . . . gods] *As F;* save the gods only *Pope.*

31. *politic*] cunning. So in l. 36. See
note on III. ii. 89 above.

 crossed himself by 't] I cannot see that
the word is used here *either* in the sense
found in I. ii. 158, of being crossed off
a list of debtors, *or, pace* Johnson, in the
sense of making the sign of the cross; it
means, simply, tricked or thwarted
himself—by making others his rivals
in unscrupulousness. Only in this
interpretation does the previous clause
make sense.

 32. *will . . . clear*] "To set clear",
a metaphor from the keeping of
accounts, has obviously been suggested to the poet's mind by "crossed"
in l. 31. But it is not certain whether
"him" refers to man or the devil. If the
former, it means "man by his own
villainies will repay the debt he owes to
Satan". But the sentence construction
suggests the latter and I confess, with
Steevens, that I am not certain what it
means. The best guess is perhaps
Malone's "will make the devil by
comparison appear clear or innocent"—but there is no suggestion of
comparison in Shakespeare's own
words.

33. *How fairly*] with what skilful
appearance of decency.

 33–5. *Takes . . . fire*] takes care to
model himself on the style of the virtuous, but only that he may work for
evil; and so is like religious fanatics
whose very zeal is used to an evil end,
in that they are willing to set kingdoms aflame (with civil war). "Takes
. . . copies" is a metaphor from the
copy-book. Warburton and others
have seen in the second half of the sentence a reference to the Puritans;
Maxwell (the "New Shakespeare")
suggests that the dramatist was thinking of the Jesuits and perhaps of the
Gunpowder Plot (1605).

 39. *wards*] locks (strictly, a ward is
only a part of the lock).

 40. *bounteous*] Either "beneficent" (as
a transferred epithet) *or* "plentiful"
("a year of plenty").

 41. *sure*] safely, securely.

 42. *liberal*] generous, or, perhaps
here, over-generous.

 43. *must . . . house*] There is, of
course, a quibble: he must *retain* his
house and keep *to* it—for fear of being
arrested for debt.

[SCENE IV]

Enter VARRO'S *two Servants, meeting other Servants of Timon's creditors, to wait for his coming out. Then enter* LUCIUS'S *Servant; then* TITUS *and* HORTENSIUS.

First Var. Serv. Well met; good morrow, Titus and Hortensius.
Tit. The like to you, kind Varro.
Hor.   Lucius!
        What, do we meet together?
Luc. Serv.   Ay, and I think
        One business does command us all; for mine
        Is money.
Tit.   So is theirs and ours.   5

Enter PHILOTUS.

Luc. Serv. And, sir, Philotus too!
Phil. Good day at once.
Luc. Serv.   Welcome, good brother.
        What do you think the hour?
Phil.   Labouring for nine.
Luc. Serv. So much?
Phil.   Is not my lord seen yet?
Luc. Serv.   Not yet.
Phil. I wonder on 't; he was wont to shine at seven.   10
Luc. Serv. Ay, but the days are wax'd shorter with him:

Scene IV

SCENE IV] *Pope; Scene II. Timon's Hall Rowe; not in F.*   S.D.] *Enter Varro's man, meeting others. All Timon's Creditors to wait for his comming out. Then enter Lucius and Hortensius F.*   1. *First Var. Serv.] As Capell; Var. man F.*   2–3. Lucius . . . together?] *As Capell; one line F.*   3, 6, 7, 9, 11, 22, 30. *Luc. Serv.] Malone; Luci. F.*   3–5. Ay . . . money] *As Capell; I . . . all. / For . . . money F.*   6. And . . . too!] And sir *Philotus* too. *F;* And Sir Philotas's too! *Pope;* and Sir Philotus too! *edd.*

6. *And . . . too!*] My punctuation of this seems to me preferable to a reading which gives the title of "Sir Philotus" to a servant, although in my reading also "sir" might be thought to be used ironically. "Philotus" is presumably the name of the master, and perhaps the whole form of address is one of mock respect. Compare II. ii. 9 S.D. and note, and II. i. 34 and note.

7. *at once*] to you all, together. Compare *Gent.*, I. i. 138.
8. *Labouring*] Perhaps, but not necessarily, with the suggestion that time is passing slowly.
11. *wax'd*] become. Originally meaning to grow *greater*, the word had come to mean "grow" or "become" in any sense and so could be used, as here, of "growing" smaller.

You must consider that a prodigal course
Is like the sun's,
But not, like his, recoverable. I fear
'Tis deepest winter in Lord Timon's purse;   15
That is, one may reach deep enough, and yet
Find little.

Phil.   I am of your fear, for that.

Tit. I'll show you how t' observe a strange event.
Your lord sends now for money?

Hort.   Most true, he does.

Tit. And he wears jewels now of Timon's gift,   20
For which I wait for money.

Hort. It is against my heart.

Luc. Serv.   Mark how strange it shows,
Timon in this should pay more than he owes:
And e'en as if your lord should wear rich jewels,
And send for money for 'em.   25

Hort. I'm weary of this charge, the gods can witness;
I know my lord hath spent of Timon's wealth,
And now ingratitude makes it worse than stealth.

First Var. Serv. Yes, mine's three thousand crowns;
What's yours?

Luc. Serv.   Five thousand mine.   30

13–14.] *As conj. Walker; one line F;* Is . . . recoverable / I fear *edd.*   14. recoverable. I fear] *As Johnson;* recouerable, I feare: *F.*   15–17. 'Tis . . . little] *As Pope;*
prose F.   26.] *As Rowe;* I'me . . . Charge, / The . . . witnesse: / *F.*   29, 31. *First*
Var. Serv.] *Malone; Varro F.*   29–30. Yes . . . yours?] *As F; one line Pope.*

---

13. *Is like the sun's*] i.e. in its mounting to its zenith and then inevitably
declining.

14. *But . . . recoverable*] but, unlike the
sun's, the course of the prodigal cannot
be retraced and so redeemed. There is
a quibble on "recover".

16–17. *That . . . little*] Steevens (1793)
thought the metaphor was carried
right through so that the comparison is
with animals digging deep for food in
winter snow and finding little.

17. *I . . . that*] I share your fears on
that question.

18. *observe*] observe and interpret.

21. *for money*] i.e. I now wait to claim

for A the money Timon cannot repay,
because he gave it in jewels to B.

22. *against my heart*] against my wish,
and grieves me.

23. *Timon . . . owes*] Timon is paying
twice; he has already given the value
of the money in gifts but is now asked
for the money also.

24–5. *And e'en . . . 'em*] i.e. whatever
the actual distribution of Timon's
jewels, the position really is that the
very man who wears them is sending
also for repayment of the money which
bought them.

26. *charge*] employment.

28. *stealth*] stealing, theft.

First Var. Serv. 'Tis much deep: and it should seem by
        th' sum,
      Your master's confidence was above mine,
      Else, surely, his had equall'd.

                    Enter FLAMINIUS.

Tit. One of Lord Timon's men.
Luc. Serv. Flaminius? Sir, a word. Pray is my lord ready   35
      to come forth?
Flam. No, indeed he is not.
Tit. We attend his lordship; pray signify so much.
Flam. I need not tell him that; he knows you are too dili-
      gent.   [*Exit.*   40

              Enter Steward in a cloak, muffled.

Luc. Serv. Ha, is not that his steward muffled so?
      He goes away in a cloud: call him, call him.
Tit. Do you hear, sir?
Second Var. Serv. By your leave, sir—
Stew. What do ye ask of me, my friend?   45
Tit. We wait for certain money here, sir.
Stew.   Ay,
      If money were as certain as your waiting,
      'Twere sure enough.
      Why then preferr'd you not your sums and bills
      When your false masters eat of my lord's meat?   50

35, 90, 94. *Luc. Serv.*] *Luc. F.*   40. *Exit*] *Steevens (1778); not in F.*   41, 57, 72, 83,
85. *Luc. Serv.*] *Luci. F.*   41–2.] *As F; prose Alexander.*   44. *Second Var. Serv.*] 2.
Varro F. sir,—] sir. *F.*   46–7. Ay . . . waiting] *As Capell; one line F.*

31. *much*] very. For Shakespeare's
frequent use of the adverb "much" to
modify a positive and not only a comparative, see Abbott 51.

32. *confidence*] faith or trust.
mine] i.e. my master's.

33. *his . . . equall'd*] his (i.e. my master's) loan to Timon would have been
as great as your master's.

39. *diligent*] Not merely "dutiful"
but (as elsewhere in Shakespeare)
"officious", only too willing to carry
out such tasks as this.

42. *in a cloud*] i.e. (1) in a state of

confusion or concern and (2) as in
covered by a cloud, because of his being muffled in a cloak. For (1) compare
Ant., III. ii. 51 and the not dissimilar
image in the words of the dying Fla-
mineo in Webster's *White Devil*: "O I
am in a mist" (v. vi. 260). Conceivably
in the second meaning there is a reference to the classical myth of Ixion's
embracing the cloud which Zeus had
created to resemble Hera, but I doubt
it.

49. *preferr'd*] proffered, brought forward (French *préférer*, Latin *prae-ferre*).

Then they could smile, and fawn upon his debts,
And take down th' int'rest into their glutt'nous maws.
You do yourselves but wrong, to stir me up;
Let me pass quietly.
Believe 't, my lord and I have made an end;   55
I have no more to reckon, he to spend.

Luc. Serv. Ay, but this answer will not serve.

Stew. If 'twill not serve, 'tis not so base as you,
For you serve knaves.   [*Exit.*

First Var. Serv. How? What does his cashier'd worship   60
mutter?

Second Var. Serv. No matter what; he's poor, and that's
revenge enough. Who can speak broader than he
that has no house to put his head in? Such may rail
against great buildings.   65

Enter SERVILIUS.

Tit. O, here's Servilius; now we shall know some answer.

Ser. If I might beseech you, gentlemen, to repair some
other hour, I should derive much from 't; for, take 't
of my soul, my lord leans wondrously to discontent.
His comfortable temper has forsook him, he's much   70
out of health, and keeps his chamber.

58. If 'twill] *F4*; If 't 'twill *F1*.   59. *Exit*] *Rowe; not in F.*

51–2. *fawn . . . maws*] The typical
Shakespearian association of flattery
with dogs is worth noting.

52. *th' int'rest*] The food Timon was
providing for them was equivalent to,
and cost as much as, paying interest on
the money he owed.

53. *You . . . up*] you do not show to
advantage, and you may even be
injuring your cause, by bothering me
thus.

56. *I have . . . spend*] The grammatical
figure is *syllepsis*: here, the understanding of a second verb in a different
person from that used in the original
one (Joseph, p. 58). "Reckon": add up
(as in "reckoning" meaning account).

60. *cashier'd*] dismissed. The retort is
prompted by the Steward's taunt that
they serve knaves; Varro's servant

suggests that the Steward no longer
serves anybody.

63. *revenge enough*] i.e. for us (simply
to know of it).

63–5. *Who . . . buildings*] who is more
given to unlimited and unmerited
criticism than the man who has
nothing of his own that can be criticized? A man who lives in the open air
will be freest in the condemnation of
large buildings; and so the Steward,
having no position himself, will criticize those who are good enough to be
in employment.

67. *repair*] come. Compare II. ii. 28 n.

68–9. *take 't of my soul*] believe it was
coming from my soul, believe that I
speak sincerely.

70. *comfortable*] In the older meaning
of "cheerful".

Luc. Serv. Many do keep their chambers are not sick;
   And if it be so far beyond his health,
   Methinks he should the sooner pay his debts,
   And make a clear way to the gods.
Ser.   Good gods!   75
Tit. We cannot take this for answer, sir.
Flam. [*Within.*] Servilius, help! My lord, my lord!

    Enter TIMON, *in a rage.*

Tim. What, are my doors oppos'd against my passage?
   Have I been ever free, and must my house
   Be my retentive enemy, my gaol?   80
   The place which I have feasted, does it now,
   Like all mankind, show me an iron heart?
Luc. Serv. Put in now, Titus.
Tit. My lord, here is my bill.
Luc. Serv. Here's mine.   85
Hort. And mine, my lord.
Both Var. Serv. And ours, my lord.
Phil. All our bills.
Tim. Knock me down with 'em: cleave me to the girdle.
Luc. Serv. Alas, my lord—   90

77. S.D.] *As F; Enter . . . rage; Flaminius following | Capell.* 77.] *Scene V Pope.*
86. *Hort.*] *Capell; 1 Var. F.* 87. *Both Var. Serv.*] *Malone; 2 Var. F.* 90. lord—]
As Capell; Lord. F.

72. *Many . . . sick*] For this common
omission of the nominative relative
pronoun, see Abbott 244.

73. *And . . . health*] Apparently "it"
is again indefinite. "If the position is
that he has known all his days of good
health".

75. *And . . . the gods*] i.e. and not be
punished by the gods for leaving un-
paid debts behind him.

77. S.D.] Most editors add "Flaminius following", for no good reason.
Alexander even gives Flaminius two
words (l. 104) which the Folio clearly
attributes to the Steward. Alexander
apparently postulates a Fla(minius)–
Fla(vius) confusion in the manuscript
—but there is no evidence that Shake-

speare wrote anything but *Stew.* except
in I. ii—and Flaminius should not be
on the stage anyway.

79. *free*] Maxwell is surely right
(p. 202) in seeing irony here, in the
double meaning of "free": unrestrained and generous.

80. *retentive*] retaining, confining.

81. *place . . . feasted*] A somewhat
forced comparison of the house itself
with a guest who has received flattery
and lavish attention and now turns
against the host.

89. *Knock . . . girdle*] Timon takes
"bills" in the sense not of "accounts"
but of "weapons" (of the halberd
type) which could cleave a man to the
belt.

Tim. Cut my heart in sums.

Tit. Mine, fifty talents.

Tim. Tell out my blood.

Luc. Serv. Five thousand crowns, my lord.

Tim. Five thousand drops pays that. What yours? And
    yours?   95

First Var. Serv. My lord—

Second Var. Serv. My lord—

Tim. Tear me, take me, and the gods fall upon you!   [*Exit.*

Hort. Faith, I perceive our masters may throw their caps
    at their money; these debts may well be call'd des-   100
    perate ones, for a madman owes 'em.   [*Exeunt.*

Re-enter TIMON *and Steward.*

Tim. They have e'en put my breath from me, the slaves.
    Creditors? Devils!

Stew.   My dear lord—

Tim. What if it should be so?

Stew.   My lord—

Tim. I'll have it so. My steward?

Stew.   Here, my lord.   105

Tim. So fitly? Go, bid all my friends again,
    Lucius, Lucullus and Sempronius: all.

95.] *As Dyce;* Fiue . . . that. / What . . . and yours? *F.*   96, 97. lord—] *As Rowe;*
Lord. *F.*   102. S.D. *Re-enter . . . Steward*] *As Rowe; Enter Timon F.*   102-3.] *As*
Steevens; prose F.   103, 104. lord—] *Johnson;* Lord. *F.*   107. Sempronius]
F3; Sempronius Vllorxa F1.

93. *Tell out*] count out. The sense
survives particularly in the modern
noun "(bank-)teller".

99-100. *may . . . money*] The modern
idiom is "may go whistle for their
money, for all the chance they have of
getting it". The proverb is explained
by reference to the custom of casting
one's cap after a runner whom one
despairs of overtaking, as a sign that
one is conceding defeat (Tilley C 62).

100-1. *desperate*] Debts in Warwick-
shire and elsewhere were classified as
either "desperate" (i.e. beyond hope
of recovery—L. *desperatus*) or "sper-
ate". (So Hilda Hulme in *English*
Studies, XXXVIII, 5, Oct. 1957, 198.)

102. *put . . . me*] put me out of breath
(with exasperation).

104. *What . . . so?*] Spoken as the
plan to give the banquet occurs to
him. The modern equivalent might be
"Can I really do it?"

106. *So fitly?*] are you at hand so
conveniently? (Is it already seeming
easy?)

107. *Sempronius: all*] The Folio's
"*Sempronius Vllorxa:* All," is one of the
most difficult problems in Shakespeare's text. Emendations include
various names (Ventidius, for example) and readings like "all luxors"
(Fleay) and "et cetera" (Deighton).
Deighton was mistaken when he

I'll once more feast the rascals.

Stew.   O my lord,
You only speak from your distracted soul;
There's not so much left to furnish out   110
A moderate table.

Tim.   Be it not in thy care.
Go, I charge thee, invite them all, let in the tide
Of knaves once more; my cook and I'll provide. [*Exeunt.*

[SCENE V]

Enter three Senators at one door, ALCIBIADES *meeting them
with Attendants.*

First Sen. My lord, you have my voice to 't; the fault's
Bloody; 'tis necessary he should die;
Nothing emboldens sin so much as mercy.
Second Sen. Most true; the law shall bruise 'em.

108–11. O . . . table] *As Pope; prose F.*   110. There's] *F; There is Capell.*   to]
F; as to Rowe.   111–12.] *As F; Be . . . go, / I . . . tide Capell.*

Scene v

SCENE V] *Capell; not in F; Scene III Rowe; Scene VI Pope.*   S.D. *Enter . . . Senators]
F: The City. | Enter . . . Senators | Rowe; the Senate-house. | Senators | Theobald.*
1–2.] *As Reed (1803); My . . . too't, / . . . Bloody: / . . . dye: / F; My . . . bloody; /
. . . dye: / Rowe.*   4. 'em] *F; him Hanmer.*

alleged that "Vllorxa" is the only
name in the Folio line in italics (they
all are). Most editors agree that the
word was intended for deletion and
may therefore simply be omitted; the
line is metrically complete without it.
The task is to explain how it got into
the text; and recent editors (e.g. Ridley
and Sisson) believe that it was an
interlineation.

110. *to furnish out*] *as* to supply.

111. *Be it . . . care*] let it (the feast) be
my responsibility, not yours.

Scene v

SCENE V] For the general interpretation of this scene, see Introduction, Section 7.

1. *my voice to 't*] my vote for, or consent to, the sentence of death under
discussion. There is no warrant for
identifying the friend in question with
Timon; commentators have misunderstood Alcibiades' later references, in Acts IV and V, to the wrongs
of Timon (i.e. the refusal of the Athenians to lend him money, and his sub-
sequent fate).

4. *bruise 'em*] crush both Alcibiades
and the man for whom he pleads, or
even sinners in general. There is no
need to adopt Hanmer's emendation,
"him". Tilley cited an old proverb
"Pardon makes offenders" (P 50).
"Bruise" (OE *brysan*) meant originally to smash or crush to pieces.

Alcib. Honour, health and compassion to the Senate!   5
First Sen. Now, captain?
Alcib. I am an humble suitor to your virtues;
        For pity is the virtue of the law,
        And none but tyrants use it cruelly.
        It pleases time and fortune to lie heavy   10
        Upon a friend of mine, who in hot blood
        Hath stepp'd into the law, which is past depth
        To those that, without heed, do plunge into 't.
        He is a man, setting his fate aside,
        Of comely virtues;   15
        Nor did he soil the fact with cowardice
        (An honour in him which buys out his fault)
        But with a noble fury and fair spirit,
        Seeing his reputation touch'd to death,
        He did oppose his foe;   20
        And with such sober and unnoted passion

14–15.] *As Johnson; one line F.*   14. fate] *F; fault Warburton.*   17. An] And *Ff.*
21. unnoted] *F; unwonted conj. Anon.*

5. *Honour . . . Senate!*] An audacious greeting, of course, which is why the First Senator is surprised. Alcibiades wishes that the Senate may enjoy not only health (a normal greeting) but also honour and pity or mercy (for his friend, the man condemned to death).

6. *Now, captain?*] May mean only "please proceed" but might more properly be paraphrased as "What was that you said?"

7 ff.] Kennedy has pointed out that this oration is characteristic of Shakespeare both in its beginning and in its construction: "the note of formality struck in the introduction serves to set the oration off at the very outset from the rest of the scene". See also Introduction, Section 7.

8. *the virtue*] the chief merit. For the sentiment, compare Portia's renowned speech in *Mer.V.,* IV. i. 184 ff ("The quality of mercy is not strain'd . . .").

12. *stepp'd . . . law*] performed an action which brings him within reach of the law. But the metaphor is of

stepping unexpectedly into a seemingly bottomless pool.

14. *his fate*] Most editors accept Warburton's emendation "fault" but that seems to me a weaker reading. Alcibiades pleads that his friend is virtuous, except for this one action which it was his unhappy fate to commit. Deighton interestingly quoted from the Chorus to Act III of Jonson's *Catiline* "So much Rome's faults (now grown her fate) do threat her"—but himself accepted Warburton's emendation.

17. *buys out*] i.e. fully redeems, as one redeems a debt.

18. *fair*] unblemished or noble.

19. *touch'd to death*] Presumably, besmirched fatally, so that, to protect it, he was justified in taking mortal vengeance. "Touch" to an Elizabethan probably had associations both with the hit in fencing (compare *Ham.,* v. ii. 297) and with defilement ("touching pitch").

21. *sober*] grave, serious, not excessive.

He did behove his anger, ere 'twas spent,
As if he had but prov'd an argument.
First Sen. You undergo too strict a paradox,
Striving to make an ugly deed look fair.   25
Your words have took such pains as if they labour'd
To bring manslaughter into form, and set quarrelling
Upon the head of valour; which indeed
Is valour misbegot, and came into the world
When sects and factions were newly born.   30
He's truly valiant that can wisely suffer
The worst that man can breathe,
And make his wrongs his outsides,
To wear them like his raiment, carelessly,
And ne'er prefer his injuries to his heart,
To bring it into danger.   35
If wrongs be evils and enforce us kill,
What folly 'tis to hazard life for ill!

22. behove] *Sisson;* behoove *Ff;* behave *Rowe.*   27.] *As F;* set / Quarrelling *edd.*
32–4.] *As F;* The . . . wrongs / . . . carelessly. / *Pope.*

unnoted] In the meaning "not specially noted or observed", recorded by *O.E.D.*, the word makes good sense. Alcibiades is insisting that his friend was not carried away by passion, that his conduct was *normal* and that of a reasonable man.

22. *behove*] Again most editors discard the Folio "behoove", in favour of Rowe's emendation "behave" (in the sense of "manage", "regulate" or "conduct", for which there is good evidence). Perhaps "behove" (or "behoove") may be retained and explained as an extension of *O.E.D.* Sense 1 ("to have use for or need of") i.e. "make use of" or "manage".

24. *undergo . . . paradox*] undertake to maintain a paradox which cannot be sustained in this forced interpretation.

27. *bring . . . form*] *Either* treat manslaughter in a purely formal way as if it were no more than one step in a rhetorical argument or a syllogism *or* (less probably) make it out to be something to be respected.

27–8. *set . . . valour*] *Either* treat quarrelling as a subdivision of valour (carrying on the parallel with logic) *or* (less probably) the same image as in "crown'd" in II. ii. 185 above: treat quarrelling as if it crowned or added distinction to valour.

28. *which*] i.e. quarrelling.

32. *breathe*] Generally explained as "utter" but might conceivably have a wider meaning, "draw in with his breath".

33. *his outsides*] i.e. mere externals (as the next line shows), not to be treated as vital.

34. *carelessly*] in a care-free way (the normal Elizabethan meaning).

35–6. *And . . . danger*] and never, as it were, promote or advance his injuries to the level at which they would be considered worthy of heartfelt concern —because that would be to bring the heart itself into danger.

37. *and . . . kill*] and force us to kill, to revenge them.

38. *What . . . ill*] how absurd it is to risk one's own life in a matter which by hypothesis involves evil.

Alcib. My lord—
First Sen.   You cannot make gross sins look clear;
          To revenge is no valour, but to bear.   40
Alcib. My lords, then, under favour, pardon me,
          If I speak like a captain.
          Why do fond men expose themselves to battle,
          And not endure all threats? Sleep upon 't,
          And let the foes quietly cut their throats   45
          Without repugnancy? If there be
          Such valour in the bearing, what make we
          Abroad? Why then, women are more valiant
          That stay at home, if bearing carry it,
          And the ass more captain than the lion,   50
          The fellow loaden with irons wiser than the judge,
          If wisdom be in suffering. O my lords,
          As you are great, be pitifully good.
          Who cannot condemn rashness in cold blood?
          To kill, I grant, is sin's extremest gust,   55

39. lord—] *As Rowe; Lord. F.*   50-1.] *As F1; And . . . fellow / . . . judge / F2.*
51. fellow] *F; felon conj. Johnson.*

39. *clear*] innocent.

40. *but to bear*] but to bear or tolerate (wrongs) *is* valour. Another form of ellipsis.

41. *under favour*] by your leave.

42. *like a captain*] i.e. as the man of war I am (rather than as a lawyer).

43. *fond*] foolish—spoken ironically, of course.

44. *Sleep upon 't*] i.e. *why do they not* sleep upon 't? (Ellipsis again.)

46. *repugnancy*] fighting back (compare L. *repugnare*).

47. *bearing*] For example, of wrongs; but there are later quibbles on "bearing children" and on "bearing (the weight of) men", the latter as in *Rom.*, II. v. 78.

49. *if . . . it*] if bearing "wins the day", comes first, is considered the most important thing. Compare *Cor.*, II. ii. 4.

50. *more captain*] For "more" as a comparative adjective, meaning "greater", see Abbott 17.

51. *fellow*] The Folio reading may

stand, as against Johnson's "felon", since "fellow" was often used as a term of contempt.

53. *As . . . good*] in the same way as you are great, be good in a pitying or merciful way. "Pitiful" is used in its active sense, "having pity", and not in the modern passive sense, "deserving pity". Compare "distasteful", II. ii. 215 n.

54. *condemn . . . blood*] Not "condemn in cold blood" but "condemn a foolish deed committed in cold blood", i.e. deliberately (as against killing in self-defence).

55. *sin's extremest gust*] With Deighton, I take this as another instance of transferred epithet and explain as "that which is tasted or relished only by the most extreme sin" and so, perhaps, "the distinguishing feature of extreme sin". Steevens and Malone took it in the sense of "violent outburst" (like a gust of wind). "Gust" is used in both these senses by Shakespeare. Shadwell played safe and

But in defence, by mercy, 'tis most just.
To be in anger is impiety;
But who is man that is not angry?
Weigh but the crime with this.
Second Sen. You breathe in vain.
Alcib.   In vain? His service done   60
At Lacedæmon and Byzantium
Were a sufficient briber for his life.
First Sen. What's that?
Alcib. Why I say, my lords, h'as done fair service,
And slain in fight many of your enemies.   65
How full of valour did he bear himself
In the last conflict, and made plenteous wounds!
Second Sen. He has made too much plenty with 'em;
He's a sworn rioter; he has a sin
That often drowns him and takes his valour
   prisoner.   70
If there were no foes, that were enough
To overcome him. In that beastly fury
He has been known to commit outrages
And cherish factions; 'tis inferr'd to us,
His days are foul and his drink dangerous.   75
First Sen. He dies.
Alcib.   Hard fate! He might have died in war.
My lords, if not for any parts in him—

60–1.] *As Pope*; In vaine? / . . . Bizantium, / *F.*   64. Why I] *F2*; Why *F1*.
h'as] *F1* (ha's), *F4*; he has *Capell*; has *Dyce.*   68. 'em] *F2*; him *F1*.   69–
70.] *As F*; He's . . . often / . . . prisoner / *Malone.*

altered it to "the extreamest guilt".

56. *by mercy*] Rather "if interpreted
mercifully" (as the law allows) than
"with your merciful leave (I say it)"
or "I call mercy herself to witness"
(Johnson).

58. *angry*] Perhaps three syllables, as
it sometimes is.

62. *briber*] giver of bribes. (The
"service" is personified.)

68. *He . . . 'em*] F2's emendation
"'em" is generally accepted and is
probably right. Presumably the F1
compositor misunderstood the abbreviation. If the lines make only feeble

sense, that may be intentional; the
Senator catches up the word "plen-
teous" and tries to score a point against
Alcibiades.

69. *a sworn rioter*] one habitually dis-
solute, one who perpetrates "riot" as
if on oath to do so.

71. *that*] i.e. that sin of drunken-
ness.

74. *cherish factions*] foster dissension.
inferr'd] alleged or implied. The
word was regularly used in both these
senses in the sixteenth and seventeenth centuries.

77. *parts*] good qualities.

Though his right arm might purchase his own time,
And be in debt to none—yet, more to move you,
Take my deserts to his, and join 'em both; 80
And for I know your reverend ages love
Security, I'll pawn my victories, all
My honour to you, upon his good returns.
If by this crime he owes the law his life,
Why, let the war receive 't in valiant gore, 85
For law is strict, and war is nothing more.

First Sen. We are for law; he dies: urge it no more,
On height of our displeasure. Friend or brother,
He forfeits his own blood that spills another.

Alcib. Must it be so? It must not be. 90
My lords, I do beseech you know me.

Second Sen.   How?

Alcib. Call me to your remembrances.

Third Sen.   What!

Alcib. I cannot think but your age has forgot me;
It could not else be I should prove so base,
To sue and be denied such common grace. 95
My wounds ache at you.

First Sen.   Do you dare our anger?
'Tis in few words, but spacious in effect:
We banish thee for ever.

81–3.] *As Capell;* And . . . Security, / . . . you / . . . returnes / *F.*   90–1. Must . . .
I] *As F;* Must . . . lords / I *Capell.*   95. denied] deny'de *F.*

---

78. *might . . . time*] might be considered to have earned him the right to die at the proper or natural time.

79. *more . . . you*] to move you still more.

80. *Take*] add.

join 'em both] Emphatic, not tautological, in Elizabethan usage.

81. *for*] because.

your reverend ages] you in your reverend old age.

83. *upon . . . returns*] as a pledge that he will make a good return for your clemency, make it a profitable investment.

88. *On . . . displeasure*] under penalty of incurring our greatest displeasure.

89. *another*] *sc.* "the blood of".

91. *know me*] recognize and remember me for what I am, take my worth into account.

92. *remembrances*] Probably pronounced as five syllables.

93. *your . . . forgot*] you, because of your age, have forgotten.

94–5. *I . . . grace*] I should be considered so worthless as to plead before you and be refused the mercy which would be any man's due.

96. *My . . . at you*] That the phrase was semi-proverbial is suggested by its occurrence also in Middleton's comedy *A Chaste Maid in Cheapside.* See Introduction, p. xxii.

Alcib.   Banish me?
   Banish your dotage, banish usury,
   That makes the Senate ugly!   100
First Sen. If after two days' shine Athens contain thee,
   Attend our weightier judgment.
   And, not to swell our spirit,
   He shall be executed presently.   [*Exeunt Senators.*
Alcib. Now the gods keep you old enough, that you may live
   Only in bone, that none may look on you!   106
   I'm worse than mad: I have kept back their foes,
   While they have told their money, and let out
   Their coin upon large interest; I myself
   Rich only in large hurts. All those, for this?   110
   Is this the balsam that the usuring Senate
   Pours into captains' wounds? Banishment!
   It comes not ill. I hate not to be banish'd;
   It is a cause worthy my spleen and fury,
   That I may strike at Athens. I'll cheer up   115
   My discontented troops, and lay for hearts.

102–3.] *As F; one line Capell.*   103. not . . . spirit] *As F;* but to swell your spirit
Theobald; now to swell your spirit *Warburton;* not to swell your spirit *Capell.*
105.] *one line Steevens (after Pope);* Now . . . enough, / . . . liue / *F.*   116. lay] *F;*
play *conj. Johnson.*

102. *Attend . . . judgment*] look out for
or expect a more severe judgment.

103. *not . . . spirit*] There have been
many emendations, most involving the
substitution of "your" for "our". The
Folio text may be interpreted satisfactorily if it is remembered that the
"spirit" was often thought of as the
seat of *angry* feeling (*O.E.D.*). So,
"without giving further rein to our
anger".

104. *presently*] immediately.

106. *Only in bone*] Conjectures like
Deighton's "bed" are so trivial as to be
hardly worth recording; and Tilley's
"at home" is not likely to have been
misread as "in bone" (he refers to a
proverb "Age should be housed").
Alcibiades' curse involves the surviving of the Senators as mere skeletons
("mere skin and bone", in the modern
idiom) and their being accordingly so

hideous that no one will be able to
bear looking at them. Timon's curse
on his flatterers "Live loath'd, and
long" (iii. vi. 89) provides the perfect
parallel.

108. *told*] counted.

111. *balsam*] A resinous preparation,
used as an ointment or salve. The
abbreviated form "balm" has replaced "balsam" in the commoner
metaphorical uses.

116. *lay for hearts*] To "lay for" was
to "waylay", "set an ambush for"
and, in military parlance, to beset.
The military sense is particularly appropriate here: Alcibiades will try
to besiege or ambush hearts, win
himself followers. Compare *2H6*, iv.
x. 3–5: "These five days have I hid
me in these woods and durst not
peep out, for all the country is laid
for me".

'Tis honour with most lands to be at odds;
Soldiers should brook as little wrongs as gods.   [*Exit.*

[SCENE VI]

Enter divers of Timon's Friends and Senators at several doors.

First Lord. The good time of day to you, sir.
Second Lord. I also wish it to you. I think this honourable
    lord did but try us this other day.
First Lord. Upon that were my thoughts tiring when we
    encounter'd. I hope it is not so low with him as he   5
    made it seem in the trial of his several friends.
Second Lord. It should not be, by the persuasion of his new
    feasting.
First Lord. I should think so. He hath sent me an earnest
    inviting, which many my near occasions did urge   10

117. lands] *F;* hands *Warburton;* lords *conj. Malone.*

Scene VI
SCENE VI] *Capell; Scene IV. Rowe;* Scene VII *Pope; not in F.*   S.D. Enter] *F;*
Timon's House. | Enter | Rowe.   S.D.] *Enter diuers Friends at seuerall doores F.*
1. *First Lord] Capell; 1 F (throughout scene); 1 Sen. Rowe.*   2. *Second Lord] Capell;*
2 F (throughout scene); 2 Sen. Rowe.

117. *lands*] Deighton and others
have felt that the text is "pointless";
but it may stand. Alcibiades, as befits
a professional man of war, judges his
honour by the number of armies he has
to meet in battle.

118. *brook . . . gods*] i.e. not endure
wrongs any more than gods endure
them.

Scene VI
S.D. divers of Timon's Friends]
Again producers, particularly, may
wish to identify the unnamed four
Lords with (for example) Lucullus,
Lucius, Sempronius and Ventidius, as
does Sisson. The identification may
well be right. My objection to making
the alteration in the text itself, however, is that, in my opinion, the dramatist had not yet decided which of these

minor characters was which. Incidentally the sum mentioned here as
owed to the First Lord (a thousand
pieces) is not the same as the fifty
talents sought from Lucullus earlier
(so far as one can tell).

4. *tiring*] From an old verb "to tire"
meaning to draw or tug; to tear flesh in
feeding, as does a bird of prey; (in
falconry) "to tear at a tough morsel
given to it [the bird] that it may
exercise itself in this way" (*O.E.D.*);
and so (as here) "to feed upon" or
"exercise upon".

7. *by the persuasion of*] on the evidence
of.

8. *feasting*] i.e. *giving* feasts.

10. *many . . . occasions*] Another example of the transposing of the possessive pronoun: my many important
engagements (strictly, "needs").

me to put off; but he hath conjur'd me beyond them,
and I must needs appear.

Second Lord. In like manner was I in debt to my importunate business, but he would not hear my excuse.
I am sorry, when he sent to borrow of me, that my   15
provision was out.

First Lord. I am sick of that grief too, as I understand how
all things go.

Second Lord. Every man here's so. What would he have
borrowed of you?   20

First Lord. A thousand pieces.

Second Lord. A thousand pieces?

First Lord. What of you?

Second Lord. He sent to me, sir—Here he comes.

Enter TIMON *and Attendants.*

Tim. With all my heart, gentlemen both; and how fare   25
you?

First Lord. Ever at the best, hearing well of your lordship.

Second Lord. The swallow follows not summer more willing than we your lordship.

Tim. [*Aside.*] Nor more willingly leaves winter; such   30
summer birds are men.—Gentlemen, our dinner
will not recompense this long stay. Feast your ears
with the music awhile, if they will fare so harshly o'

---

19. here's] *F4;* heares *F1-2;* heare *F3.*   30. *Aside*] *Johnson; not in F.*

11. *conjur'd . . . them*] implored
me in a way so pressing as to persuade
me to forgo them, as less important.
Compare I. i. 7 and n.

13–14. *in debt . . . business*] under the
necessity of attending to my business,
which was as demanding as a creditor
seeking payment of debts.

16. *provision was out*] supply (of
money) had run out.

17–18. *I . . . go*] A rather cryptic
comment—perhaps intentionally so.
"I share your grief (at not having been
able to help him)—particularly now
that I understand the position of
affairs" (i.e. *either* that others could
not help him *or* that he is now in a

position to entertain again).

21. *pieces*] Perhaps, sovereigns; but
the word may again be vague because
Shakespeare intended to check all
these figures. The change from
"talents" to "crowns" to "pieces"
certainly adds to the confusion.

25. *With . . . heart*] i.e. greetings
from my heart.

27. *hearing well*] when (as now) we
hear good news.

30–1. *Nor . . . men*] Timon's retort
depends upon the proverb "Swallows,
like false friends, fly away upon the
approach of winter" (Tilley S 1026).

32. *stay*] wait.

33–4. *if . . . sound*] if they can receive

th' trumpet's sound; we shall to 't presently.

First Lord. I hope it remains not unkindly with your lord-   35
ship that I return'd you an empty messenger.

Tim. O sir, let it not trouble you.

Second Lord. My noble lord—

Tim. Ah my good friend, what cheer?

> [*The banquet brought in.*

Second Lord. My most honourable lord, I am e'en sick of   40
shame, that when your lordship this other day sent
to me I was so unfortunate a beggar.

Tim. Think not on't, sir.

Second Lord. If you had sent but two hours before—

Tim. Let it not cumber your better remembrance.   45
—Come, bring in all together.

Second Lord. All cover'd dishes.

First Lord. Royal cheer, I warrant you.

Third Lord. Doubt not that, if money and the season can
yield it.   50

First Lord. How do you? What's the news?

Third Lord. Alcibiades is banish'd: hear you of it?

First and Second Lords. Alcibiades banish'd?

Third Lord. 'Tis so, be sure of it.

First Lord. How? How?   55

Second Lord. I pray you, upon what?

Tim. My worthy friends, will you draw near?

Third Lord. I'll tell you more anon. Here's a noble feast
toward.

Second Lord. This is the old man still.   60

---

38. lord—] *Hanmer;* Lord. *F.*   39. S.D.] *As F; after 46 Dyce.*   44. before—]
Rowe; before. *F.*   49. *Third Lord*] *As Capell; 3 F (throughout scene); 3 Sen. Rowe.*
53. *First and Second Lords*] *As Malone; Both F.*

nourishment from anything as un-
palatable as the harsh sound of the
trumpet.

34. *shall to 't presently*] shall sit down
to the meal immediately.

35. *remains not unkindly*] does not
remain as a memory of ingratitude.

42. *so . . . beggar*] so unlucky as to be,
at the time, as poor as a beggar.

45. *Let . . . remembrance*] do not let it
remain as an unpleasant load on your

mind, which has better things to think
about. Or perhaps, as Steevens (1793)
suggested, the comparative "better"
is used for the positive "good", in a
normal Elizabethan manner.

47. *cover'd dishes*] Which would normally mean good food.

56. *upon what?*] for what reason?

59. *toward*] forthcoming.

60. *This . . . still*] this is the old
Timon, as he formerly was (the fre-

Third Lord. Will 't hold? Will 't hold?
Second Lord. It does; but time will—and so—
Third Lord. I do conceive.
Tim. Each man to his stool, with that spur as he would to
the lip of his mistress. Your diet shall be in all places   65
alike. Make not a City feast of it, to let the meat cool
ere we can agree upon the first place. Sit, sit. The
gods require our thanks.

You great benefactors, sprinkle our society with thankful-
ness. For your own gifts, make yourselves prais'd; but   70
reserve still to give, lest your deities be despis'd. Lend to each
man enough, that one need not lend to another; for were your
godheads to borrow of men, men would forsake the gods.
Make the meat be belov'd, more than the man that gives it.
Let no assembly of twenty be without a score of villains. If 75
there sit twelve women at the table, let a dozen of them be as
they are. The rest of your fees, O gods, the Senators of
Athens, together with the common leg of people—what is

---

62. will—and so—] *Steevens* (*1778*); will, and so. *F.*   66. City feast] Citie
Feast *F*; city feast *edd.*   71. *despis'd*] despised *F.*   74. *belov'd*] beloued *F.*
77. *fees*] *F*; *foes Hanmer.*   78. *leg*] *F4*; legge *F1–3*; lag *Rowe*; tag *conj. Anon.*
people—] People, *F.*

---

quent meaning of "still" as "without change"). Cf. *Eph.*, iv. 22? (Noble).

61. *Will 't hold?*] *Either* will it last? *or* is it (this interpretation of Timon's position) valid?

62. *time . . . so*—] i.e. time will alter all things, and therefore one cannot be too sure.

63. *conceive*] understand you.

64. *that . . . would to*] the same speed (induced by the spur) as he would show if hurrying to . . .

65. *diet*] food.

66. *City feast*] i.e. a formal banquet such as would be given in the City (of London) with places allotted in order of precedence. (An anachronism, of course.) I suspect that the real point of the comparison is missed when "city" is spelt without the capital.

68. *require*] demand.

71. reserve . . . give] always keep something in reserve, for future gifts.

77. fees] The Folio reading makes sense if, as Sisson suggests (*New Readings*, p. 173), it is taken in the sense of property (as in law) and might have special point if one could believe that Shakespeare knew the slightly earlier use of the word to mean cattle or livestock.

78. leg] Most editors prefer Rowe's "lag"—that which comes at the end; but the word is not found elsewhere in Shakespeare as a noun. There is a further presumption in favour of the F1 reading in that its preservation by the later Folios perhaps means that it made sense to a seventeenth-century reader. Diffidently, I suggest comparison with *Cym.*, v. iii. 92–3: "A leg of Rome shall not return to tell / What crows have peck'd them here" where although "leg" probably means only the limb, it is possibly also a term of contempt as used by the British cap-

> *amiss in them, you gods, make suitable for destruction. For*
> *these my present friends, as they are to me nothing, so in no-*　80
> *thing bless them, and to nothing are they welcome.*
>
> Uncover, dogs, and lap.
>
> 　　[*The dishes are uncovered and seen to be full of warm water.*

Some. What does his lordship mean?

Others. 　　　　　　　　　I know not.

Tim. May you a better feast never behold,
　　　You knot of mouth-friends! Smoke and lukewarm water
　　　Is your perfection. This is Timon's last;　　　86
　　　Who, stuck and spangled with your flatteries,
　　　Washes it off, and sprinkles in your faces
　　　Your reeking villainy. 　　[*Throwing the water in their faces.*
　　　　　　　　　Live loath'd, and long,
　　　Most smiling, smooth, detested parasites,　　　90
　　　Courteous destroyers, affable wolves, meek bears,
　　　You fools of fortune, trencher-friends, time's flies,

---

82. S.D.] *As Johnson; not in F.*　　83. *Some*] *Some speake. F.*　　*Others*] *Some other. F.*
87. with your flatteries] *Hanmer;* you with Flatteries *F;* you with flattery *Dyce.*
89. S.D.] *As Johnson; not in F.*

---

tain. Alternatively Phillips suggests
(p. 128) that it is part of the normal
analogue between the human body
and the body politic. Menenius similarly compares the plebeians of Rome
to the "members" or limbs of the body
and one particular citizen to "the
great toe". In any case, it is clear that
it is the worthlessness of the common
people that is in question. Compare
also "cap-and-knee slaves" in l. 93.

78–9. people . . . them] The construction breaks off, and the thought
seems to be: "As for the Senators and
the common people—because of what
is wrong with them (i.e. everything)—
make them . . ."

79. For] as for.

82. S.D.] Perhaps stones also are in
the dishes. See note on l. 97 S.D.
below.

85. *mouth-friends*] Schmidt paraphrased as "one who professes friendship without entertaining it"; and
"mouth-honour" in *Mac.*, v. iii. 27 is
an interesting parallel. But surely it

also means friends who can be won by
the mouth—by mere feeding of them.
Compare "trencher-friends" in l. 92.

86. *Is your perfection*] is all you are fit
for, *or* is all you are even in your perfect state *or* is a perfect likeness of you
(Warburton).

87. *stuck . . . flatteries*] The construction and the following words make
Hanmer's emendation "with your
flatteries" almost certain; and the
Folio reading "you with Flatteries"
may be explained either as an instance
of Shakespeare's pen running ahead of
his thought, or as a scribe's or compositor's error of a common enough
kind. As printed here the words mean
"bespattered, and sprinkled as if with
spangles, with your flatteries".

92. *fools of fortune*] Deighton suggested an allusion to the proverb "Fortune favours fools" and explained as
"empty-handed worshippers of fortune". But perhaps they are also, in
Timon's eyes, the dupes of fortune in
the long run—if, for example, they

Cap-and-knee slaves, vapours, and minute-jacks!
Of man and beast the infinite malady
Crust you quite o'er! What, dost thou go?   95
Soft, take thy physic first—thou too—and thou!
Stay, I will lend thee money, borrow none.
                                        [*Drives them out.*
What? All in motion? Henceforth be no feast,
Whereat a villain's not a welcome guest.
Burn, house! Sink, Athens! Henceforth hated be   100
Of Timon, man and all humanity!   [*Exit.*

Re-enter the Lords and Senators.

First Lord. How now, my lords?
Second Lord. Know you the quality of Lord Timon's fury?
Third Lord. Push, did you see my cap?
Fourth Lord. I have lost my gown.   105
First Lord. He's but a mad lord, and nought but humours
          sways him. He gave me a jewel th' other day, and

93. minute-jacks!] *Camb. edd.; * Minute Iackes. *F1; * Minute Iackes *F2–4 (subst.).*
97. S.D.] *not in F; Throwing the Dishes at them, and drives' em out Rowe.*   101. S.D.]
Enter the Senators, with other Lords F.   105. *Fourth Lord*] *Malone; 4 F; 4 Sen.*
Rowe.

"live loath'd and long". Compare
"O, I am fortune's fool!" *Rom.*, III. i.
141.
     trencher-friends] friends won by feed-
ing. Compare "mouth-friends", l. 85.
     time's flies] insects who come only in
summer or good times. Compare II. ii.
175–6.
     93. *Cap-and-knee slaves*] mere slaves
always raising their caps or on their
knees.
     vapours] i.e. unsubstantial as air.
     minute-jacks] A jack was the figure
striking the bell in a clock (compare
R2, v. v. 60, and, particularly, *R3*,
IV. ii. 111–19). "Jack" was also a frequent term of contempt. Accordingly
the phrase means "contemptible villains who adjust their feelings by the
clock, adapt their alleged friendship to
the circumstances".
     94. *infinite*] *Either* worst conceivable
or limitless.

95. *Crust*] Also used for the vile
scabbing sores of disease in *Ham.*, v. i.
72 (Deighton).
     96. *physic*] medicine.
     97. *borrow*] *sc.* "I will".
     S.D.] The final line of the scene may
imply that Timon here throws stones
after them. In the old *Timon* play,
stones were served at the mock-
banquet, painted to look like artichokes. See Introduction, Section 5.
     101. *Of*] by. "Man and all human-
ity" is the subject of the verb.
     104. *Push*] An exclamation of fussy
impatience. Wells and Sykes found it
characteristic of Middleton, and
Sykes pointed out triumphantly that
it was not elsewhere used by Shakespeare.
     106. *humours*] For "humours" ("cap-
rices"), compare I. ii. 26 and note.
     107. *He . . . day*] The gift of the jewel
does seem to identify this "First Lord"

now he has beat it out of my hat. Did you see my
    jewel?
Third Lord. Did you see my cap?   110
Second Lord. Here 'tis.
Fourth Lord. Here lies my gown.
First Lord. Let's make no stay.
Second Lord. Lord Timon's mad.
Third Lord.   I feel 't upon my bones.   114
Fourth Lord. One day he gives us diamonds, next day stones.
                                            [*Exeunt.*

110. *Third Lord*] *As Capell; 2 F.*   111. *Second Lord*] *As Capell; 3 F.*

with the "First Lord" of I. ii; but there
is nothing to make it certain that either
is identifiable with the Lucullus of III. i.

114. *upon my bones*] i.e. where
Timon's blows (or the stones he has
thrown) have made impact.

[ACT IV

SCENE I]

Enter TIMON.

Tim. Let me look back upon thee. O thou wall
That girdles in those wolves, dive in the earth
And fence not Athens! Matrons, turn incontinent!
Obedience fail in children! Slaves and fools,
Pluck the grave wrinkled senate from the bench,   5
And minister in their steads! To general filths
Convert, o' th' instant, green virginity!
Do 't in your parents' eyes! Bankrupts, hold fast;
Rather than render back, out with your knives,
And cut your trusters' throats! Bound servants, steal! 10
Large-handed robbers your grave masters are,
And pill by law. Maid, to thy master's bed;
Thy mistress is o' th' brothel! Son of sixteen,

ACT IV

Scene 1

ACT IV SCENE I] *Act IV Sc. I. Without the Walls of Athens Rowe; not in F.*
1. thee.] *F;* thee, *Pope.*   2. wolves,] *F;* wolves! *Pope.*   6. steads! To general
filths] *As Johnson;* steeds, to generall Filthes. *F;* steads: to general filths *Pope*
(*ed. 2*).   8–9. Bankrupts ... knives] *As Theobald;* Bankrupts ... fast / Rather ...
backe; ... Kniues *F.*   13. o' th'] *F;* i' th' *Hanmer;* at the *Keightley.*   Son] *F4;*
Some *F1;* Sonne *F2–3.*

2. *girdles*] Variously explained as the
use of the third person, in agreement
with "wall" rather than "thou"
(Abbott 412), and as an alternative
form of the second person.

6. *minister*] act, govern.

filths] "Filth" is used both of a vile
person such as a harlot and of an
immoral act or a state of corruption.
Either meaning is possible here. Compare *Tp.*, I. ii. 346, *Oth.*, v. ii. 231.

7. *Convert*] turn, used intransitively.
(Compare Malcolm's "Let grief /

Convert to anger", *Mac.*, IV. iii. 229.)

green] young, innocent.

9. *render back*] give back, repay
debts.

10. *your trusters*] those who have
trusted you.

Bound servants] servants under bond
to serve for a given number of years.

12. *pill*] plunder.

13. *o' th' brothel*] Emendation to "in
the" actually weakens the meaning
here. She is in it and *of* it—belongs
there.

Pluck the lin'd crutch from thy old limping sire;
With it beat out his brains! Piety and fear,   15
Religion to the gods, peace, justice, truth,
Domestic awe, night-rest and neighbourhood,
Instruction, manners, mysteries and trades,
Degrees, observances, customs and laws,
Decline to your confounding contraries;   20
And yet confusion live! Plagues incident to men,
Your potent and infectious fevers heap
On Athens ripe for stroke! Thou cold sciatica,
Cripple our senators, that their limbs may halt
As lamely as their manners! Lust and liberty   25
Creep in the minds and marrows of our youth,
That 'gainst the stream of virtue they may strive,
And drown themselves in riot! Itches, blains,
Sow all th' Athenian bosoms, and their crop
Be general leprosy! Breath infect breath,   30
That their society, as their friendship, may
Be merely poison! Nothing I'll bear from thee
But nakedness, thou detestable town!
Take thou that too, with multiplying bans!

20. contraries;] *As Reed;* contraries. *F.*   21. yet] *F;* let *Hanmer.*   34.] *Throw-*
ing away his raiment | conj. Delius.

14. *lin'd*] padded.
16. *Religion to*] religious respect for.
17. *Domestic awe*] the respect appropriate in the home, to parents.
neighbourhood] neighbourliness (the
original meaning, before the word was
applied to place).
18. *mysteries*] crafts, or callings. Me-
dieval Latin *misterium* (ministerium),
not *mysterium.*
20. *your confounding contraries*] oppo-
sites which will "confound", or bring
all to ruinous confusion.
21. *And yet . . . live!*] Hanmer's "let"
is unsatisfactory both because it is unlikely to have been misread as "yet"
and because it weakens the meaning:
"And yet, in spite of all this destruction, may destruction *still* continue!"
incident to] natural to; or perhaps (in
a more literal meaning) falling upon.
23. *cold*] *Either* as inducing cold *or*

as being due to it (but it was commonly
thought of as a concomitant of venereal
disease).
25. *liberty*] licence, licentiousness (as
elsewhere in Shakespeare). "Riot" in
l. 28 means much the same.
28. *blains*] blisters or pustules. (The
same word as in "chilblain".)
29. *Sow*] i.e. sow themselves in.
31. *their*] The antecedent is "th'
Athenian bosoms" in l. 29.
32. *merely poison*] poison unadultre-
ated.
bear] carry away.
33. *detestable*] In the normal Elizabethan pronunciation, with the principal stress on the first syllable and
another stress on the third.
34. *that too*] Apparently some of
his clothing, as Delius conjectured.
(Ingleby pictured him tearing out his
hair!) Alternatively, "that" may refer

Timon will to the woods, where he shall find   35
Th' unkindest beast more kinder than mankind.
The gods confound—hear me, you good gods all—
Th' Athenians both within and out that wall;
And grant, as Timon grows, his hate may grow
To the whole race of mankind, high and low!   40
Amen.   [*Exit.*

[SCENE II]

Enter Steward, with two or three Servants.

First Serv. Hear you, master steward, where's our master?
Are we undone, cast off, nothing remaining?
Stew. Alack, my fellows, what should I say to you?
Let me be recorded by the righteous gods,
I am as poor as you.
First Serv.   Such a house broke?   5
So noble a master fall'n, all gone, and not
One friend to take his fortune by the arm,
And go along with him.
Second Serv.   As we do turn our backs
From our companion thrown into his grave,
So his familiars to his buried fortunes   10

Scene II

SCENE II] *Sc. II. Timon's House Rowe; not in F.*   1. master] M. *F.*   6. fall'n]
falne *F.*   10. to his] *F;* from his *Hanmer.*

back to "nakedness", in which case
the phrase means "May nakedness be
your condition as well as mine".

multiplying bans] curses that multiply
(or, simply, multiplied or multiple
curses). The active participle sometimes has a passive effect and vice
versa. See, for example, IV. iii. 2.

36. *more kinder*] For the double comparative, see Abbott 11; and for the
pun ("more kin") compare II. ii. 221
and n.

38. *within and out*] within and *without*: a common ellipsis.

Scene II

S.D. two or three Servants] The

"permissive" S.D. again points to
author's manuscript or to transcript as
the printer's "copy".

3. *Alack*] A common exclamation of
regret, from "O"+"lack" (deficiency,
need).

4–5. *Let . . . you*] let me go on record
before the just gods (as avowing that)
I am as poor as you.

7. *his fortune*] i.e. him in his ill-
fortune.

10–11. *his familiars . . . away*] A
highly concentrated way of saying:
Timon's friends, close to him in fortune
or in his better days, slink away from
him now those fortunes are buried and
are no more.

Slink all away, leave their false vows with him,
Like empty purses pick'd; and his poor self,
A dedicated beggar to the air,
With his disease of all-shunn'd poverty,
Walks like contempt, alone. More of our fellows.   15

Enter other Servants.

Stew. All broken implements of a ruin'd house.
Third Serv. Yet do our hearts wear Timon's livery,
That see I by our faces; we are fellows still,
Serving alike in sorrow. Leak'd is our bark,
And we, poor mates, stand on the dying deck,   20
Hearing the surges threat; we must all part
Into this sea of air.
Stew.   Good fellows all,
The latest of my wealth I'll share amongst you.
Wherever we shall meet, for Timon's sake
Let's yet be fellows. Let's shake our heads, and say,   25
As 'twere a knell unto our master's fortunes,
"We have seen better days". Let each take some;
                              [*Giving them money.*
Nay, put out all your hands. Not one word more;
Thus part we rich in sorrow, parting poor.
                    [*Embrace, and part several ways.*
O the fierce wretchedness that glory brings us!   30

---

14. all-shunn'd] *As Pope;* all shunn'd *F.*   27. S.D.] *As Rowe; not in F.*

13. *dedicated . . . air*] a beggar vowed or doomed to the open air. The construction, with the adjective ("dedicated") preceding the noun, and the adverbial part of the phrase ("to the air") following it, is normal in Elizabethan English. See Abbott 419 a.

15. *like contempt*] as if he were contempt or contemptibility itself.

16. *implements*] "Furnishings" might be the best paraphrase, to preserve the metaphor.

17. *Yet . . . livery*] but our hearts still wear the uniform of Timon's servants, i.e. are still at his service.

18. *fellows*] colleagues, fellow-workers. So in l. 25 below.

19. *bark*] a small sailing vessel.

20. *the dying deck*] the deck of death, or, perhaps, the deck which is itself sinking towards death.

21. *part*] depart.

22. *sea of air*] i.e. the open air affords us as little comfort as the sea does to sailors who must take to it when their ship founders. Ingleby, in a passage incomprehensible to me (*The Still Lion*, p. 87), seems to imagine that the wrecked ship is the body from which the soul is taking flight.

23. *latest*] last (by derivation, the same word).

28. *put out all*] i.e. all put out.

30. *fierce*] violent, excessive. (So

Who would not wish to be from wealth exempt,
Since riches point to misery and contempt?
Who would be so mock'd with glory, or to live
But in a dream of friendship,
To have his pomp and all what state compounds   35
But only painted like his varnish'd friends?
Poor honest lord, brought low by his own heart,
Undone by goodness; strange, unusual blood,
When man's worst sin is he does too much good!
Who then dares to be half so kind again?   40
For bounty, that makes gods, do still mar men.
My dearest lord, bless'd to be most accurs'd,
Rich only to be wretched—thy great fortunes
Are made thy chief afflictions. Alas, kind lord,
He's flung in rage from this ingrateful seat   45
Of monstrous friends;
Nor has he with him to supply his life,
Or that which can command it.

---

33. or to] *F;* as to *Rowe.*   35. what] *F;* that *conj. Grant White.*   compounds] *F;*
comprehends *Collier (edn 2);* comprends *Deighton.*   46–8.] *As F;* Of . . . to /
Supply . . . it / *Pope.*

Knight, comparing a similar use of it
in Ben Jonson.)

32. *point to*] lead to (as a line
"points" in a given direction).

33–4. *Who . . . friendship*] who would
wish to be so deceived by false glory or
would wish to live merely in the dream
or illusion that he had friends? (See
too Abbott 350.) This whole speech by
the Steward seems to be a draft, never
worked over by Shakespeare. See
Introduction, Section 3.

35. *all . . . compounds*] For "what",
meaning "that which", compare
Abbott 252. "Compounds" is a rather
odd but not unique use of the active
for the passive (compare Abbott 294,
295): "is compounded (or composed)
of". "State", of course, means the
splendour attaching to a position of
wealth or importance.

36. *But only painted*] i.e. only a
painted imitation of the real thing,
just as Timon's friends are not

genuine but have only the "varnish"
or outside gloss of friends.

38. *blood*] Schmidt explained as
"disposition", "temper", and most
editors agree. "Blood" can also mean,
however, the physical or animal
nature of man, and that may be what
is referred to here.

40. *half . . . again*] Not "as kind and
half as kind again" but "even half as
kind (as Timon) in future".

41. *do*] For the attraction of the verb
into the plural by the proximity of
"gods", see Abbott 412.

42. *to be*] only to be.

45. *seat*] centre or residence. Compare "seat of government", "country
seat".

47. *to . . . life*] that with which to
supply, or provide the food of, life.

48. *Or . . . it*] or that which can ob-
tain or purchase such food (i.e. money
or anything for sale). "It" is again
general, with no clear antecedent.

I'll follow and enquire him out.
I'll ever serve his mind, with my best will;   50
Whilst I have gold I'll be his steward still.   [*Exit.*

[SCENE III]

Enter TIMON *in the Woods.*

Tim. O blessed breeding sun, draw from the earth
          Rotten humidity; below thy sister's orb
          Infect the air! Twinn'd brothers of one womb,
          Whose procreation, residence and birth
          Scarce is dividant—touch them with several fortunes,   5
          The greater scorns the lesser. Not nature,
          To whom all sores lay siege, can bear great fortune,
          But by contempt of nature.
          Raise me this beggar, and deny 't that lord,

Scene III

SCENE III] *Rowe; not in F.*   S.D.] *As F; The Woods. Enter Timon | Rowe; Wood;
a Cave in View. Enter Timon, with a Spade. Capell; Woods and cave near the Sea-shore.
Enter Timon, from the cave. Camb. edd.*   1. blessed breeding] *F; blessed-breeding
Warburton.*   3. Twinn'd] *Pope;* Twin'd *Ff.*   9. deny 't] *F;* denude *Theobald;*
degrade *Hanmer.*

Scene III
S.D. Enter . . . Woods] Another
interesting S.D. that seems to come
from author's manuscript.
   1. *blessed breeding*] Warburton wanted to read "blessed - breeding"
("breeding blessings") but the emendation is unnecessary.
   2. *Rotten*] Perhaps means "rotting"
—humidity which causes rot. Compare IV. i. 34 n.
   2–3. *below . . . air!*] According to the
Ptolemaic cosmology, only the re-
gion below the moon was subject to
change, all above it being incorrup-
tible. Timon calls on the sun (which
is normally associated with "breeding" or creation) to reverse its nature
and destroy by infection (such as
the plague) the entire sublunary
sphere.

   5. *dividant*] divisible, separable.
   touch] (if you) test, try. For "touch"
compare III. iii. 7 and note.
   several] different.
   7. *To whom . . . siege*] which is constantly beset by all kinds of sores (and
might therefore be expected to bear
yet another—great fortune).
   8. *But . . . nature*] except by acting in
defiance of nature and natural affection (by despising its kind). There may
be a quibble on "nature" in the senses
of "human nature" and "beings of the
same nature or kind", as Deighton suggested.
   9. *deny't*] Emendations (such as "degrade") are unnecessary. "It" is again
general, referring to the whole preceding phrase and meaning, roughly,
"the privilege of being raised by
wealth".

The senators shall bear contempt hereditary,   10
The beggar native honour.
It is the pasture lards the brother's sides,
The want that makes him lean. Who dares, who dares,
In purity of manhood stand upright,
And say this man's a flatterer? If one be,   15
So are they all, for every grise of fortune
Is smooth'd by that below: the learned pate
Ducks to the golden fool; all's obliquy;
There's nothing level in our cursed natures

---

10. senators] *As F;* Senator *Rowe.*   12. pasture] *As Rowe;* Pastour *F1;* Pastor
F2–4.   lards] *Rowe;* Lards, *F1;* Lords, *F2–4.*   brother's] Brothers *Ff;*
Beggar's *Rowe;* weather's (wether's) *Warburton;* rother's *Singer.*   13. lean]
leaue *F1? (—see note);* leane *F2.*   16. grise] grize *F;* greeze *Pope.*   18. all's
obliquy] *F1* (All's oblique) *; All is oblique *Pope.*

---

10. *contempt hereditary*] the contempt
that is inherited with a low station (as
against the honour that is "native" to a
high one).

12–13. *It . . . lean*] A notorious
crux. Collier's suggested emendation
to "rother's" (a "rother" is a horned
beast) is almost as famous as Theobald's "a' babbled of green fields" in
H5, II. ii. 18; but neither it nor Warburton's (and Sisson's) "weather's"
("wether's")—which is a rather more
credible misreading of an Elizabethan
hand—seems to me to make good
enough sense (though Warburton
added "the similitude is extremely
beautiful"). Timon is not uttering
platitudes about fat and lean animals;
he is deploring the fact that mere
chance of birth or wealth puts one of
two "twinn'd brothers" above another. Surely the Folio text is right and
means, as Malone and Knight virtually suggested: "It is the (possession
of) pasture that makes one brother fat
(like the cattle on it); and the want of
it that makes the brother (the younger
one) lean". Compare Hamlet's jibe
that the landed Osric is "spacious in
the possession of dirt" (v. ii. 90).
There is no difficulty about "lean": I
believe a close inspection of the Folio
reveals that the alleged reading

"leaue" is really "leane" with an "n"
turned upside-down. For "Pastors"
probably meaning "pastures", compare Folio *R2,* III. iii. 100.

16. *grise*] A variant of "grece" (ME
grese): a step or stair (or a flight of
stairs). Compare, e.g., *Tw.N.,* III. i.
134–5.

17. *smooth'd*] flattered, softened with
flattery. The metaphor is frequent in
Elizabethan literature and survives,
of course, today; but it may have a
special significance here as used of
smoothing the *step.*

pate] head (which "ducks" or
inclines).

18. *golden*] i.e. favoured with gold,
rich.

all's obliquy] Pope altered to "All is
oblique", no doubt on the reasoning
that there was no such word as
"obliquy". *O.E.D.* does in fact record
it but as a common spelling of
"obloquy" (slander), perhaps by confusion with "obliquity". "Obliquity"
seems to be the word required here;
perhaps "obliquy" is Shakespeare's
own version of it.

19. *level*] Could mean (in addition to
its present meanings) either "steady"
or "direct, in a straight line". The
context seems to demand the latter
here.

But direct villainy. Therefore be abhorr'd   20
All feasts, societies, and throngs of men!
His semblable, yea himself, Timon disdains.
Destruction fang mankind! Earth, yield me roots.

                                            [*Digging.*

Who seeks for better of thee, sauce his palate
With thy most operant poison. What is here?   25
Gold? Yellow, glittering, precious gold?
No, gods, I am no idle votarist.
Roots, you clear heavens! Thus much of this will make
Black, white; foul, fair; wrong, right;
Base, noble; old, young; coward, valiant.   30
Ha, you gods! Why this? What this, you gods? Why, this
Will lug your priests and servants from your sides,
Pluck stout men's pillows from below their heads.
This yellow slave
Will knit and break religions, bless th'accurs'd,   35
Make the hoar leprosy ador'd, place thieves,
And give them title, knee and approbation

---

23. fang] *Johnson;* phang *Ff.*   S.D.] *As Rowe; not in F.*   26–30.] *As F;* Gold
... Gods / ... heavens / ... fair / ... valiant / *Hanmer.*

20. *direct*] The stress, as often, is on the first syllable.

22. *His semblable*] anything like himself. The word is also used as a noun in *Ham.* (v. ii. 124): "his semblable is his mirror", but in a passage where Hamlet is parodying Osric's affected speech.

23. *fang*] The most probable interpretation of the Folio "phang". The verb, meaning "grasp", "seize", is now found only in dialect. Caroline Spurgeon saw it as an extension of the "dog" imagery so common in the play.

24. *of*] from.

25. *operant*] operative, potent.

26–30. *Gold? . . . valiant*] An interesting example of a Folio line-division that seems to have a certain rhetorical force that is lost in the mechanical rearrangement made by Hanmer and adopted by most modern editors.

27. *no idle votarist*] not one who has

idly taken a vow, meaning not to keep it.

28. *clear*] pure. But Rolfe noted a suggestion that it is used as if equivalent to the Latin *clarus*, glorious.

33. *Pluck . . . heads*] A method of killing by sudden deprivation of breath. So Mosca proposes to Volpone (II. vi. 86–8): "In his next fit we may let him go. / 'Tis but to pluck the pillow from his head, / And he is throttled".

35. *knit . . . religions*] i.e. bind men together or divide them even where religion is in question.

36. *hoar leprosy*] So called because it leaves shining white scales on the skin. To forestall emendation, it may be mentioned that the Folio does seem to distinguish between "hoar" ("hoare") and "whore" (used in this same speech at l. 43).

place] elevate or appoint to a place of dignity.

37. *knee*] the right to be kneeled to.

With senators on the bench. This is it
That makes the wappen'd widow wed again:
She whom the spital-house and ulcerous sores   40
Would cast the gorge at, this embalms and spices
To th' April day again. Come, damn'd earth,
Thou common whore of mankind, that puts odds
Among the rout of nations, I will make thee
Do thy right nature.   [*March afar off.*
          Ha? A drum? Th'art quick,   45
But yet I'll bury thee. Thou'lt go, strong thief,
When gouty keepers of thee cannot stand.
Nay, stay thou out for earnest.   [*Keeping some gold.*

39. wappen'd] *F;* wapper'd *conj. Malone;* wained *conj. Johnson;* weeping *conj.*
Steevens (1785).   41. at, this] *Pope;* at. This *Ff.*   43. puts] puttes *F;* puttest
Rowe; putt'st *Pope.*   45. Do . . . quick] *As Pope;* Do . . . Nature. / . . . quicke / *F.*
48. S.D. *Keeping some gold] Pope; not in F.*

39. *makes . . . wed again*] helps to a
second marriage.

wappen'd] A very rare, possibly dia-
lectal, word, generally explained as
"worn out" or "stale", but Steevens
cited uses of "wappening" and
"wapping" which suggest that it was a
cant word meaning
"sexually exhausted". Malone proposed the slightly commoner "wapper'd" ("fatigued" or "weary").
Shadwell altered to "warp'd and
wither'd".

40. *She*] Emphatic, for the objective
case "her".

the spital-house] (inhabitants of) a
hospital. The word "spital" (an
aphetic form of "hospital" and originally spelt "spittle") was most commonly applied to an institution for low
persons or for those afflicted with horrible diseases and particularly leprosy.

ulcerous sores] Apparently, those
afflicted with ulcerous sores. So Shadwell took it, altering to "ulcerous
Creatures".

41. *Would . . . at*] would vomit
merely to look at.

41–2. *this . . . again*] this gold preserves (in the same way as bodies are
embalmed) and perfumes (spice was
used both for embalming and for per-

fuming) to make her as fresh as a day
in spring. Compare *Wiv.*, III. ii. 68–70
where it is said of Fenton that "he
has eyes of youth . . . he speaks holi-
day, he smells April and May";
Knight also compared from Sonnet 3:
"Calls back the lovely April of her
prime".

43–4. *puts . . nations*] For the form
"puts", see note on IV. i. 2 above.
There is no call for emendation. The
phrase means "sets the mob of
nations at each other's throats". Compare "set into odds", l. 394 below.
"Rout" clearly has a derogatory
sense, "disorderly herd".

44–5. *make . . . nature*] make you act
according to your true nature, i.e.
cause trouble (Deighton rightly rejected Johnson's explanation "lie in
the earth where nature laid thee").

45. *quick*] A pun (1) sudden, (2)
alive, or (possibly) pregnant—but
nevertheless to be buried. Compare
Wint., IV. iv. 132.

46. *go*] move (carrying on the
quibble in "quick").

48. *earnest*] Strictly, a part payment
to seal a bargain; hence, instalment,
or pledge. (ME *ernes,* perhaps con-
fused with "earnest" in the sense of
"seriousness".)

Enter ALCIBIADES, *with drum and fife, in warlike manner;*
and PHRYNIA *and* TIMANDRA.

Alcib. What art thou there? Speak.
Tim. A beast as thou art. The canker gnaw thy
    heart,   50
    For showing me again the eyes of man!
Alcib. What is thy name? Is man so hateful to thee
    That art thyself a man?
Tim. I am *Misanthropos*, and hate mankind.
    For thy part, I do wish thou wert a dog,   55
    That I might love thee something.
Alcib.   I know thee well;
    But in thy fortunes am unlearn'd and strange.
Tim. I know thee too, and more than that I know thee
    I not desire to know. Follow thy drum;
    With man's blood paint the ground, gules, gules.   60
    Religious canons, civil laws are cruel;
    Then what should war be? This fell whore of thine
    Hath in her more destruction than thy sword, ˗
    For all her cherubin look.
Phry.   Thy lips rot off!

49.] *Scene IV Pope.*   54. *Misanthropos*] *F2; Misantropos F1.*

S.D. Timandra] The name is taken
from North's *Plutarch*, where it is related that Timandra, one of Alcibiades' concubines, "buried him as
honorably as she could possible" after
he had been murdered.

50. *canker*] Virtually the same word
as "cancer". "Canker", now practically confined in medicine to cancer
of the mouth, was used originally of
any spreading growth or sore. Alternatively, it may mean here, as often in
Shakespeare, the canker-worm, which
lives by gnawing buds and leaves.

54. Misanthropos] A hater of mankind. Shakespeare would have read in
North's translation of Plutarch, after
the account of the defeat at Actium,
this marginal note: "*Antonius followeth
the life and example of Timon Misanthropos the Athenian. Plato and Aristo-*

*phanes testimony of Timon Misanthropos,
what he was.*" The paragraph thus sum-
marized was apparently Shakespeare's
principal source for the play and makes
quite unnecessary any suggestion (such
as Deighton's) of a verbal borrowing
from Lucian here.

56. *something*] somewhat.

57. *unlearn'd and strange*] uninformed
and ignorant. But commentators note
some uncertainty on the dramatist's
part about Alcibiades' exact knowledge of Timon's misfortunes.

60. *gules*] red (the regular term in
heraldry).

62. *fell*] virulent, destructive. Now
chiefly *dial.* or *poet.*

64. *cherubin look*] angelic face. The
noun "cherubin", strictly a plural,
was treated as a singular and is here, of
course, used as an adjective.

Tim. I will not kiss thee; then the rot returns   65
　　To thine own lips again.

Alcib. How came the noble Timon to this change?

Tim. As the moon does, by wanting light to give.
　　But then renew I could not like the moon;
　　There were no suns to borrow of.   70

Alcib. Noble Timon, what friendship may I do thee?

Tim. None, but to maintain my opinion.

Alcib. What is it, Timon?

Tim. Promise me friendship, but perform none. If thou
　　wilt not promise, the gods plague thee, for thou art   75
　　a man! If thou dost perform, confound thee, for
　　thou art a man!

Alcib. I have heard in some sort of thy miseries.

Tim. Thou saw'st them when I had prosperity.

Alcib. I see them now; then was a blessed time.   80

Tim. As thine is now, held with a brace of harlots.

Timan. Is this th' Athenian minion whom the world
　　Voic'd so regardfully?

Tim.　　　　　　　　Art thou Timandra?

Timan.　　　　　　　　　　　　　Yes.

Tim. Be a whore still. They love thee not that use thee.

65. thee;] *Steevens;* thee, *F.*   71.] *As F;* Timon, / What *Capell.*   72.] *As F;* to /
Maintain *Capell.*   84–8.] *As Pope;* prose *F.*

65–6. *I . . . again*] Editors accept
Johnson's explanation of a belief that
if venereal disease was transmitted to
another it "left the infecter free". The
verb "returning" seems odd but Timon is
"returning" Phrynia's curse that *his*
lips may rot off: "I won't kiss you; and
by not kissing you, I've left the rot
where it started and belongs".

68. *wanting*] lacking.

69. *renew*] Used intransitively, "to
become new, or grow again", with a
pun on the renewing of a loan, as the
following line shows. For the repetition
of this image from III. iv. 12–14, see the
Introduction, Section 2.

72. *but . . . opinion*] i.e. except to help
me retain my opinion (of mankind).

76–7. *If . . . man*] i.e. even if you do
both promise and carry out your pro-

mise, may you still be damned, for you
are still a man.

78. *in some sort*] Compare the modern
"in a sort of way": imperfectly, indirectly.

81. *held with*] tied with, or, perhaps,
held back, retarded by. Compare
1H6, v. iii. 13, "O, hold me not with
silence over-long!"

82. *minion*] favourite, darling (often
used scornfully).

83. *Voic'd so regardfully*] spoke of with
such regard, acclaimed with such high
praise. H. C. Goddard (*The Meaning of
Shakespeare*) well compared the thought
and idiom of Lodovico's "Is this the
noble Moor, whom our full Senate /
Call all in all sufficient?" *Oth.*, IV. i.
275–6.

84–8. *Be . . . diet*] The Folio prints

Give them diseases, leaving with thee their lust.   85
Make use of thy salt hours; season the slaves
For tubs and baths; bring down rose-cheek'd youth
To the tub-fast and the diet.
Timan.   Hang thee, monster!
Alcib. Pardon him, sweet Timandra, for his wits
Are drown'd and lost in his calamities.   90
I have but little gold of late, brave Timon,
The want whereof doth daily make revolt
In my penurious band. I have heard and griev'd
How cursed Athens, mindless of thy worth,
Forgetting thy great deeds, when neighbour states,   95
But for thy sword and fortune, trod upon them—
Tim. I prithee beat thy drum, and get thee gone.
Alcib. I am thy friend, and pity thee, dear Timon.
Tim. How dost thou pity him whom thou dost trouble?
I had rather be alone.
Alcib.   Why, fare thee well: 100
Here is some gold for thee.
Tim. Keep it, I cannot eat it.

---

88. tub-fast] *Theobald (Warburton)*; Fubfast *Ff.*   96. them—] *Rowe;* them. *F.*

---

this as prose, but the page shows some signs of having been squeezed up by the compositor to save space.

85. *leaving*] i.e. they leaving, while they leave.

86. *salt*] lecherous, salacious (used of bitches in heat).

season] spice.

87. *tubs and baths*] the sweating-tubs (compare "tub-fast" in l. 88) and hot baths used for the treatment of sexual disease.

88. *diet*] the curative diet. Fasting was still part of the treatment as late as James Boswell's day.

89 ff.] While I have argued in the Introduction that Alcibiades is not *as* noble as Timon, his attitude throughout this scene shows his many worthy qualities also. And yet even here he can explain Timon's distress and his hatred of mankind only on the presumption of madness. That is exact-

ly what glib critics say of the Swift who wrote Book IV of *Gulliver's Travels*.

93. *penurious*] Not "niggardly" but "needy" (Latin *penuria*).

94–6. *How . . . them*] The suggestion here that Timon had rendered important military services to Athens is repeated at v. i. 145–6 and 158–62 but is not linked with anything else in the play. Perhaps Shakespeare himself was uncertain about it. The only mention of military prowess in the possible known sources is, I think, in Lucian, in the lawyer Demeas' exaggerated claim (written into his decree) that Timon cut two Peloponnesian companies to pieces—to which Timon replies (Fowler's translation) "Good work that, considering that my name was not on the muster-rolls, because I could not afford a suit of armour".

96. *trod*] i.e. would have trodden.

Alcib. When I have laid proud Athens on a heap—
Tim. Warr'st thou 'gainst Athens?
Alcib.   Ay, Timon, and have cause.
Tim. The gods confound them all in thy conquest,   105
       And thee after, when thou hast conquer'd!
Alcib. Why me, Timon?
Tim.   That by killing of villains
       Thou wast born to conquer my country.
       Put up thy gold. Go on. Here's gold. Go on.
       Be as a planetary plague, when Jove   110
       Will o'er some high-vic'd city hang his poison
       In the sick air. Let not thy sword skip one.
       Pity not honour'd age for his white beard:
       He is an usurer. Strike me the counterfeit matron:
       It is her habit only that is honest,   115
       Herself's a bawd. Let not the virgin's cheek
       Make soft thy trenchant sword: for those milk-paps,
       That through the window-bars bore at men's eyes,

---

103. heap—] *As Rowe (edn 3);* heape. *F.*   118. window-bars] *conj. Johnson;* window Barne *F.*

104–8. *Warr'st . . . country*] These lines have worried even commentators who have seen no difficulty in printing other passages as poor verse. One can see something like a five-stress pattern in the lines, but the verse is exceptionally "free".

105. *in thy conquest*] during, or as a result of, your conquest of them.

109. *Put up thy gold*] i.e. put away thy gold (the gold Alcibiades was offering to Timon).

110. *planetary plague*] a plague induced by the planets, either because of their evil influence or because disorder in heaven was reflected by dislocation of the moral and physical order on earth.

111. *Will*] determines to.

112. *sick*] infected. Plague was commonly held to have been caused by poison in the air, even in ancient times (J. A. K. Thomson, *Shakespeare and the Classics,* 1952, p. 152).

114. *Strike me*] An interesting example of the pleonastic pronoun.

"Me" is almost meaningless, unless it faintly suggests "so far as I am concerned".

115. *habit*] dress, costume.

honest] unpolluted. ("Honest" often means "chaste" in Elizabethan usage.)

117. *trenchant*] In its original, literal, sense: sharp, cutting.

118. *window-bars*] Johnson's emendation for the Folio's "window Barne" is generally accepted. It is an easy misreading and the compositor may have been influenced by the next word "bore" and perhaps thought of "borne" while carrying the line in his head. The "window-bars" would probably be the open-work squares of the bodice of the woman's frock—another anachronism. If the literal meaning is to be preserved, then there could be a memory of the proverb that a woman at a window is like grapes on the highway, "everybody will be plucking, and gathering, and reaching at them" (Tilley W 647).

Are not within the leaf of pity writ,   119
But set them down horrible traitors. Spare not the babe
Whose dimpled smiles from fools exhaust their mercy:
Think it a bastard, whom the oracle
Hath doubtfully pronounc'd the throat shall cut,
And mince it sans remorse. Swear against objects.
Put armour on thine ears and on thine eyes   125
Whose proof nor yells of mothers, maids, nor babes,
Nor sight of priests in holy vestments bleeding
Shall pierce a jot. There's gold to pay thy soldiers.
Make large confusion; and, thy fury spent,
Confounded be thyself! Speak not, be gone.   130
Alcib. Hast thou gold yet? I'll take the gold thou givest me,
     Not all thy counsel.
Tim. Dost thou, or dost thou not, heaven's curse upon thee!
Phry., Timan. Give us some gold, good Timon: hast thou
     more?
Tim. Enough to make a whore forswear her trade,   135

---

123. pronounc'd] *Pope;* pronounced, *F.*   the] *F;* thy *Pope.*   124. objects] *F;*
abjects *Collier (ed. 2).*   131-2.] *As Capell; prose F.*   134, 151, 169. Phry.,
Timan.] *Both. F.*

119. *within . . . writ*] included on the
list of things to be pitied and spared.
   121. *exhaust*] draw off or out. Latin
ex + *haurire* to draw. (Compare the
"exhaust" of the modern car.)
   123. *Hath . . . cut*] "Doubtfully"
means "ambiguously"—yet editors
remove the ambiguity by reading "thy
throat" for the Folio's "the throat".
The oracle is apparently to be thought
of as "pronouncing" ambiguously, in
the manner of classical oracles, so that
it is not clear whose throat is to be cut.
Timon cynically advises Alcibiades to
act like a man faced with a prediction
that might mean either that he would
kill the child or that the child would
kill him—i.e. to get in first. This point
has been obscured by commentators
who refer to the story of Laius in-
formed by the oracle that he would
perish at the hands of his own son
(Oedipus).
   124. *sans*] without. The preposition

is used several times by Shakespeare,
notably in the "Seven Ages of Man"
speech in *AYL.*
   objects] Emendations (none of them
satisfactory anyway) are now known
to be quite unnecessary: Sisson has
pointed out (*New Readings*, p. 174) that
"objects" meant "objections" (or, as
O.E.D. puts it, "a statement intro-
duced in opposition"). Timon bids
Alcibiades, then, not to be put off
by protests; and the following lines
develop this idea.
   126. *Whose proof*] the tested power of
which. . . The antecedent of "whose"
is "armour"; and "proof" is the technical term for the quality of armour
which has been tested to withstand
blows. Hence, *fig.*, "proof" came to
mean "invulnerability".
   133. *Dost . . . not*] whether you do or
not. For the subjunctive construction
with verb before subject, see Abbott
361.

And to make whores a bawd. Hold up, you sluts,
Your aprons mountant. You are not oathable,
Although I know you'll swear, terribly swear
Into strong shudders and to heavenly agues
Th' immortal gods that hear you. Spare your oaths: 140
I'll trust to your conditions. Be whores still;
And he whose pious breath seeks to convert you,
Be strong in whore, allure him, burn him up;
Let your close fire predominate his smoke,
And be no turncoats: yet may your pains, six months,
Be quite contrary. And thatch   146

146-50.] *As F;* Be . . . roofs / . . . hang'd / . . . still / . . . face / *Capell.*

136. *And . . . a bawd*] Emendation
again seems to miss the point, which I
take to be that whores with money
enough will leave that part of the
trade—and set themselves up, as many
have done, in the more profitable business of organizing others. The singular
"bawd" is a difficulty, but does not,
I think, make this interpretation
impossible. Johnson's interpretation
"enough to make a whore leave whor-
ing and a bawd leave making whores"
wrenches the syntax beyond belief.

137. *mountant*] always in process of
being raised. Timon is coining a word
on the model of heraldic terms describing position such as "couchant" and
"rampant"; he requires that the
aprons be held up this time to receive
his gold.

not oathable] not able to be placed on
oath in the expectation that you will
keep that oath, however strongly you
express it.

141. *conditions*] quality, nature or,
possibly, vocations (Mason).

144. *close . . . smoke*] The phrase begins from the proverb "Where there's
smoke, there's fire". Schmidt explained "smoke" in the sense of "phrases,
idle words" and took it to refer back
to l. 142: so, "may the secret fire
(of your sexual ardour or disease)
dominate over, defeat his idle attempts to convert you". But I

suspect further sexual connotations.

145. *turncoats*] The word was used in
the same sense as it has today but
could also be applied to anything or
anyone that changed in appearance or
colour (*O.E.D.*); both senses could be
involved here. The principal meaning,
at any rate, is that they must not be unfaithful to their profession as prostitutes and must therefore turn the
would-be converter into a client—and,
of course, infect him.

145-6. *yet . . . contrary*] On this clause
one receives little help from previous
editors. There is no obvious justification either for Warburton's suggestion
that for the second six months of the
year the prostitutes were to follow
different or *contrary* labours and repair
the disorders resulting from their profession, or for Steevens's that for six
months at least they were to undergo
punishment in a house of correction.
Deighton argued that no imprecation
upon the courtesans is involved (and
went on to most improbable emendation); but, as Johnson suggested,
Timon "is afraid lest the whores
should imagine that he wishes well to
them", and therefore, although he
favours the harm they do to mankind,
he puts in a special curse for them. It
may be only the obvious one: that for
six months their menstrual pains may
be abnormal.

Your poor thin roofs with burthens of the dead—
Some that were hang'd, no matter;
Wear them, betray with them. Whore still;
Paint till a horse may mire upon your face: 150
A pox of wrinkles!
Phry., Timan.   Well, more gold. What then?
Believe 't that we'll do anything for gold.
Tim. Consumptions sow
In hollow bones of man; strike their sharp shins,
And mar men's spurring. Crack the lawyer's voice,   155
That he may never more false title plead,
Nor sound his quillets shrilly. Hoar the flamen,
That scolds against the quality of flesh,

---

158. scolds] *Rowe;* scold'st *F.*

147. *with . . . dead*] with loads (of
hair) taken from dead people. Loss of
hair, a normal result of sexual disease
—or believed to be so—had to be
covered up by a wig. "Burthen" was a
regular alternative form of "burden".

150. *till . . . face*] Schmidt explained
as "until a horse may sink in the mud
upon your face" (because of the depth
of the cosmetics); Deighton as "until
a horse may bespatter your face without washing off the thick paint" (compare *Ado,* iv. i. 135).

151. *A pox of wrinkles!*] A pox on
wrinkles! i.e. let them be abolished for
ever (by paint and powder). But I
cannot help wondering whether the
Folio colon is not misleading and
whether "a pox of wrinkles" is not the
object of the verb "mire".

152. *Believe 't*] For the quasi-
redundant object "it", see Abbott
414.

153–4. *Consumptions . . . man*] "Consumption" was used not only of pul-
monary consumption, as it is now, but
also of other forms of wasting disease:
here, of course, particularly V.D.
"Hollow" is probably used prolep-
tically, i.e. sow disease in the bones of
man so as to make them hollow.

154. *sharp*] Deighton cited from Dr
Bucknill's *Shakespeare's Medical Know-*

ledge the belief that Shakespeare is referring to "painful nodes on the shin
bones" also caused by syphilis.

155. *spurring*] Commentators seem
satisfied to take this literally: by hurt-
ing men's shins, lessen their power to
apply the spur (or perhaps, in the
commonest figurative sense, to hasten). There may be a sexual innuendo.

Crack . . . voice] Another effect of
syphilis: ulcerations of the larynx
(Bucknill).

157. *quillets*] quibbles, over-subtle
verbal distinctions. Compare *1H6,* ii.
iv. 17.

Hoar] whiten (with disease). Compare note on iv. iii. 36 above; but the
reference is more probably here to
sexual disease than to leprosy: perhaps
to the whitish sores, perhaps, as
Deighton suggested, to the whitening
of the hair.

flamen] priest (strictly, a Roman
priest).

158. *That . . . flesh*] Sisson (*N.R.,*
p. 175) rightly casts doubt on Deighton's explanation of this as "Who is
angry when the flesh of the victim refuses to give a good omen" (on the
altar). The priest is pretending to
decry the flesh generally ("flesh and
the devil") and sexual pleasure in particular—but doesn't believe himself.

And not believes himself. Down with the nose,
Down with it flat, take the bridge quite away   160
Of him that, his particular to foresee,
Smells from the general weal. Make curl'd-pate ruffians
    bald,
And let the unscarr'd braggarts of the war
Derive some pain from you. Plague all,
That your activity may defeat and quell   165
The source of all erection. There's more gold.
Do you damn others, and let this damn you,
And ditches grave you all!

Phry., Timan. More counsel with more money, bounteous
    Timon.

Tim. More whore, more mischief first; I have given you
    earnest.   170

Alcib. Strike up the drum towards Athens! Farewell, Timon:
    If I thrive well, I'll visit thee again.

Tim. If I hope well, I'll never see thee more.

Alcib. I never did thee harm.

Tim. Yes, thou spok'st well of me.

Alcib.   Call'st thou that harm?

Tim. Men daily find it. Get thee away, and take   176
    Thy beagles with thee.

171-2. Strike . . . again] *As Pope; prose F.*   176-7.] *As Dyce;* Men . . . away, / . . . thee. / *F;* Men . . . it. / . . . thee. *Steevens.*

159. *Down . . . nose*] The decay of the nose-bridge was perhaps the most commonly known of all the symptoms of syphilis.

161-2. *his . . . weal*] Johnson explained this as a somewhat "incongruous" metaphor from hunting: "to provide for his private advantage . . . leaves the right scent of public good". The change from "fore-*see*" to "smells" is abrupt—but no more so than many image sequences in Shakespeare, and, for that matter, "foresee" had lost most of its literal meaning and had come to mean "make provision for", "look after". "Particular" was often used in the sense of personal or private profit. "Weal" = "welfare".

163. *the . . . war*] those who boast

of their part in the war although in fact they have never been close enough to the fighting to be in any danger. Compare *H5,* iii. vi. 70–85.

168. *grave*] bury, entomb.

170. *earnest*] The "consideration" that makes the contract binding. Compare l. 48 above, and note.

173. *If I hope well*] if I hope successfully, if my hopes are realized.

175. *Yes . . . me*] Malone suggested another probable Biblical echo: "Woe unto you when all men shall speak well of you! for so did their fathers to the false prophets", *Luke,* vi. 26. This seems more likely than the allusion Tilley saw to the proverb "Praise by evil men is dispraise" (P 540).

177. *beagles*] small hunting dogs.

Alcib.   We but offend him. Strike!

  [*Drum beats. Exeunt Alcibiades, Phrynia and Timandra.*

Tim. That nature, being sick of man's unkindness,
 Should yet be hungry! Common mother, thou [*Digging.*
 Whose womb unmeasurable and infinite breast   180
 Teems and feeds all; whose self-same mettle,
 Whereof thy proud child, arrogant man, is puff'd,
 Engenders the black toad and adder blue,
 The gilded newt and eyeless venom'd worm,
 With all th' abhorred births below crisp heaven   185
 Whereon Hyperion's quick'ning fire doth shine:
 Yield him, who all the human sons do hate,
 From forth thy plenteous bosom, one poor root.
 Ensear thy fertile and conceptious womb;

---

177. S.D.] *As Johnson; Exeunt F.*   178.] *Scene V Pope.*   179. S.D.] *As Johnson* (*before 178*); *not in F.*   187. the] *Ff;* thy *Pope.*   do] *F;* do's *Rowe;* doth *Capell.*

The word came to be used as a term of contempt, applied particularly to spies and informers. The only other character to use it in Shakespeare, however, is the sporting Sir Toby, who employs it, incongruously, as a compliment (*Tw. N.*, II. iii. 191).

 178. *being sick of*] being made ill by (an overdose of) . . .

 181. *Teems*] Deighton described this as a transitive use of the verb; I think not. "Bears prolifically".

 mettle] Originally a variant of "metal" and probably used in a double sense: (1) essence, (2) spirit, in the sense of high spirits.

 182. *Whereof*] with which. "Of" was regular in Elizabethan English with "verbs of fulness" (Abbott 171).

 puff'd] inflated (in pride).

 184. *newt*] Originally "an ewt": an aquatic salamander, thought of as poisonous (e.g. in *Bartholomew Fair*, II. iii. 24–5). "Gilded" presumably of its colour, but compare *Mer.V.*, II. vii. 69. "Gilded tombs do worms enfold".

 eyeless . . . worm] Generally explained as "the blind-worm" (which is not blind but has particularly small eyes). "Worm" could also mean "serpent",

however, as notably in several passages of *Ant.* and, presumably, in *Cym.*, III. iv. 35–7, "Slander . . . whose tongue / Outvenoms all the worms of Nile"; and one wonders whether "eyeless" may not be used, exceptionally, to mean lacking eye*lids*, as does a serpent traditionally. The adder was also known as the blind-worm.

 185. *crisp*] *O.E.D.* cites this passage and Fletcher's "neat crisp Claret" (*Bloody Brother*, IV. ii) as presumptive evidence for thinking that the word may have meant "shining" or "clear", as perhaps it does also in *Tp.*, IV. i. 130, "You nymphs . . . Leave your crisp channels". Steevens and others take it in the normal Elizabethan sense of "curling" and explain it as a reference to the folds of the clouds.

 186. *Hyperion*] Sometimes the father of the Sun, here the sun itself.

 quick'ning] life-giving.

 187. *do*] The number of the verb is again influenced by the nearest noun, the plural "sons".

 188. *thy plenteous bosom*] Perhaps an ironical echo of the application of the phrase to Timon at I. ii. 120–1.

 189. *Ensear*] dry up, wither away,

Let it no more bring out ingrateful man.   190
Go great with tigers, dragons, wolves and bears;
Teem with new monsters, whom thy upward face
Hath to the marbled mansion all above
Never presented. O, a root; dear thanks!
Dry up thy marrows, vines and plough-torn leas,   195
Whereof ingrateful man, with liquorish draughts
And morsels unctuous, greases his pure mind,
That from it all consideration slips—

                Enter APEMANTUS.

More man? Plague, plague!
Apem. I was directed hither. Men report   200
   Thou dost affect my manners, and dost use them.
Tim. 'Tis then because thou dost not keep a dog
   Whom I would imitate. Consumption catch thee!
Apem. This is in thee a nature but infected,
   A poor unmanly melancholy sprung   205
   From change of future. Why this spade? This
      place?
   This slave-like habit, and these looks of care?
   Thy flatterers yet wear silk, drink wine, lie soft,
   Hug their diseas'd perfumes, and have forgot
   That ever Timon was. Shame not these woods   210

---

195. marrows, vines,] Marrowes, Vines, *F;* Marrows, Veins, *Rowe;* marrowie
vines *conj. Dyce.*   197. unctuous] *Johnson;* Vnctious *F.*   199.] *Scene VI Pope.*
206. future] *F;* Fortune *Rowe.*   210. woods] *F;* weeds *Theobald (Warburton).*

---

a rare prosthetic form of the commoner "sear".

conceptious] conceiving, prolific (another very rare form).

191. *great*] pregnant.

193. *marbled mansion*] i.e. Heaven,
either because of its colour or because
it is thought of as being rich and wonderful, as is a city of marble. Compare *Oth.*, III. iii. 460 and *Cymb.*, v. iv.
120.

197. *unctuous*] fat or oily (hence
"greases").

198. *consideration*] reflection, ability
to think.

201. *affect*] imitate in an unnatural

or "affected" way, or lay claim to.

203. *Consumption*] See l. 153 above,
and note.

204. *infected*] Perhaps both "infected
as with a disease" and "not implanted
by nature, but, as it were, caught;
factitious" (Schmidt). Rowe read
"affected" and was followed by most
early editors.

206. *future*] This Folio reading seems
to make perfect sense (a change in
Timon's prospects) and Rowe's emendation to "fortune" is therefore
quite unnecessary.

209. *perfumes*] i.e. perfumed mistresses (Malone).

By putting on the cunning of a carper.
Be thou a flatterer now, and seek to thrive
By that which has undone thee. Hinge thy knee,
And let his very breath whom thou'lt observe
Blow off thy cap; praise his most vicious strain,   215
And call it excellent. Thou wast told thus.
Thou gav'st thine ears, like tapsters that bade welcome,
To knaves, and all approachers. 'Tis most just
That thou turn rascal; hadst thou wealth again,
Rascals should have 't. Do not assume my likeness.   220
Tim. Were I like thee I'd throw away myself.
Apem. Thou hast cast away thyself, being like thyself
A madman so long, now a fool. What, think'st
That the bleak air, thy boisterous chamberlain,
Will put thy shirt on warm? Will these moist trees,   225
That have outliv'd the eagle, page thy heels
And skip when thou point'st out? Will the cold brook,
Candied with ice, caudle thy morning taste
To cure thy o'er-night's surfeit? Call the creatures

---

217. bade] bad *F1;* bid *F2–4.*   222. like thyself] As *F;* like thyself, *Pope.*
225. moist] *F3–4;* moyst *F1–2;* moss'd *Hanmer.*

211. *cunning*] knowledge (without derogatory implication); or perhaps, as Schmidt suggested, an extension of the sense of "art or skill" and so "profession".
carper] fault-finder, cynic.
214–15. *And . . . cap*] and cringe so obsequiously before the person you want to court (observe) that his breath could blow off your cap.
215. *strain*] quality (inherited); perhaps, even, family, race.
216. *Thou . . . thus*] this is what others told you.
217–18. *like . . . approachers*] The necessity for tapsters to answer every call and be at every man's service provides the humour of part of a long scene in *1H4* (II. iv).
219. *rascal*] With a pun on "rascal" in the sense of the inferior member of the herd (which tends to keep by itself) as well as "rascal" in the modern sense of "rogue".

224. *chamberlain*] the officer in charge of the private apartments or, more generally, a personal servant.
225. *moist*] damp—carrying on the idea of the lack of comfort and, as Knight pointed out, contrasting the trees with the *warm* shirt. Hanmer's "moss'd" is unnecessary.
226. *That . . . eagle*] Tradition had it that the eagle lived to a great age.
226–7. *page . . . out*] i.e. walk at your heels like a page and "jump to it" when you point out something you want.
228. *Candied*] encrusted, as if with sugar.
228–9. *caudle . . . surfeit*] provide a caudle (orig. a warm drink, later a spiced medicinal one) for your taste in the morning, to counteract the effects of your previous evening's indulgence. Probably with a quibble on "taste" in the sense of "nip of liquor".

Whose naked natures live in all the spite   230
Of wreakful heaven, whose bare unhoused trunks,
To the conflicting elements expos'd,
Answer mere nature; bid them flatter thee.
O thou shalt find—

Tim.   A fool of thee. Depart.
Apem. I love thee better now than e'er I did.   235
Tim. I hate thee worse.
Apem.   Why?
Tim.   Thou flatter'st misery.
Apem. I flatter not, but say thou art a caitiff.
Tim. Why dost thou seek me out?
Apem.   To vex thee.
Tim. Always a villain's office, or a fool's.
Dost please thyself in 't?
Apem.   Ay.
Tim.   What, a knave too?   240
Apem. If thou didst put this sour cold habit on
To castigate thy pride 'twere well; but thou
Dost it enforcedly. Thou'dst courtier be again
Wert thou not beggar. Willing misery
Outlives incertain pomp, is crown'd before;   245
The one is filling still, never complete,

---

234. find—] *Rowe;* finde. *F.*   241. sour cold] sowre cold *Ff;* sour-cold *Steevens*
(*1793*).   245. Outlives incertain] *As Rowe;* Out-liues: incertaine *F.*

230–1. *Whose . . . heaven*] who, in
their natural state of nakedness, are
exposed to the spite of the vengeful
skies.

233. *Answer mere nature*] have to endure nature in its undiluted, unmiti-
gated form. Deighton compared *Lr.,*
III. iv. 105–7: "Why, thou wert better
in thy grave than to answer with thy
uncovered body this extremity of the
skies". This interpretation certainly
seems preferable to Hudson's "have
no more than the absolute necessities
of nature".

234. *of*] in (Abbott 172).

237. *caitiff*] O.N.F. *caitif,* Latin *cap-
tivus.* Orig. a captive; hence, one in a
pitiful state, a mere wretch.

240. *a knave too*] i.e. for not merely

vexing, like a villain or a fool, but
actually enjoying doing so.

241. *habit*] Probably not merely
"garment" here, but also "appearance" and "manner".

244–5. *Willing . . . before*] want that
is accepted without complaint lasts
longer (or is more satisfactory in the
long run) than mere parade or show
that may be lost at any time; and such
poverty achieves glory first. Perhaps
there is a reference to the Voluntary
Poverty of, e.g., the monastic order.

246. *still*] always. Commentators
see here a reference to the punishment
of the Danaids in Hades, ever trying to
fill with water a jar with holes in the
bottom. It may be so, although the
classical allusion is not as probable as

The other, at high wish. Best state, contentless,
Hath a distracted and most wretched being,
Worse than the worst, content.
Thou shouldst desire to die, being miserable.　　250
Tim. Not by his breath that is more miserable.
Thou art a slave, whom Fortune's tender arm
With favour never clasp'd, but bred a dog.
Hadst thou like us from our first swath proceeded
The sweet degrees that this brief world affords　　255
To such as may the passive drugs of it
Freely command, thou wouldst have plung'd thyself
In general riot, melted down thy youth
In different beds of lust, and never learn'd
The icy precepts of respect, but followed　　260

256. drugs] *F4*; drugges *F1–2*; druggs *F3*; drudges *Delius*.　　257. command]
Rowe; command'st *F*.

in *Cym.*, I. vi. 47–9, which is quoted as a
parallel.

247. *at high wish*] as high or complete
as one could wish.

247–9. *Best . . . content*] The expression is concentrated but the meaning
clear, once the opposition of "best
state contentless" and "worst, content" is grasped. "The man most
favoured by Fortune, if he is not content, lives a disordered and divided
life of wretchedness which is worse
than the life lived by the man least
favoured by Fortune but content".

250. *being miserable*] since you are
so completely miserable (neither fortunate nor content).

251. *by . . . miserable*] at the suggestion of one who is more wretched still.

253. *but bred*] but (whom Fortune)
bred. A typical Shakespearian ellipsis.
Warburton suggested an allusion to
"cynic" (which is derived from the
Greek for "dog"), Apemantus being
one of the Cynic school of philoso-
phers. More interesting, however, is
the way in which during the following
lines there develops the typical Shakespearian association of flattery with
fawning dogs licking melted sugar-
icing or sweetmeats: "dog . . . sweet

degrees . . . melted . . . icy precepts . . .
sugar'd game . . . confectionary . . .
mouths . . . tongues . . . flatter'd" (see
Spurgeon's analysis, p. 199) and then
the further association of these with
barked trees (as pointed out by Armstrong, pp. 186–7).

254. *our first swath*] our swaddling
clothes. (*Swaddling* and *swath* derive
from the same O.E. root.)

254–5. *proceeded . . . degrees*] advanced
from one stage to the next. This is
technical academic language: "proceeding" Bachelor and Master, e.g.,
with the world itself represented as
conferring the degrees on those who
tyrannize over others.

256. *drugs*] I preserve the Folio
"drugges" in this modernized form in
the text, as an alternative Elizabethan
form of "drudges", menial household
servants. Maxwell (p. 203) suggests a
conscious pun ("drug" also meaning
poison). One would need to know, of
course, whether the spelling "drugge"
was Shakespeare's or the compositor's.

260. *The icy . . . respect*] the chilling
commands to be obeyed by one who
wishes to hold a place of respect in a
social hierarchy or (more probably)
one who acquires circumspection and

The sugar'd game before thee. But myself—
Who had the world as my confectionary,
The mouths, the tongues, the eyes and hearts of men
At duty, more than I could frame employment:
That numberless upon me stuck, as leaves   265
Do on the oak, have with one winter's brush
Fell from their boughs and left me open, bare,
For every storm that blows—I, to bear this,
That never knew but better, is some burthen.
Thy nature did commence in sufferance, time   270
Hath made thee hard in 't. Why shouldst thou hate
     men?
They never flatter'd thee. What hast thou given?
If thou wilt curse, thy father (that poor rag)
Must be thy subject, who in spite put stuff
To some she-beggar and compounded thee   275
Poor rogue hereditary. Hence, be gone!
If thou hadst not been born the worst of men,
Thou hadst been a knave and flatterer.

261. sugar'd] Sugred *F*.   273. rag] *F4*; ragge *F1–3*; rogue *conj. Johnson.*

sees all things in proportion (not merely the "sugar'd game" before him). Compare *Mer.V.*, v. i. 99 and *Rom.*, III. i. 128.

261. *sugar'd*] i.e. outwardly sweet and attractive.

261–9. *But myself . . . burthen*] The construction begins "but as for myself who had", then changes when "these", understood from a subordinate clause, becomes the subject of a principal verb "have", and then returns to something like its original form with "I"—i.e. "for me".

262. *my confectionary*] the place to make sweetmeats merely for me.

263. *The mouths . . .*] sc. (I) who had . . .

264. *At duty*] dutifully ready to obey my command.

more . . . employment] more of them than I could invent employment *for.*

265. *That . . . stuck*] A pronoun like "these" has to be understood as the antecedent of "that" and the subject

of "have". "Numberless"= innumerable.

266. *one winter's brush*] even one wintry sweeping of the trees.

267. *Fell*] For this form of the past participle see Abbott 344.

268. *I*] The original construction is resumed here: "for me to bear".

269. *That . . . better*] who knew only better things.

270. *sufferance*] enduring hardship.

271. *hard*] hardened.

273. *rag*] Johnson's "rogue" may well be right, in view of l. 276, but "rag" was a common term of contempt and probably suggested "stuff" (which, of course, is used as a sexual euphemism).

276. *rogue hereditary*] rogue by heredity, because your father was one.

277. *worst*] lowest (in the social scale); but Johnson took the line to mean that Timon is telling Apemantus "he had not virtue enough for the vices he condemns".

Apem.   Art thou proud yet?
Tim. Ay, that I am not thee.
Apem.   I, that I was
    No prodigal.
Tim.   I, that I am one now.   280
    Were all the wealth I have shut up in thee,
    I'ld give thee leave to hang it. Get thee gone.
    That the whole life of Athens were in this!
    Thus would I eat it.   [*Eating a root.*
Apem.   Here, I will mend thy feast.
                                        [*Offering food.*
Tim. First mend my company, take away thyself.   285
Apem. So I shall mend mine own, by th' lack of thine.
Tim. 'Tis not well mended so, it is but botch'd;
    If not, I would it were.
Apem. What wouldst thou have to Athens?
Tim. Thee thither in a whirlwind. If thou wilt,   290

279-80. I, that . . . prodigal] *As Capell; one line F.*   284. *Eating a root*] *Rowe;
not in F.   Offering food*] *not in F; offering him another | Johnson; Throwing him a
crust Capell.*   285. my] *Rowe; thy Ff, Rowe (edns 2 and 3).*

278. *yet*] still, even now.

279. *Ay . . . thee*] An ironical reversal
of their positions at their first meeting,
I. i. 189-90. For "thee" after the verb
"to be" see Abbott 213.

280-1. *now. | Were*] The punctuation
is as in the Folio. Some editors place a
colon after "now". If the former is
right, Timon's prodigality would be
his willingness to give people gold with
which to damn themselves; if the
latter, his readiness to have Apemantus
hang himself even if it meant losing his
own wealth at the same time.

283. *That*] would that.

285. *my company*] The alteration of
"thy" to "my" here can hardly be
questioned (and it is an easy slip for a
compositor to make since "thyself"
occurs in the same line and "thy" in
the preceding one). Timon requests
Apemantus to mend his company before he mends his feast; and Apemantus replies that by mending Timon's
company he will automatically mend
his own. Steevens (1778) pointed out

that there is here another probable
reminiscence of North's *Plutarch*: "On
a time . . . *Apemantus* said unto the
other: O here is a trim Banquet *Timon*.
Timon answered again: Yea, said he,
so thou wert not here." Painter also
tells the story.

287. *but botch'd*] only clumsily re-
paired (because he will still have to put
up with himself).

288. *If . . . were*] This is a difficult
line. I do not see how we can take the
"it" to refer back to *Timon's* company
(as Rolfe took it). Perhaps "it" refers
to Apemantus' having to put up with
his own company: "if it isn't botched
—i.e. if you don't find it so—I only
wish you did" (because he would
rather have Apemantus discontent
than not). Alternatively, "even if it
were not *well mended*, I still wish it were
botched—namely, by your taking yourself off."

289. *What . . . Athens?*] Presumably,
what would you like taken to
Athens?

Tell them there I have gold; look, so I have.

Apem. Here is no use for gold.

Tim.   The best and truest;
For here it sleeps, and does no hired harm.

Apem. Where liest a nights, Timon?

Tim.   Under that's above me.
Where feed'st thou a days, Apemantus?   295

Apem. Where my stomach finds meat; or, rather, where
I eat it.

Tim. Would poison were obedient and knew my mind!

Apem. Where wouldst thou send it?

Tim. To sauce thy dishes.   300

Apem. The middle of humanity thou never knewest, but
the extremity of both ends. When thou wast in thy
gilt and thy perfume, they mock'd thee for too much
curiosity; in thy rags thou know'st none, but art
despis'd for the contrary. There's a medlar for thee;   305
eat it.

Tim. On what I hate I feed not.

Apem. Dost hate a medlar?

Tim. Ay, though it look like thee.

Apem. And th' hadst hated meddlers sooner, thou   310
shouldst have loved thyself better now. What man

305. medlar] medler *F.*   308. medlar] Medler *F.*   310. meddlers] Medlers *F.*

301-2. *The middle . . . ends*] Apemantus surely scores a point here; and in scoring it gives us further good reason for not confusing Shakespeare's view of the world with Timon's. Tilley thought there might be an allusion to a proverb "Virtue is found in the middle".

304. *curiosity*] delicacy, fastidiousness.

305. *medlar*] A fruit like a small apple, not ripe till it is brown with decay. Compare *AYL.*, III. ii. 126-8.

307. *hate*] The retort was "smarter" when "hate" and "eat" were perhaps pronounced with the same vowel (Kökeritz, pp. 103-4).

309. *though . . . thee*] There is no need to interpret—or try to interpret— "though" as "since". Timon's remark

has a typical double-edge—for to be told that one looks like a medlar (which is generally eaten only when decayed) is no compliment.

310. *And*] if.

meddlers] Compare *Meas.*, IV. iii. 184 for the pun on medlar (the fruit) and meddler (one who meddles or intrigues); also, one who over-indulges in sexual intercourse).

311-13. *What . . . means?*] This is a difficult sentence. Apparently, "What man who was loved in accordance with his means did you ever know to be unthrifty?" i.e. the unthrifty ones— like you—are those who are loved not in accordance with their true means but according to what they are thought or hoped to have. Most editors explain "after" as "later than", "after the loss

didst thou ever know unthrift that was beloved after
his means?

Tim. Who, without those means thou talk'st of, didst
thou ever know belov'd?　　　　　　　　　　　　315

Apem. Myself.

Tim. I understand thee; thou hadst some means to keep
a dog.

Apem. What things in the world canst thou nearest compare to thy flatterers?　　　　　　　　　　　　320

Tim. Women nearest, but men—men are the things
themselves. What wouldst thou do with the world,
Apemantus, if it lay in thy power?

Apem. Give it the beasts, to be rid of the men.

Tim. Wouldst thou have thyself fall in the confusion of 325
men, and remain a beast with the beasts?

Apem. Ay, Timon.

Tim. A beastly ambition, which the gods grant thee
t' attain to. If thou wert the lion, the fox would beguile thee; if thou wert the lamb, the fox would eat 330
thee; if thou wert the fox, the lion would suspect thee,
when peradventure thou wert accus'd by the ass; if
thou wert the ass, thy dulness would torment thee,
and still thou liv'dst but as a breakfast to the wolf; if
thou wert the wolf, thy greediness would afflict thee, 335
and oft thou shouldst hazard thy life for thy dinner;
wert thou the unicorn, pride and wrath would confound thee and make thine own self the conquest of
thy fury; wert thou a bear, thou wouldst be kill'd by

of"—but, as Deighton pointed out,
there is no parallel to this use of "after",
while "according to" is its regular
Elizabethan meaning. Timon's reply
perhaps fits in with either of the above
interpretations.

317-18. *thou . . . dog*] you had just
means enough to keep a dog—who
loved you; nobody else would.

325-6. *fall . . . men*] fall when mankind in general fell (was "confounded"
or overthrown); i.e. cease to be a man
and become a beast.

329-30. *beguile*] defeat by guile.

332. *when peradventure*] if it chanced

that. "Peradventure" is an adverb,
ME *paraventure*, from OF *per aventure*,
by chance.

334. *and . . . but*] and into the bargain
you would live merely to become.

338-9. *and . . . fury*] Alluding to the
tradition, recorded e.g. by Topsell in
his *History of Four-footed Beasts*, that the
unicorn in his blind fury to get at the
treed lion would run his horn into the
tree so firmly that he would be at the
lion's mercy.

339-40. *wert . . . horse*] Topsell
similarly mentions the "mortal hatred
betwixt a horse and a beare".

the horse; wert thou a horse, thou wouldst be seiz'd   340
by the leopard; wert thou a leopard, thou wert germane to the lion, and the spots of thy kindred were
jurors on thy life. All thy safety were remotion, and
thy defence absence. What beast couldst thou be
that were not subject to a beast? And what a beast   345
art thou already, that seest not thy loss in transformation!

Apem. If thou couldst please me with speaking to me,
thou mightst have hit upon it here; the common-
wealth of Athens is become a forest of beasts.   350

Tim. How has the ass broke the wall, that thou art out of
the city?

Apem. Yonder comes a poet and a painter. The plague of
company light upon thee! I will fear to catch it, and
give way. When I know not what else to do, I'll see   355
thee again.

Tim. When there is nothing living but thee, thou shalt be
welcome. I had rather be a beggar's dog than Apemantus.

348–50.] *As Pope;* If . . . please me / . . . might'st / . . . heere. / . . . become / . . .
Beasts. /*F.*   353–6.] *As Pope (who transfers to end of scene);* Yonder . . . Painter: /
. . . thee: / . . . way. / . . . do, / . . . againe. / *F.*   357–9.] *As Pope (at end of
scene);* When . . . thee, / . . . welcome. / . . . Dogge, / . . . *Apemantus.* / *F.*

341–2. *germane*] closely related, akin.

342–3. *and . . . life*] i.e. the world
being what it is, you would suffer not
because of your own spots but because
of the "spots" (faults or vices) of your
relation, the lion—which would be
held to be your responsibility and
so would condemn you to death. For
this metaphorical use of "spot" cf.
v. iv. 35. By putting a semi-colon instead of the Folio full-stop after "life",
editors make the following words refer
only to the leopard and the lion,
whereas they are surely a summary of
all that Timon has said.

343. *All . . . remotion*] all your safety
would depend on removal of yourself
(to a distance).

346–7. *that . . . transformation*] if you
can't see that you would be worse off
still if transformed into a beast.

349–50. *the . . . beasts*] The remark
perhaps has further point if it is remembered that the Elizabethans commonly contrasted the ordered com-
monwealth with the lawlessness of the
lives of beasts (Phillips, pp. 136–7).

353. *Yonder . . . painter*] The Poet and
Painter do not enter for some time;
and critics have assumed dislocation
or the intrusion of another writer's
work. But one may believe *either* that
the Poet and Painter have been seen
some distance off merely making their
way towards Timon *or* that the bandits who enter first were the author's
afterthought. If the latter, it is a much
less serious change of mind than the
double announcement of the death of
Portia in *Cæs.*!

355. *give way*] retire, leave the place
to others.

Apem. Thou art the cap of all the fools alive.   360
Tim. Would thou wert clean enough to spit upon!
Apem. A plague on thee, thou art too bad to curse.
Tim. All villains that do stand by thee are pure.
Apem. There is no leprosy but what thou speak'st.
Tim. If I name thee.   365
    I'll beat thee, but I should infect my hands.
Apem. I would my tongue could rot them off!
Tim. Away, thou issue of a mangy dog!
    Choler does kill me that thou art alive;
    I swound to see thee.   370
Apem. Would thou wouldst burst!
Tim. Away, thou tedious rogue, I am sorry I shall lose a
    stone by thee.   [*Throwing a stone at him.*
Apem. Beast!
Tim. Slave!   375
Apem. Toad!
Tim. Rogue, rogue, rogue!
    I am sick of this false world, and will love nought
    But even the mere necessities upon 't.
    Then, Timon, presently prepare thy grave;   380

360–70.] *As Capell (Pope);* Thou . . . Cap / . . . enough / . . . thee, / . . . Villaines /
. . . Leprosie, / . . . beate thee; / . . . tongue / . . . dogge, / . . . me, / . . . thee. / *F.*
370. swound] swoond *F.*   371–7.] *As F;* Would . . . Away! / . . . lose / . . . rogue! /
Capell.   373. S.D.] *As Capell; not in F.*   376.] *Apem. retreats backward, as going.*
Theobald.

360. *cap*] summit, apex, and, so,
chief. Perhaps, as Malone suggested,
there is further point in it since a cap
was one of the distinguishing marks
of a fool: then one might paraphrase
"you are the very essence of fool".

362. *A . . . curse*] Early editors re-
distributed the lines (giving "A
plague on thee!" to Timon) because
they maintained it was inconsistent
for Apemantus to curse Timon and
then say he was too bad to curse. But
"a plague on thee" is probably not, to
an Apemantus, a *real* curse; and he
invokes a plague on Timon for being
immune from curses, by being too bad
to curse.

363. *that . . . pure*] that may be compared to you are shown, by compari-

son, to be pure, virtually without fault.

366. *I'll*] I'd. The irregularity with
sequence of tenses is not unusual.

370. *swound*] An alternative form of
"swoon", now *dial.*

378. *I am . . .*] Here Timon begins to
speak as if Apemantus had already
gone; and perhaps one could mark an
"exit" for Apemantus after l. 377 and
have him re-enter about l. 392, over-
hear Timon's final words and inter-
rupt to bring the news of the approach
of the bandits. Theobald inserted
"Apemantus retreats backward, as
going". But again it seems unlikely
that the doubt would have been left in
a fully revised play.

379. *mere*] bare.

380. *presently*] immediately.

Lie where the light foam of the sea may beat
Thy grave-stone daily: make thine epitaph,
That death in me at others' lives may laugh.
[*Looking on the gold.*] O thou sweet king-killer, and
    dear divorce
'Twixt natural son and sire, thou bright defiler   385
Of Hymen's purest bed, thou valiant Mars,
Thou ever young, fresh, loved and delicate wooer,
Whose blush doth thaw the consecrated snow
That lies on Dian's lap! Thou visible god,
That sold'rest close impossibilities,   390
And mak'st them kiss; that speak'st with every tongue,
To every purpose! O thou touch of hearts,
Think thy slave Man rebels, and by thy virtue
Set them into confounding odds, that beasts
May have the world in empire!

Apem.   Would 'twere so!   395
But not till I am dead. I'll say th' hast gold.
Thou wilt be throng'd to shortly.

Tim.   Throng'd to?

Apem.   Ay.

Tim. Thy back, I prithee.

Apem.   Live, and love thy misery.

384. S.D.] *Pope; not in F.*   385. son and sire] *Rowe;* Sunne and fire *F1–3;* Sun
and Fire *F4.*   389.] *As Rowe;* That . . . lap. / . . . God, / *F.*   393. slave Man]
Rowe; slave-man *Ff.*   395.] *Advancing* / *Capell.*   398–9. *Apem.* Live . . .
misery. / *Tim.* Long] *F;* Live . . . misery. / Long *Hanmer.*

383. *death in me*] The modern idiom
would be rather "I in death" or "death
through me".

385. *natural*] related by blood (*not*, as
in modern usage, illegitimate).

386. *Mars*] An allusion to the adul-
tery of Mars with the goddess of love
herself.

388. *blush*] The shine on the metal.

388–9. *thaw . . . lap*] "consecrated",
"snow", and "Dian" all connote chas-
tity. Diana was the *virgin* huntress.

390. *close*] Not an adjective governing "impossibilities" but an adverb
modifying "sold'rest" — i.e. solder
close together.

impossibilities] i.e. things otherwise

irreconcilable or incompatible.

392. *touch*] touchstone.

393–4. *Think . . . odds*] believe that
Man, your slave, is in rebellion; and
by your power, set men at odds so that
they will destroy each other. For
"odds" see IV. iii. 43–4 above and note;
and for "confounding" cf. IV. i. 20.

394–5. *that . . . empire*] Here, by
notable dramatic irony, Timon repeats the very wish for which he had
so harshly reprimanded Apemantus
a few minutes before: another proof
that Timon is being viewed critically
by the dramatist and that Apemantus
does not always have the worst of the
argument.

Tim. Long live so, and so die! I am quit.   399
Apem. Moe things like men! Eat, Timon, and abhor them.

[*Exit.*

Enter the Banditti.

First Bandit. Where should he have this gold? It is some
    poor fragment, some slender ort of his remainder.
    The mere want of gold, and the falling-from of his
    friends, drove him into this melancholy.
Second Bandit. It is nois'd he hath a mass of treasure.   405
Third Bandit. Let us make the assay upon him. If he care
    not for 't, he will supply us easily; if he covetously
    reserve it, how shall's get it?
Second Bandit. True; for he bears it not about him: 'tis
    hid.   410

399–400.] *As F;* Long . . . quit. [*Exit Apem.*] / . . . them. *Hanmer.*   400.] *As Pope;*
Mo . . . men, / Eate *Timon*, and abhorre then. *F.*   401. S.D. *Enter the Banditti*]
Enter the Bandetti. F; Scene VII. Enter Thieves. Pope.   *First Bandit*] *1 F (throughout
scene).*   403. falling-from] *Capell;* falling from *F.*   405. *Second Bandit*] *2
F (throughout scene).*   405.] *As Pope;* It . . . nois'd / . . . Treasure. / *F.*   406.
Third Bandit] *3 F (throughout scene).*   409–10.] *As Pope;* True . . . him: / 'Tis
hid. *F.*

399. *I am quit*] I am rid of him at last.

400. *Moe . . . them*] This line is given
by Hanmer and most editors to
Timon, and the exit of Apemantus
transferred to l. 399 after "die!"—
partly because editors will not understand that a line may be spoken as a
character leaves the stage and not only
after he has left it. Similarly Apemantus is able here to refer to the Bandits
because he can see them approaching
before they actually come on the
stage.

abhor] Not merely "detest" but
"shrink from with loathing". If F
"then" is correct, the verb must be intransitive, as often.

S.D. Banditti] Many editors, following Pope, print "Thieves" for the
Folio's "Bandetti". If the Italianate
plural (which is also a collective singular) must be replaced by a different
word, "outlaws" would be more
accurate.

401. *Where . . . have*] Either where is

he likely to have *or* whence is he likely
to have had? For "should" thus used
in questions, see Abbott 325.

402. *ort*] The word is usually found
in the plural "orts" and means
strictly "fragments of food left over
from a meal". So here "ort of his
remainder" is almost tautology; but
it could be paraphrased as "fraction of
what he has left" (after he has given so
much to others).

403. *mere*] "sheer" or "very" rather
than the modern sense. Cf. l. 233.

falling-from] falling off or falling
away. A normal prepositional com-
pound (Abbott 431).

405. *nois'd*] rumoured. (The verb
survives in this sense but is rare.)

406. *make . . . him*] put him to the
test, as one tries an alloy to determine
the percentage of metal in it.

407. *for 't*] i.e. for the gold.

408. *shall's*] For this colloquialism,
compare, e.g., *Cym.*, IV. ii. 233 and
Cor., IV. vi. 148.

First Bandit. Is not this he?
All. Where?
Second Bandit. 'Tis his description.
Third Bandit. He; I know him.
All. Save thee, Timon.   415
Tim. Now, thieves?
All. Soldiers, not thieves.
Tim.   Both too; and women's sons.
All. We are not thieves, but men that much do want.
Tim. Your greatest want is, you want much of meat.
    Why should you want? Behold the earth hath roots;   420
    Within this mile break forth a hundred springs;
    The oaks bear mast, the briers scarlet hips;
    The bounteous housewife nature on each bush
    Lays her full mess before you. Want? Why want?
First Bandit. We cannot live on grass, on berries, water,   425
    As beasts and birds and fishes.
Tim. Nor on the beasts themselves, the birds and fishes;
    You must eat men. Yet thanks I must you con
    That you are thieves profess'd, that you work not
    In holier shapes; for there is boundless theft   430
    In limited professions. Rascal thieves,

418.] *As Pope;* We ... men / ... want. / *F.*   419. much of meat] *F;* much.—Of meat *Rann;* much of men *Hanmer.*   422. hips] *F2;* Heps *F1.*

415. *Save thee*] may God save (or preserve) thee.

416. *Now*] well? A bare acknowledgment of a greeting, perhaps short for "how now?"

418. *want*] need, lack.

419. *Your . . . meat*] If the Folio pointing is thus preserved, Timon's reply means "Your greatest want (need) comes about because you want *so much* meat or food", i.e. your requirements are confined to your stomachs and are excessive. I cannot accept Farmer's conjecture (adopted by Sisson, for example) of a stop after "much", so that Timon's question becomes "Of meat why should you want?", for Timon goes on to talk of the springs as well.

422. *mast*] The fruit of forest trees,

such as the oak and beech (generally used as food for swine).

hips] The "hip" is the fruit of the rose or (as here) wild rose. Such references as these seem to come from Shakespeare's own observation of nature and not from mere literary convention.

424. *mess*] a serving of food. The modern idiom would no doubt be "her full menu".

428. *thanks . . . con*] To "con thanks" (OE *þanc cunnan*) is "to acknowledge one's gratitude", "to offer thanks".

431. *limited*] As opposed to "boundless", and so must be used of professions which would claim to be exclusive, to limit the number of members and control their activities (such as a

Here's gold. Go, suck the subtle blood o' th' grape,
Till the high fever seethe your blood to froth,
And so 'scape hanging. Trust not the physician;
His antidotes are poison, and he slays   435
Moe than you rob. Take wealth and lives together.
Do villainy, do, since you protest to do 't,
Like workmen. I'll example you with thievery:
The sun's a thief, and with his great attraction
Robs the vast sea; the moon's an arrant thief,   440
And her pale fire she snatches from the sun;
The sea's a thief, whose liquid surge resolves
The moon into salt tears; the earth's a thief,
That feeds and breeds by a composture stol'n
From gen'ral excrement; each thing's a thief.   445
The laws, your curb and whip, in their rough power

---

437. villainy] *As Rowe;* Villaine *F1–2;* villain *F3–4.*   437–8. do't, Like work-men.] *As Pope;* doo't. Like workemen, *F.*   443. moon] Moone *F;* mound *Theobald.*

City guild). Warburton paraphrased as "legal", Knight "legalized".

432. *subtle*] treacherous, working harm unobtrusively.

433. *high fever*] Presumably, of in-toxication (perhaps with the suggestion that the thirst of the drunkard like that of fever is insatiable).

434. *Trust . . . physician*] The transi-tion is abrupt; but apparently dying of fever puts physicians in Timon's mind, and he advises the thieves not to believe they can escape death by con-sulting physicians; and in the mean-time to imitate them, since they both kill and rob.

437. *protest*] profess.

438. *example . . . thievery*] "Example" as a transitive verb normally means in Shakespeare "to give precedent for" (compare, e.g. *LLL.,* I. ii. 121). The exact meaning here would therefore be "afford you justification for your thievery by quoting other instances of it".

439. *attraction*] In the literal sense, drawing-up.

440. *arrant*] A variant of "errant" (wandering) but because of the fre-quency of phrases like "arrant thief" it came to be understood as a mere inten-sive, "pure", "genuine", "unmiti-gated" and is used to intensify com-plimentary words as well as words like "thief" (*O.E.D.*).

442. *resolves*] melts (L. *re + solvere,* to loosen or dissolve). The tides of the sea, affected by the moon, are spoken of as stolen from it (rather than from the clouds). Theobald, protesting that "the *Sea* melting the *Moon* into tears is, I believe, a Secret in Philosophy, which nobody but *Shakespeare's* deep Editors ever dream'd of'', read "mounds", explaining by reference to a belief that the saltness of the sea is caused by mounds of rock-salt under-neath it. Malone, however, aptly com-pared *R3,* II. i. 68–70; compare also *MND.,* II. i. 103–5 where the moon is thought of as creating moisture.

444. *composture*] compost. Not else-where found in Shakespeare; possibly *dial.,* as now.

446. *your . . . whip*] which curb and whip you.

Has uncheck'd theft. Love not yourselves; away,
Rob one another. There's more gold. Cut throats.
All that you meet are thieves. To Athens go;
Break open shops: nothing can you steal   450
But thieves do lose it. Steal less for this I give you,
And gold confound you howsoe'er!   Amen.
                        [*Withdrawing.*

Third Bandit. H'as almost charm'd me from my profes-
    sion, by persuading me to it.

First Bandit. 'Tis in the malice of mankind that he thus 455
    advises us; not to have us thrive in our mystery.

Second Bandit. I'll believe him as an enemy, and give over
    my trade.

First Bandit. Let us first see peace in Athens. There is no
    time so miserable but a man may be true.   460
                        [*Exeunt Bandits.*

450–2.] *As Delius;* Breake . . . you steale / . . . give you, / . . . Amen. / *F;* Break . .
you steal / . . . this / . . . howso'er / . . . Amen. *Capell;* Break . . . thieves / . . . give
you / . . . Amen. / *Sisson.*   451. less] *as F;* no less *Collier (edn 2);* not less *Rowe.*
452. S.D.] *not in F; Retiring towards his Cave Capell.*   453. H'as] *F3;* Has *F1–2.*
456. us; not] *As Rowe;* vs not *F.*   457–8.] *As Pope;* Ile . . . Enemy, / . . . Trade. /
F.   459. There] *F (subst.); 2 Thief.* There *Warburton.*   460. *Exeunt
Bandits*] *Exit Theeues F.*

447. *Has . . . theft*] The verb is, as
before, attracted into the singular by
the nearest noun "power"; and the
words seem to mean "have an unrestrained power to thieve", to take as
they will from those who offend against
them.

451–2. *Steal . . . howsoe'er*] Maxwell
(the "New Shakespeare") argues con-
vincingly that Collier's emendation
"no less" (which ruins the metre) is
seen to be unnecessary once the Elizn.
construction is understood. A paraphrase would be: "*Even if* you steal
less because of what I am giving you,
may gold damn you just the same".

452. *howsoe'er*] in any case. Deighton
well compared "however" in *Gent.,*
I. i. 34.

455. *in . . . mankind*] in (because of)
the malice he bears towards mankind.

456. *mystery*] profession, as in IV. i. 18
above. Cf. "trade" in l. 458.

457. *I'll . . . enemy*] *Either,* as Deighton explained, a reference to the Latin
proverb "it is lawful to learn even
from an enemy" *or,* as Maxwell now
suggests, "I'll do the opposite of what
he advises, since he is an enemy".

459–60. *There . . . true*] Most editors
follow Warburton in giving these
words to the Second Bandit: an emendation which may, of course, be
right, the Second Bandit replying in
effect that there is no need to wait for
peace before living honestly. But I take
the First Bandit to mean much what
Falstaff meant when he advised Prince
Hal "Repent at idle times as thou
mayest" (*2H4,* II. ii. 140–1): there is
no time so miserable that it isn't time
enough for being true (or honest);
there's no hurry about reforming
while there are better things to do.
Such a sentiment certainly seems to fit
the context better. Shakespeare can

Enter Steward.

Stew. O you gods!
　　Is yond despis'd and ruinous man my lord?
　　Full of decay and failing? O monument
　　And wonder of good deeds evilly bestow'd!
　　What an alteration of honour has desp'rate want made!
　　What vilder thing upon the earth than friends　　466
　　Who can bring noblest minds to basest ends!
　　How rarely does it meet with this time's guise,
　　When man was wish'd to love his enemies!
　　Grant I may ever love, and rather woo　　470
　　Those that would mischief me than those that do!
　　H'as caught me in his eye: I will present
　　My honest grief unto him; and, as my lord,
　　Still serve him with my life. My dearest master!

TIMON *comes forward.*

Tim. Away! What art thou?
Stew.　　　　　　　　Have you forgot me, sir?　　475

461.] *Scene IV Reed; Act V Sc. I Rowe; Act V Theobald.*　　S.D. *Enter Steward]*
Enter the Steward to Timon F.　　461-5.] *As F; prose Sisson;* O . . . gods / . . . lord /
. . . monument / . . . bestow'd / . . . honour / . . . made / *Malone.*　　472. H'as] *F4;*
Has *F1-3*.　　472-4. H'as . . . life] *As Pope; prose F.*　　474. S.D.] *Theobald; not
in F.*

---

hardly have wanted at this stage of the
play to give a repentant thief the last
word.

462. *ruinous*] ruined, in ruins.

463. *failing*] weakness (presumably
the word is a verbal noun governed by
"of", and not a participle).

463-4. *monument / And wonder*] An
instance of hendiadys: "wonderful
monument" (or memorial).

465. *What . . . made!*] The line is not
scannable and must be thought of as
prose or as a line which would in revision have been reduced to metre.
Merely dividing it into two, as do some
editors, is no help; while to print
ll. 462-5 as prose is to disguise what
seems to me to be their true nature,
roughed-out verse.

of] in.

466. *vilder*] viler. Cf. i. i. 15 and
note.

468. *How . . . guise*] how admirably it
(the fact that friends destroy noble
minds such as Timon's) fits in with the
way of the world—how admirably
when (one pauses to think that) . . . The
words are spoken with bitter irony.
"Rarely" is here used in the colloquial
sense "splendidly", "excellently".

469. *wish'd*] admonished, desired.

471. *Those . . . do*] those who make it
plain that they would (intend to) do
me harm rather than those who in fact
do me harm (though professing the
opposite). So Johnson, who compared
the proverb "Defend me from my
friends, for from my enemies I will
defend myself" (compare Tilley
F 739).

Tim. Why·dost ask that? I have forgot all men.
    Then, if thou grant'st th'art a man,
    I have forgot thee.
Stew. An honest poor servant of yours.
Tim. Then I know thee not.   480
    I never had honest man about me, I; all
    I kept were knaves, to serve in meat to villains.
Stew. The gods are witness,
    Ne'er did poor steward wear a truer grief
    For his undone lord than mine eyes for you.   485
Tim. What, dost thou weep? Come nearer; then I love
      thee,
    Because thou art a woman, and disclaim'st
    Flinty mankind, whose eyes do never give
    But thorough lust and laughter. Pity's sleeping.
    Strange times, that weep with laughing, not with
      weeping!   490
Stew. I beg of you to know me, good my lord,
    T'accept my grief and whilst this poor wealth lasts
    To entertain me as your steward still.
Tim. Had I a steward
    So true, so just, and now so comfortable?   495
    It almost turns my dangerous nature mild.
    Let me behold thy face. Surely this man
    Was born of woman.
    Forgive my general and exceptless rashness,

477–8.] *As F; one line Capell.*   477. grant'st] grunt'st, *Ff.*   481.] *As F;* me, I; /
All *Alexander.*   me, I; all] *Steevens (1778);* me, I all *F;* me; ay, all *Delius.*
486.] *As Rowe;* What . . . weepe? / . . . thee / *F.*   494–8.] *As F;* Had . . . just /
. . . turns / . . . behold / . . . woman *Capell.*   496. mild] *Hanmer;* wilde *F.*

---

481. *I; all*] The Folio "I" might
stand either for the reading given here
or (as often) for "ay". Fortunately the
meaning is not affected seriously.

482. *knaves*] In both senses, "servants" and "villains".

488. *Flinty*] as hard as flint.

give] yield (tears), flow.

489. *But thorough*] Except through.

493. *entertain*] retain.

495. *comfortable*] comforting, lending
strength (compare "Be of good com-

fort"). Many adjectives in "able" and
"ible" which have only a passive
meaning today had an active one as
well in Shakespeare's English. See
Abbott 3 and compare *Lr.*, I. iv. 327–8:
"Yet have I left a daughter / Who, I
am sure, is kind and comfortable".

496. *mild*] The Folio "wilde", if retained, could perhaps be interpreted
as "insane".

499. *exceptless*] Also in the active
sense: making no exceptions.

You perpetual-sober gods! I do proclaim   500
One honest man. Mistake me not, but one.
No more, I pray—and he's a steward.
How fain would I have hated all mankind,
And thou redeem'st thyself. But all, save thee,
I fell with curses.   505
Methinks thou art more honest now than wise;
For, by oppressing and betraying me,
Thou mightst have sooner got another service;
For many so arrive at second masters
Upon their first lord's neck. But tell me true—   510
For I must ever doubt, though ne'er so sure—
Is not thy kindness subtle, covetous,
A usuring kindness, and as rich men deal gifts,
Expecting in return twenty for one?

Stew. No, my most worthy master, in whose breast   515
Doubt and suspect, alas, are plac'd too late!
You should have fear'd false times when you did
    feast;
Suspect still comes where an estate is least.
That which I show, heaven knows, is merely love,
Duty and zeal to your unmatched mind,   520
Care of your food and living; and believe it,
My most honour'd lord,

---

500. perpetual-sober] *Hanmer;* perpetuall sober *F.*   513. A usuring kindness]
Pope; If not a Vsuring kindnesse *F;* is't not . . . *Rowe.*

504. *And . . . thyself*] but now you save or deliver yourself from that (hate)—and so prevent my saying I hate *all.*

505. *fell*] cut or knock down.

507. *oppressing*] distressing; or perhaps in the now obsolete sense of "reducing to dire straits".

508. *service*] position in a household.

510. *Upon . . . neck*] by mounting on the neck (shoulders, in the modern idiom) of their first master.

511. *For . . . sure*] for I by nature must always retain a doubt, however convincing the evidence.

513. *A . . . kindness*] The Folio "If not" at the beginning of the line has been generally omitted since Pope, except, notably, by Kittredge and Alexander. Metre indicates that the two words are superfluous (and this, no doubt, was why Pope omitted them). The compositor would seem to have caught up "is not" from the preceding line.

516. *suspect*] The word was common as a noun (="suspicion") until the seventeenth century.

518. *Suspect . . . least*] suspicion always comes (as it has come to you) when a man's estate is least—and then it is too late.

519. *merely*] purely. Compare l. 233 above and note.

> For any benefit that points to me,
> Either in hope, or present, I'd exchange
> For this one wish, that you had power and wealth   525
> To requite me, by making rich yourself.

Tim. Look thee, 'tis so. Thou singly honest man,
> Here, take: the gods out of my misery
> Has sent thee treasure. Go, live rich and happy,
> But thus condition'd: thou shalt build from men;   530
> Hate all, curse all, show charity to none,
> But let the famish'd flesh slide from the bone
> Ere thou relieve the beggar; give to dogs
> What thou deniest to men; let prisons swallow 'em,
> Debts wither 'em to nothing; be men like blasted
> woods;   535
> And may diseases lick up their false bloods!
> And so farewell, and thrive.

Stew. O let me stay and comfort you, my master.

Tim. If thou hat'st curses
> Stay not; fly, whilst thou art bless'd and free: 540
> Ne'er see thou man, and let me ne'er see thee.

> [*Exit Steward; Timon withdraws into his Cave.*

---

529. Has] Ha's *Ff;* Have *Rowe;* Ha' *Fletcher.*   538–9. O . . . curses] *As F;* O . . . stay / . . . curses / *Capell;* O . . . stay / . . . hat'st / *Malone.*   541. S.D.] *As Collier (edn 2); Exit F; Exeunt severally Theobald.*

523. *For any benefit*] There is a change of construction here. The sentence begins "(As) for any benefit . . . I'd exchange (it)" but ends as if it had begun simply with "Any benefit" (as object of "exchange").

525–6. *For . . . yourself*] The two lines are perhaps to be thought of as another couplet, "wealth" and "yourself" forming a half-rhyme.

526. *requite*] Perhaps stressed on the first syllable.

527. *Look thee*] Abbott regards "thee" in this construction not as a reflexive but as an unemphatic pronoun (212).

singly] The word may be used here

in both the senses it then had: (1) solely—i.e. you alone being honest; and (2) truly, really.

529. *Has*] The verb is again singular by attraction to the nearest noun "misery".

530. *But . . . condition'd*] but bound or restricted by this condition.

from] away from.

535. *blasted woods*] Timon is carrying on from the previous phrase the idea of withering.

536. *lick up*] A further example noted by Caroline Spurgeon (pp. 198–9) of Shakespeare's association of dogs with what is sickening and detestable.

[ACT V   SCENE I]

Enter Poet and Painter.

Pain. As I took note of the place, it cannot be far where he
abides.

Poet. What's to be thought of him? Does the rumour hold
for true that he's so full of gold?

Pain. Certain. Alcibiades reports it; Phrynia and Timan-   5
dra had gold of him. He likewise enrich'd poor
straggling soldiers with great quantity. 'Tis said he
gave unto his steward a mighty sum.

Poet. Then this breaking of his has been but a try for his
friends.   10

Pain. Nothing else. You shall see him a palm in Athens
again, and flourish with the highest. Therefore 'tis
not amiss we tender our loves to him, in this suppos'd

ACT V

Scene 1

ACT V SCENE I] *Capell; not in F; Scene II Pope.*   S.D. *Enter*]*F; The Woods before
Timon's Cave. | Enter | Camb. edd.*   3–4.] *As Pope;* What's ... him? | ... true, | F.*
5–38.] *As Pope;* Certaine. | ... *Timandylo* | ... enrich'd | ... quantity. | ... Stew-
ard | ... his, | ... else: | ... againe, | ... highest | ... loues | ... his: | ... vs, |
... purposes | ... for, | ... goes | ... now | ... time | ... him | ... too; | ... him. |
... best. | ... Time; | ... Expectation. | ... acte, | ... people, | ... vse. | ...
fashionable; | ... Testament | ... iudgement | ... Workeman, | ... badde |
... thinking | ... him: | ... himselfe: | ... Prosperity, | ... Flatteries | ... needes |
... Worke? | ... men? | F.   5. Phrynia] *Phrinia F2; Phrinica F1.*   5–6. Ti-
mandra] *F2; Timandylo F1.*

ACT V] The traditional division is
noted here only for convenience of
reference. The action is, in fact, continuous. See Introduction.

7. *soldiers*] i.e. the bandits, who
averred to Timon that they were
soldiers (IV. iii. 417).

7–8. *'Tis . . . sum*] Earlier editors,
wishing to justify their irrational division between "Acts" IV and V, claim-
ed that the act interval allowed time
for the Poet and Painter to learn of
Timon's gift to the Steward. But there
would have been no interval here on
the Elizabethan stage; and the Poet
and Painter have apparently been

seen approaching in the distance by
Apemantus (IV. iii. 353) before the
Steward has visited Timon. No audience would be aware of any difficulty
in this knowledge of the gift to the
Steward; but readers may, if they
wish, believe that this, too, would have
been "tidied up" in revision.

9. *breaking*] going bankrupt. (The
word is still used.)   *try*] test.

11–12. *You . . . highest*] Perhaps, as
Steevens (1793) suggested, another
Biblical allusion: "The righteous shall
flourish like a palm-tree" (*Psalms,*
xcii. 11).

13. *tender*] offer.

distress of his: it will show honestly in us, and is very
likely to load our purposes with what they travail for,   15
if it be a just and true report that goes of his having.

Poet. What have you now to present unto him?

Pain. Nothing at this time but my visitation; only I will
promise him an excellent piece.

Poet. I must serve him so too, tell him of an intent that's   20
coming toward him.

Pain. Good as the best. Promising is the very air o' th'
time; it opens the eyes of expectation. Performance
is ever the duller for his act; and, but in the plainer
and simpler kind of people, the deed of saying is quite   25
out of use. To promise is most courtly and fashion-
able; performance is a kind of will or testament
which argues a great sickness in his judgment that
makes it.

Enter TIMON *from his cave.*

Tim. [*Aside.*] Excellent workman, thou canst not paint a   30
man so bad as is thyself.

Poet. I am thinking what I shall say I have provided for
him. It must be a personating of himself; a satire
against the softness of prosperity, with a discovery of
the infinite flatteries that follow youth and opulency.   35

30, 36, 46. *Aside*] *Capell; not in* F.

14. *show honestly*] look honourable.

15. *load*] i.e. with gifts or with
reward.

travail] *Travail* and *travel* are doublets, and "travail" may therefore mean
simply "travel". But already in ME it
could also mean "exert oneself" or
"labour", and more probably has that
meaning here.

16. *having*] possessions (as in II. ii.
148).

24. *his act*] its act, the fact that it has
been put in execution ("his" as the
neuter possessive pronoun).

25. *the . . . saying*] the doing of what
one says one will do. Malone compared *Ham.*, I. iii. 25–7: "so far to believe it / As he in his particular act and

place / May give his saying deed".

26. *use*] custom.

27–9. *is . . . it*] i.e. is, like the making
of a will, a sign that the person per-
forming the deed fears that he is ill and
may soon die.

30–1. *Excellent . . . thyself*] Timon
here accepts the opinion which
Apemantus advanced at I. i. 198–
9.

33. *personating of himself*] represen-
tation of Timon's own situation
(abandoned by his friends).

34. *softness of prosperity*] effeminacy
induced by a life of luxury.

discovery] revealing, as the drawing
of a curtain "discovers" what is
behind it.

Tim. [*Aside.*] Must thou needs stand for a villain in thine
    own work? Wilt thou whip thine own faults in other
    men? Do so, I have gold for thee.
Poet. Nay, let's seek him:
    Then do we sin against our own estate,   40
    When we may profit meet, and come too late.
Pain. True.
    When the day serves, before black-corner'd night
    Find what thou want'st, by free and offer'd light.
    Come.   45
Tim. [*Aside.*] I'll meet you at the turn. What a god's gold,
    That he is worshipp'd in a baser temple
    Than where swine feed?
    'Tis thou that rigg'st the bark and plough'st the foam,
    Settlest admired reverence in a slave: 50
    To thee be worship; and thy saints for aye
    Be crown'd with plagues, that thee alone obey!
    Fit I meet them.   [*Coming forward.*
Poet. Hail, worthy Timon!
Pain.   Our late noble master!
Tim. Have I once liv'd to see two honest men?   55

43. black-corner'd] *As F;* black-curtain'd *Singer.*   night] night; *F.*   46–8.]
As Capell; Ile . . . turne: / . . . worshipt / . . . feede? / *F.*   51. worship] *Rowe;*
worshipt *Ff.*   aye] *Rowe (edn 3);* aye: *F.*   53. S.D.] *not in F.*   55–6.] *As
Reed;* Haue . . . liu'd / . . . Sir: / *F.*

36. *stand for*] serve as a model for (a
frequent use in Shakespeare). The
point of Timon's remark is that the
very satire the Poet proposes to write
against false friendship will itself be an
example of it.

40–1. *Then . . . late*] we do wrong to
our own fortune or possessions if we
come late at a time when there is profit
to be had.

43. *serves*] is available, or is con-
venient.

43–4. *before . . . light*] The many emendations proposed for "black-corner'd
night" are unconvincing and probably
unnecessary, since it is natural enough
to think of "night" as having the properties of the black corners which it
creates. The night of black corners is,
then, the opposite to "free and offer'd

light", i.e. light that is offered freely,
without restriction.

46. *turn*] Deighton explained as "the
turn in the path"; Schmidt glossed "as
soon as it will seem proper" taking
"turn" in the sense of "occasion". But
I suspect an idiomatic use connected
with hunting (as a hound gives a hare
a turn). It might then mean that
Timon will intercept them and turn
their plot back upon themselves.

47. *baser temple*] i.e. the human body.
Compare *I Cor.,* vi. 19.

50. *Settlest . . . slave*] causes a slave to
admire and reverence his master
("admired" with the active force
"admiring" perhaps in the sense of
"wondering at").

55. *once*] Used as an intensive, meaning "actually" or "indeed". So

Poet. Sir,
 Having often of your open bounty tasted,
 Hearing you were retir'd, your friends fall'n off,
 Whose thankless natures (O abhorred spirits!)
 Not all the whips of heaven are large enough— 60
 What, to you,
 Whose star-like nobleness gave life and influence
 To their whole being! I am rapt, and cannot cover
 The monstrous bulk of this ingratitude
 With any size of words. 65
Tim. Let it go naked, men may see 't the better.
 You that are honest, by being what you are,
 Make them best seen and known.
Pain.   He and myself
 Have travail'd in the great show'r of your gifts,
 And sweetly felt·it.
Tim.   Ay, you are honest men. 70
Pain. We are hither come to offer you our service.
Tim. Most honest men! Why, how shall I requite you?

---

60. enough—] *Rowe;* enough. *F.* 66.] *As Pope;* Let . . . go, / . . . better: / *F.*
go naked, men] *Theobald;* go, Naked men *F.* 70. men] *F2;* man *F1.* 71–5.]
As Pope; We . . . come / . . . men: / . . . you? / . . . no? / . . . can do, / . . . men, /
. . . Gold, *F.*

Schmidt, who compared the German *einmal.*

 57. *Having*] Possibly scanned as one syllable. See Abbott 466.

 open] generous, liberal.

 58. *retir'd*] withdrawn.

 59–61. *Whose . . . you*] Another typical mingling of constructions, but one with psychological point: the poet pretends to be lost for words and breaks off, so great is his (assumed) indignation. The full construction would be *"for* whose thankless natures . . . not all the whips of heaven are large enough, since they were thankless to you, you whose . . ."

 62. *influence*] Used in its astronomical sense, following the reference in "star-like": the supposed emanation from the stars of an ethereal fluid which affects the actions and condition of men ("influenza" was originally any

epidemic disease thought to be so caused). So Timon's nobility cast a glow over the characters of his associates.

 63. *rapt*] so moved as to be lost for words. Compare I. i. 19.

 65. *any size*] There is a quibble on "size" in the senses of (1) magnitude, and (2) a covering glue. Compare *Ham.,* II. ii. 484.

 66. *Let it go naked*] Timon is punning on "bulk" in the sense of trunk or body, as found, for example, in *Ham.,* II. i. 95. His answer takes the form of the proverb "The Truth shows best being naked" (Tilley T 589).

 68. *them*] the thankless natures of others.

 69. *travail'd*] See note on l. 15 above; here used in the sense of "walked" or "travelled", as one walks in a light rain or mist and finds it "sweet".

Can you eat roots and drink cold water, no?
Both. What we can do, we'll do, to do you service.
Tim. Y'are honest men. Y' have heard that I have gold;   75
    I am sure you have; speak truth, y'are honest men.
Pain. So it is said, my noble lord; but therefore
    Came not my friend nor I.
Tim. Good honest men! Thou draw'st a counterfeit
    Best in all Athens: th' art indeed the best;   80
    Thou counterfeit'st most lively.
Pain.   So, so, my lord.
Tim. E'en so, sir, as I say. And, for thy fiction,
    Why, thy verse swells with stuff so fine and smooth
    That thou art even natural in thine art.
    But, for all this, my honest-natur'd friends,   85
    I must needs say you have a little fault;
    Marry, 'tis not monstrous in you, neither wish I
    You take much pains to mend.
Both.   Beseech your honour
    To make it known to us.
Tim.   You'll take it ill.
Both. Most thankfully, my lord.
Tim.   Will you indeed?   90
Both. Doubt it not, worthy lord.
Tim. There's never a one of you but trusts a knave,
    That mightily deceives you.
Both.   Do we, my lord?

85. honest-natur'd] *Rowe;* honest Natur'd *F.*

79. *counterfeit*] reproduction or picture (the normal Elizabethan meaning); but in Timon's mind, of course, the word has the sense of *false* reproduction, which it also commonly had then.

81. *most lively*] in the most life-like way.

So, so] indifferently (spoken in mock-modesty).

82. *fiction*] imaginative invention (this to the Poet).

83. *stuff*] matter, particularly intellectual matter. (The word is not necessarily derogatory.)

smooth] without rough edges; but to Timon the word also implies smoothness in the sense of flattery.

84. *That . . . thine art*] To the Poet the words imply only the usual contrast of "art" and "nature": he achieves the appearance of being natural even when in fact his art is only imitating nature; his art is concealing art. But what Timon really means is that he is his natural self, shows himself in his true colours, in his art—since he is lying. There may even be a further quibble on "natural" in the sense of "foolish".

Tim. Ay, and you hear him cog, see him dissemble,
　　Know his gross patchery, love him, feed him,   95
　　Keep in your bosom; yet remain assur'd
　　That he's a made-up villain.
Pain. I know none such, my lord.
Poet.　　　　　　　　　　　Nor I.
Tim. Look you, I love you well; I'll give you gold,
　　Rid me these villains from your companies;   100
　　Hang them or stab them, drown them in a draught,
　　Confound them by some course, and come to me,
　　I'll give you gold enough.
Both. Name them, my lord; let's know them.
Tim. You that way and you this, but two in company;   105
　　Each man apart, all single and alone,
　　Yet an arch-villain keeps him company.
　　[*To one.*] If, where thou art, two villains shall not be,
　　Come not near him. [*To the other.*] If thou wouldst not
　　　　reside
　　But where one villain is, then him abandon.   110
　　Hence, pack! There's gold; you came for gold, ye
　　　　slaves.
　　[*To Poet.*] You have work for me, there's payment:
　　　　hence!
　　[*To Painter.*] You are an alchemist, make gold of that!

94.] *As Rowe;* I, . . . cogge, / . . . dissemble, / *F.*   99.] *As Pope;* Looke you, /
. . . Gold / *F.*   105.] *As Pope;* You . . . this: / . . . Company: / *F.*   108. *To one*]
This ed.; not in F; To the Painter / *Pope.*   109. *To the other*] *This ed.; not in F; To
the Poet* / *Pope.*   112. *To Poet*] *This ed.; not in F; To Painter Globe.*   113. *To
Painter*] *This ed.; not in F; To Poet Globe.*

94. *cog*] cheat. A term probably
derived from dicing.

95. *patchery*] knavery, the conduct of
a "patch" (a fool, a rogue). The word
is similarly used by Thersites in *Troil.*,
II. iii. 77.

97. *made-up*] In the obsolete sense of
"fully made", "complete", "consum-
mate" (not, as Johnson thought,
"hypocritical"). Compare *R3*, I. i. 21.

101. *draught*] a sink or privy. Compare *Troil.*, v. i. 82, *Matt.*, xv. 17 and
Mark vii. 19.

102. *Confound*] bring to ruin,
destroy.

105. *but . . . company*] Because, as he
goes on to explain, wherever either of
them is, there is not only a poet (or
painter) but also a villain.

108. *shall not be*] are not to be *or* are
not intended to be.

110. *But*] except.

111. *pack!*] be off! The intransitive
form survives only in "to send someone packing"; the transitive "to pack
someone off" is, of course, common.

112. *work*] i.e. the poem which he
overheard the Poet plan to offer him.

113. *You . . . that*] The Painter is presumably called an alchemist because

Out, rascal dogs!

[Drives them out and then retires into his cave.

Enter Steward and two Senators.

Stew. It is vain that you would speak with Timon;   115
    For he is set so only to himself,
    That nothing but himself, which looks like man,
    Is friendly with him.
First Sen.   Bring us to his cave.
    It is our part and promise to th' Athenians
    To speak with Timon.
Second Sen.   At all times alike   120
    Men are not still the same. 'Twas time and griefs
    That fram'd him thus: time with his fairer hand
    Offering the fortunes of his former days
    The former man may make him. Bring us to him,
    And chance it as it may.
Stew.   Here is his cave.   125
    Peace and content be here! Lord Timon! Timon!
    Look out, and speak to friends. Th' Athenians
    By two of their most reverend senate greet thee.
    Speak to them, noble Timon.

Re-enter TIMON *from his cave.*

Tim. Thou sun, that comforts, burn! Speak and be hang'd;
    For each true word, a blister; and each false   131
    Be as a cauterizing to the root o' th' tongue,

114. *Drives . . . cave*] As Staunton; *Exeunt F.*   115.] *Scene II Capell; Scene III Pope.*
vain] *F1–2;* in vain *F3–4.*   125. chance] *F3–4;* chanc'd *F1;* chanc'e *F2.*
129. S.D.] *Enter Timon out of his Caue F.*   130.] *As Hanmer;* Thou . . . burne, /
. . . hang'd: / *F.*   132. cauterizing] *Rowe;* Cantherizing *F1;* Catherizing *F2–4.*

he changes one colour into another
by blending. Timon scornfully invites
him to change into gold the stones or
dirt which he hurls after them.

116. *set . . . himself*] his interests are
concentrated so completely on himself. "Only" is intensified by "so" as
any other adverb might be (but as
usage does not permit today).

119. *part and promise*] role and promise; almost hendiadys for "the role
we promised to play".

125. *chance it*] let things happen.
"It" is indefinite. The Folio reading
exemplifies the common e:d confusion.

130. *comforts*] For the form, see note
on IV. i. 2.

132. *cauterizing*] searing with a hot
iron or caustic. The Cambridge editors (in their note xvi) referred to *The
questyonary of Cyrurgens* (1541), where
the form "canterisynge" was found
"very frequently". If not simply a
misprint, it must be a form arrived at

Consuming it with speaking!

First Sen.   Worthy Timon—

Tim. Of none but such as you, and you of Timon.

First Sen. The senators of Athens greet thee, Timon.   135

Tim. I thank them; and would send them back the plague,
    Could I but catch it for them.

First Sen.   O forget
    What we are sorry for ourselves in thee.
    The senators, with one consent of love,
    Entreat thee back to Athens, who have thought   140
    On special dignities which vacant lie
    For thy best use and wearing.

Second Sen.   They confess
    Toward thee forgetfulness too general gross;
    Which now the public body, which doth seldom
    Play the recanter, feeling in itself   145
    A lack of Timon's aid, hath sense withal
    Of it own fall, restraining aid to Timon,
    And send forth us, to make their sorrowed render

134.] *As Pope;* Of . . . you, / . . . *Timon.* / *F.*   136.] *As Pope;* I thanke them, /
. . . plague, / *F.*   143. general gross] *As F;* general, gross *Pope;* general-gross
Dyce (edn 2).   146. sense] *As Rowe;* since *Ff.*   147. it] *F;* it's *Rowe;* its
edd.   fall] *F;* fail *Capell;* fault *Hanmer.*   restraining] *F;* refraining *conj.*
Johnson.

by false analogy with "cantharidize".
O.E.D. does not recognize "canter-
ize"; but if it did exist, the Folio
"Cantherizing" ought to be preserved
in the text.

138. *What . . . in thee*] "In thee" must
mean, as Deighton suggested, "in
regard to you" or "in your case" (the
closest parallel being, as J. C. Maxwell
points out to me, "my blemishes in
thee", *Wint.,* v. i. 8). The whole
phrase thus means "the wrongs that
we regret causing you".

139. *consent*] Probably, as Malone
pointed out, in the sense of "concent"
(L. *concentus*): harmony or concord of
voices. The distinction between "concent" and "consent" was not always
made.

142. *For . . . wearing*] until such time
as you, who can best do so, assume

and maintain them with distinction.

146. *Timon's aid*] See notes on iv. iii.
94–6 above.

withal] along with it, at the same
time.

147. *it*] An older form of the genitive
"its", often used, instead of the common "his", in contempt. See Abbott
228 and compare *John,* ii. i. 160.

fall] This, the Folio reading, may be
preserved in the sense of "fall from
grace", "deterioration".

restraining] (in) checking or restrict-
ing. This is a normal meaning of the
word and emendation is unnecessary.

148. *sorrowed render*] "Render" is
generally explained either as "confession of fault" (Steevens, 1778, and
Deighton) or "rendering of an account" (*O.E.D.*), in each case with

Together with a recompense more fruitful
Than their offence can weigh down by the dram—   150
Ay, even such heaps and sums of love and wealth
As shall to thee blot out what wrongs were theirs,
And write in thee the figures of their love,
Ever to read them thine.

Tim.   You witch me in it;
Surprise me to the very brink of tears.   155
Lend me a fool's heart and a woman's eyes,
And I'll beweep these comforts, worthy senators.

First Sen. Therefore so please thee to return with us,
And of our Athens, thine and ours, to take
The captainship, thou shalt be met with thanks,   160
Allowed with absolute power, and thy good name
Live with authority. So soon we shall drive back
Of Alcibiades th' approaches wild,
Who like a boar too savage doth root up
His country's peace.

Second Sen.   And shakes his threat'ning sword
Against the walls of Athens.

First Sen.   Therefore Timon—   166

Tim. Well, sir, I will; therefore, I will, sir, thus:
If Alcibiades kill my countrymen,
Let Alcibiades know this of Timon,

---

166. Timon—] *Rowe*; *Timon. F.*

reference to *Cym.*, IV. iv. 11. But *O.E.D.*
also lists the legal meanings, such as a
return in money or service payable by
a tenant to his landlord, which also
makes good sense: the Athenians return what is strictly due to Timon and
(as the Senator goes on to say) something more. "Sorrowed", of course,
means "sorrowful", "expressing regret".

150. *Than . . . dram*] than their
offence (against you) can counterpoise, even if measured to the last
dram (a particularly small unit of
weight—in liquid measure, one eighth
of a fluid ounce).

153. *figures*] Probably with a quibble on the senses of "numerals"
(or "letters") as written in a ledger

and "images" (or "representations").

154. *Ever . . . thine*] so that from
these "figures" you will be able to read
that they (the Athenians) are always
yours.

witch] bewitch.

157. *comforts*] Probably "joys"
rather than "consolations", although
the latter sense is not impossible.

161. *Allowed*] endowed (L. *allocare*).

162. *Live with authority*] (shall) continue (as if it had never been questioned) and you shall have authority
as well.

164–5. *Who . . . peace*] Steevens
(1793) pointed out the Biblical phras-
ing (*Psalms*, lxxx. 13): "The wild boar
out of the wood doth root it up"
("waste it" *A.V.*).

That Timon cares not. But if he sack fair Athens,   170
And take our goodly aged men by th' beards,
Giving our holy virgins to the stain
Of contumelious, beastly, mad-brain'd war,
Then let him know (and tell him Timon speaks it,
In pity of our aged and our youth)   175
I cannot choose but tell him, that I care not,
And let him take 't at worst—for their knives care not
While you have throats to answer. For myself,
There's not a whittle in th' unruly camp
But I do prize it at my love before   180
The reverend'st throat in Athens. So I leave you
To the protection of the prosperous gods,
As thieves to keepers.
Stew.   Stay not; all's in vain.
Tim. Why, I was writing of my epitaph;
It will be seen to-morrow. My long sickness   185
Of health and living now begins to mend,
And nothing brings me all things. Go, live still;

177. worst—for] worst: For *F;* worst; for *Rowe.*   181. reverend'st] As *F2;*
reuerends *F1.*   184. Why,] Why *F.*

173. *contumelious*] overbearingly insolent (in that it pays no respect to
persons).
177. *And . . . worst*] and let him put
whatever interpretation he wishes
upon it. Throughout this speech
Timon tantalizes the Senators by
speaking as if he were about to offer
them aid and defy Alcibiades.
177–8. *for . . . answer*] If the Folio
colon is correctly represented here by
the dash, then Timon is saying that *he*
does not care about the knives of Alcibiades' men so long as the Athenians
can provide throats for the knives to
cut. Some editors put a full-stop and
assume that Timon is advising the
Senators not to worry about the
knives.
179. *whittle*] a carving-knife; also
used of a clasp-knife.
th' unruly camp] Presumably, the
camp of those revolting against the rule
and discipline of Athens.

180–1. *But . . . Athens*] that I do not
value as worthy of my love and so
above (more valuable than) the
throat of the most venerable Athenian.
182. *prosperous*] favourable or pro-
pitious. Interestingly in *Oth.*, I. iii. 245,
F reads "prosperous" where Q has
"gracious".
183. *As . . . keepers*] as I would leave
thieves to the (doubtful) mercy of their
gaolers.
184. *Why . . . epitaph*] Deighton
pointed out that "it is not easy to
supply the suppressed connection
here". I take it that Timon disregards
—or perhaps does not hear—the
Steward's comment and explains why
he has said he will "leave" the Senators (l. 181). "Writing" is a verbal
noun (as in the surviving construction
"I was a-writing of my epitaph")
rather than a participle. See Abbott
178.
187. *nothing*] i.e. oblivion.

Be Alcibiades your plague, you his,
And last so long enough.

First Sen.   We speak in vain.

Tim. But yet I love my country, and am not   190
One that rejoices in the common wrack,
As common bruit doth put it.

First Sen.   That's well spoke.

Tim. Commend me to my loving countrymen.

First Sen. These words become your lips as they pass through
      them.

Second Sen. And enter in our ears like great triumphers   195
In their applauding gates.

Tim.   Commend me to them,
And tell them that, to ease them of their griefs,
Their fears of hostile strokes, their aches, losses,
Their pangs of love, with other incident throes
That nature's fragile vessel doth sustain   200
In life's uncertain voyage, I will some kindness do them:
I'll teach them to prevent wild Alcibiades' wrath.

First Sen. I like this well; he will return again.

Tim. I have a tree which grows here in my close,

---

191. wrack] *F3–4;* wracke *F1–2;* wreck *Hanmer.*   194. through] thorow *F;*
thro' *Rowe.*   199. throes] *F4;* throwes *F1–3.*

189. *And . . . enough*] Timon's curses
on the Senators are similar to those of
Alcibiades at III. v. 105–6, in that he
wishes them a long life of suffering
rather than early death.

191. *wrack*] Most editors adopt
Hanmer's "wreck"; but "wrack" is a
distinct word, sharing some of the
ordinary meanings of "wreck" (but
also meaning, for example, the rubbish
washed down or deposited by moving
water).

192. *bruit*] report.

194. *become*] befit, do credit to. The
word survives chiefly in the participial
or adjectival form "becoming".

195. *triumphers*] those making a
triumphal entry into a city. The
accent is on the second syllable.

196. *applauding*] A personification or
more probably a transferred epithet
("thronged by applauding citizens").

198. *aches*] Two syllables, as before.

200. *sustain*] *Either* endure *or* (in a
more literal sense) carry or contain
(L. *sustinere, sub + tenere*).

202. *prevent*] anticipate. But the
Senators take it in the other sense, now
the usual one, of "counteract" or
"avoid".

204–11. *I have . . . greeting*] This passage is more closely modelled on
North's *Plutarch* (see Appendix A)
than any other in the play. It is also
a good illustration of the rhetorical
figure *hirmus*, when the sense is sus-
pended until the end of a long sentence or paragraph (Joseph, p. 60).

204. *close*] enclosure (normally
about a building). The word is not
elsewhere used by Shakespeare. It survives in "cathedral close" and other
similar uses.

That mine own use invites me to cut down,   205
And shortly must I fell it; tell my friends,
Tell Athens, in the sequence of degree,
From high to low throughout, that whoso please
To stop affliction, let him take his haste,
Come hither, ere my tree hath felt the axe,   210
And hang himself. I pray you, do my greeting.

Stew. Trouble him no further; thus you still shall find him.

Tim. Come not to me again; but say to Athens,
Timon hath made his everlasting mansion
Upon the beached verge of the salt flood,   215
Who once a day with his embossed froth
The turbulent surge shall cover. Thither come,
And let my grave-stone be your oracle.
Lips, let four words go by and language end:
What is amiss, plague and infection mend!   220
Graves only be men's works and death their gain;
Sun, hide thy beams, Timon hath done his reign.   [*Exit.*

First Sen. His discontents are unremoveably
Coupled to nature.

Second Sen. Our hope in him is dead. Let us return,   225

212.] *As Pope;* Trouble . . . shall / . . . him. *F.*   219. four] *As Ff;* sour *Rowe.*
223–4. His . . . nature] *As Capell; one line F.*

207. *in . . . degree*] paying proper
attention to the degrees of precedence.

208–9. *that . . . haste*] There is again
a mingling of two grammatical constructions: "that whoso please . . . is to
take haste" and "to let whoso please
. . . take haste". "Take haste" is unusual for "make haste", presumably
by parallel with "take leave", "take
horse", etc.

212. *still*] always.

215. *beached verge . . . flood*] beach
that is the edge or limit of the sea. Compare "the beached margent of the
sea", *MND.*, II. i. 85.

216. *Who*] For the Shakespearian
use of "who" see Abbott 258, 259 and
264. Here the antecedent is more
probably "verge" than "mansion" or
"Timon"; in any case, "who" is the
object of the verb "cover".

his] its.

embossed] covered with foam (ME
embose). *O.E.D.* gives one meaning of
"embossed" as "foaming from exhaus-
tion"—an extension of the use of
"emboss" meaning to drive a hunted
animal to extremity. Rolfe and
Deighton thought it was an extension
of the other word "emboss" meaning
to cover with protuberances. Spen-
ser uses it to mean "encase with armour".

218. *be your oracle*] be consulted by
you as a fount of wisdom.

219. *four*] Presumably used in-
definitely, as we should say "two or
three". Rowe's emendation "sour"
hardly makes sense, since Timon proceeds to further curses.

224. *Coupled to nature*] part of *his*
nature.

And strain what other means is left unto us
In our dear peril.
First Sen.　　　　　It requires swift foot.　　　[*Exeunt.*

[SCENE II]

Enter two other Senators with a Messenger.

Third Sen.　Thou hast painfully discover'd; are his files
　　As full as thy report?
Mess.　　　　　I have spoke the least;
　　Besides, his expedition promises
　　Present approach.
Fourth Sen.　We stand much hazard if they bring not Timon. 5
Mess.　I met a courier, one mine ancient friend,
　　Whom, though in general part we were oppos'd,
　　Yet our old love made a particular force,
　　And made us speak like friends. This man was riding
　　From Alcibiades to Timon's cave,　　　　　　　10
　　With letters of entreaty, which imported

Scene II

SCENE II] *Dyce; not in F; Scene III Capell; Scene IV Pope.*　S.D. *Enter*] *F; The Walls of Athens. | Enter | Rowe; Before the Walls of Athens. | Enter | Camb. edd.*　1, 13. *Third Sen.*] *Sisson; 1 F.*　3–4.] *As Pope; one line F.*　5. *Fourth Sen.*] *Sisson; 2 F.* 7. *Whom*] *F; Who Pope; And Hanmer; When Singer (ed. 2).*　8. *made*] *F; had Hanmer.*

227. *dear*] extreme, grievous (O.E. *déor*). Compare *Ham.*, I. ii. 282.

Scene II

1. *Third Sen.*] I follow Sisson in numbering the Senators "3" and "4" here to distinguish them from "1" and "2" who later return from their mission to Timon.

1. *Thou . . . discover'd*] You have revealed what it is painful for us to hear.

1–2. *are . . . full*] i.e. are his troops as numerous. Compare "rank and file".

2. *spoke the least*] given the lowest estimate.

3–4. *his . . . approach*] the speed of his movements makes it probable

that he will be here immediately.

7–9. *Whom . . . friends*] There is again a change of construction. "Whom" becomes, as it were, part of the later object "us". Emendation is unnecessary.

7. *in general part*] on matters of general or public concern.

8. *made . . . force*] exercised a strong *personal* influence ("particular" is opposed to "general" in the preceding line).

11–13. *which . . . mov'd*] which aimed at inducing him to join the expedition against Athens, since it was in a cause that had been begun partly for his sake. Some commentators have seen in this and in v. iv. 56 a hint that Timon

His fellowship i' th' cause against your city,
In part for his sake mov'd.

Enter the two other Senators.

Third Sen.   Here come our brothers.
First Sen. No talk of Timon, nothing of him expect.
　　The enemy's drum is heard, and fearful scouring   15
　　Doth choke the air with dust. In, and prepare.
　　Ours is the fall, I fear; our foes' the snare.   [*Exeunt.*

[SCENE III]

Enter a Soldier in the Woods seeking Timon.

Sold. By all description this should be the place.
　　Who's here? Speak, ho! No answer? What is this?
　　Timon is dead, who hath outstretch'd his span:
　　Some beast read this; there does not live a man.

13. S.D. *two*] *not in F.*   14. *First Sen.*] *3 F.*   15. enemy's] *Delius;* enemies *Ff;*
enemies' *Theobald (edn. 2).*   17. foes'] Foes *F;* foe's *Johnson.*

SCENE III] *Dyce; not in F; Scene IV. The Woods. A Rude Tomb seen. Capell; om.
whole scene Pope.*   3–4.] *F (roman).*   4. *read*] *F3;* reade *F1–2;* rear'd *Theobald
(Warburton).*

was the friend for whom Alcibiades
pleaded in vain to the Athenian
Senators in III. v; I think it more likely
that their refusal of financial assistance
to Timon is regarded by Alcibiades as
further justification for his rebellion
against Athens.

　　13. S.D. Enter the two other Sena-
tors] Capell and later editors have
taken the Folio S.D. to mean that
these are the Senators who have been
to Timon. This seems almost certain,
provided that "no talk of Timon" in
l. 14 is explained as "do not talk of
Timon" rather than as "there is no
talk (or news) of Timon".

　　15. *scouring*] hasty movement to and
fro (particularly, as here, in preparation for fighting).

　　17. *foes'*] The possessive form,

whether in the plural or singular,
better preserves the parallel of construction than "foes". The enemy are
thought of as possessing or setting the
snare which will cause the downfall of
Athens.

Scene III

　　S.D. Enter . . . Timon] Another
good instance of an author's S.D. as
distinct from one added in a prompt-
book, since it explains *why* the
character appears.

　　3–4. Timon . . . man] With Staunton, I take these two lines, although
they are not italicized in the Folio, to
be some kind of inscription or notice
which Timon has left, distinct from the
epitaph for the tomb, but equally mis-
anthropic, since it says, virtually, that

Dead, sure; and this his grave. What's on this tomb   5
I cannot read. The character I'll take with wax;
Our captain hath in every figure skill,
An ag'd interpreter, though young in days.
Before proud Athens he's set down by this,
Whose fall the mark of his ambition is.   [*Exit.* 10

[SCENE IV]

Trumpets sound. Enter ALCIBIADES *with his Powers before Athens.*

Alcib. Sound to this coward and lascivious town
Our terrible approach.   [*Sounds a parley.*

Scene IV

SCENE IV] *Dyce; not in F; Scene II Rowe; Scene V Pope.*   S.D. *Trumpets*] F; *Before the Walls of Athens.* | *Trumpets edd.*

there are no true men, only beasts. The soldier can read this first piece of writing, which is in the language of his country (no doubt, so far as Shakespeare was concerned, English!); he says that he cannot read the other, presumably because (like most Elizabethan epitaphs) it is in Latin. Johnson unconvincingly interpreted "some beast read this" as an exclamation of annoyance, meaning "I wish some beast would read it, since I cannot". If Warburton's emendation "rear'd" is adopted, then the lines are not an inscription but merely part of the running commentary by the soldier, who sees the tomb, infers from it that Timon is dead and says that a beast must have erected the tomb since there is no evidence of any man who could have done so. The couplet form makes it more probable that the lines are an inscription; see also the separate note on l. 3. In either case, presumably Timon has erected his own tombstone and has lain down to die in a grave dug in the beach sand; and the sea has subsequently washed sand over it. See

v. i. 214–18. North's *Plutarch* says simply that "He died in the City of Hales, and was buried upon the Sea side. Now ... the sea getting in, it compassed his Tomb round about, that no man could come to it". (For the full passage, see Appendix A.) I do not think we are intended to believe that Timon commits suicide.

3. outstretch'd his span] lived beyond his (desired) time. The sentiment is obviously far more appropriate to Timon than to the soldier.

6. *character*] lettering or symbols cut on the tomb.

take] take an impression of.

7. *figure*] system of lettering or linguistic form.

8. *ag'd*] i.e. experienced.

9. *he's set down*] he has already laid his siege, pitched his tents.

10. *Whose fall*] the fall of which— "whose" being used with an impersonal antecedent, as often.

mark] goal.

Scene IV

2. *terrible*] terrifying.

The Senators appear upon the walls.

Till now you have gone on, and fill'd the time
With all licentious measure, making your wills
The scope of justice; till now, myself and such   5
As slept within the shadow of your power
Have wander'd with our travers'd arms, and breath'd
Our sufferance vainly. Now the time is flush,
When crouching marrow, in the bearer strong,
Cries, of itself, "No more". Now breathless wrong   10
Shall sit and pant in your great chairs of ease,
And pursy insolence shall break his wind
With fear and horrid flight.
First Sen.   Noble, and young:
When thy first griefs were but a mere conceit,
Ere thou hadst power or we had cause of fear,   15

---

10. Cries, of itself, "No more".] *As Rowe;* Cries (of it selfe) no more: *F.*

4. *With . . . measure*] with every form of licentious or unrestrained conduct.

5. *scope*] measure or aim (preserving its original meaning of a shooting-mark, a target). Alcibiades claims that what was called justice in Athens was merely the satisfying of the judges' own wishes.

6. *slept*] Perhaps "lived" or "dwelt" but possibly "remained passive".

7. *with our travers'd arms*] Generally explained as meaning "with our arms folded in dejection" but must mean "with our (military) arms in a crossed position as for drill", not threatening warfare. See M. R. Ridley's note on *Oth.*, I. iii. 371 in the "New Arden" edition.

7-8. *breath'd . . . vainly*] in vain expressed (or uttered complaints about) our sufferings. For "breathe" in this sense, compare III. v. 60 above.

8. *flush*] full or in flood. The modern idiom would be "ripe".

9. *crouching marrow*] courage which has previously crouched or remained inactive. The marrow was once thought of as the source of vitality and strength; also (as in "pith and mar-

row") it was the vital part or essence.

10. *of itself*] on its own initiative, without further provocation.

breathless wrong] the wronged ones who were out of breath (*either* from their flight from injustice *or*, less probably, because they "breath'd" so long in vain).

11. *your great chairs of ease*] the chairs (of state) in which you at present recline at your ease.

12-13. *And . . . flight*] and, conversely, the short-winded tyrants shall gasp for breath as they flee in fear and terror. "Pursy" is a later form of "pursif" or "pursive", breathing with difficulty. "Insolence" is used particularly of arrogant contempt for inferiors; and "horrid" has much the sense of the modern colloquial "hair-raising". Compare *Mac.*, I. i. 134-7, "that suggestion / Whose horrid image doth unfix my hair / And make my seated heart knock at my ribs, / Against the use of nature" (L. *horridus*).

14. *griefs*] grievances.

conceit] idea, something conceived in the mind (and not yet transferred into action).

We sent to thee, to give thy rages balm,
To wipe out our ingratitude, with loves
Above their quantity.
Second Sen.   So did we woo
Transformed Timon to our city's love
By humble message and by promis'd means.   20
We were not all unkind, nor all deserve
The common stroke of war.
First Sen.   These walls of ours
Were not erected by their hands from whom
You have receiv'd your grief; nor are they such   24
That these great tow'rs, trophies, and schools should fall
For private faults in them.
Second Sen.   Nor are they living
Who were the motives that you first went out;
Shame, that they wanted cunning in excess,
Hath broke their hearts. March, noble lord,
Into our city with thy banners spread;   30
By decimation and a tithed death,
If thy revenges hunger for that food
Which nature loathes, take thou the destin'd tenth,

24. grief] *As F;* griefs *Theobald.*   25. tow'rs] *F* (Towres), *Pope;* Towers *Rowe.*
28.] *As Rowe;* (Shame that they wanted, cunning in excesse) *F1;* Shame (that
they wanted cunning in excess) *F2–4;* Shame, that they wanted cunning, in
excess *Theobald.*

16. *sent to thee*] i.e. sent messages to
thee.

18. *their*] The antecedent is either
"griefs" or "rages" (or both): the
loving redress offered by the Senators
was thought by them to be greater
than was strictly necessary to satisfy
the complaints of the aggrieved.

19. *Transformed*] changed by his
sense of injustice, as you were by
yours.

20. *means*] Probably used here, as
frequently, to mean terms or conditions of peace. It might also mean
"middle courses", "compromises" or
even "wealth".

21. *all*] Perhaps in an adverbial
sense, "altogether", although the
First Senator continues as if it meant
simply "all of us".

24. *they*] i.e. those from whom you
received your grief.

25. *trophies, and schools*] monuments
and public buildings. "School" in this
sense (L. *schola*) is not recorded after
1601 by *O.E.D.*

26. *private*] individual.

27. *motives . . . out*] causes or instruments of your original banishment.

28. *Shame . . . excess*] Not, *pace* Theobald, excess of shame for their lack of
cunning but (as the compositors or
editors of the later Folios understood
it) shame because they lacked the final
extremes of cunning. "Cunning" here
has its later pejorative sense of "crafty
deceit".

31. *decimation and a tithed death*] A
doublet: the killing of one person in
every ten.

And by the hazard of the spotted die
Let die the spotted.
First Sen.   All have not offended.   35
For those that were, it is not square to take
On those that are, revenge: crimes, like lands,
Are not inherited. Then, dear countryman,
Bring in thy ranks, but leave without thy rage;
Spare thy Athenian cradle and those kin   40
Which in the bluster of thy wrath must fall
With those that have offended; like a shepherd,
Approach the fold and cull th' infected forth,
But kill not all together.
Second Sen.   What thou wilt,
Thou rather shalt enforce it with thy smile   45
Than hew to 't with thy sword.
First Sen.   Set but thy foot
Against our rampir'd gates, and they shall ope,
So thou wilt send thy gentle heart before,
To say thou 'lt enter friendly.
Second Sen.   Throw thy glove,
Or any token of thine honour else,   50
That thou wilt use the wars as thy redress
And not as our confusion, all thy powers
Shall make their harbour in our town, till we
Have seal'd thy full desire.
Alcib.   Then there's my glove.

44. all together] *F3;* altogether *F1.*

34. *die*] dice (strictly "die" is the singular, "dice" the plural).
35. *the spotted*] those marked with the spots or taint of guilt (with a quibble on "spotted" as used in l. 34).
36. *square*] just or equitable (the normal meaning of the adjective when applied to actions).
39. *without*] outside.
41. *in . . . fall*] must die if thy wrath is allowed to storm its way uncontrolled. The noun "bluster" means boisterous storm or tempest.
47. *rampir'd*] strengthened against

attack (e.g. by ramparts) or blocked up (by piling earth behind them). "Rampire" in either sense is now archaic (Fr. *remparer*).
48. *So*] provided that.
50. *token*] pledge or guarantee.
52. *confusion*] ruin (as in Gray's famous lines "Ruin seize thee, ruthless King! / Confusion on thy banners wait!").
powers] forces, army.
53. *make their harbour*] have safe lodging.
54. *seal'd*] i.e. completely satisfied.

Descend, and open your uncharged ports.   55
Those enemies of Timon's and mine own
Whom you yourselves shall set out for reproof
Fall, and no more; and, to atone your fears
With my more noble meaning, not a man
Shall pass his quarter or offend the stream   60
Of regular justice in your city's bounds
But shall be remedied to your public laws
At heaviest answer.
Both.   'Tis most nobly spoken.
Alcib. Descend, and keep your words.

Enter a Soldier.

Sold. My noble general, Timon is dead,   65
Entomb'd upon the very hem o' th' sea;
And on his grave-stone this insculpture which
With wax I brought away, whose soft impression
Interprets for my poor ignorance.
Alcib. [*Reading the Epitaph*] *Here lies a wretched corse, of*
    wretched soul bereft: 70

55. Descend] *F2;* Defend *F1.*   62. remedied to] *F1;* remedied by *F2-4;*
render'd to *Dyce, conj. Chedworth.*   64. S.D.] *Theobald;* Enter a Messenger *F.*
70. S.D.] *Alcibiades reades the Epitaph. F.*

55. *uncharged*] unassailed. Deighton
took the phrase as proleptic and explained "open your gates so that they
will no longer be fastened up"—perhaps not impossible, in view of
"rampir'd" in l. 47, but tautological.

57. *reproof*] disgrace or condemnation; the Elizabethan meaning was
stronger than the modern one.

58–9. *atone . . . meaning*] appease
your fears by telling you of my nobler
intentions. "Atone", a back formation
from "atonement" ("at + onement")
retains something of its literal meaning, "make one" or "reconcile".

60. *quarter*] Perhaps "billet" (as in
modern "quarters") but more probably "area of military duty". Com-
pare *Ant.,* IV. iii. 22 and *1H6,* II. i. 63–8.

62. *remedied to*] Emendation hardly

seems necessary, since the meaning
"handed over for remedy (or punishment)" would be in line with many
such constructions in Shakespearian
English.

63. *At heaviest answer*] to pay the
heaviest penalty you may wish to
inflict. For the use of "at" see Abbott
143 and 144; the construction here is,
I think, that described as "the *at* of
price".

67. *insculpture*] inscription.

68–9. *whose . . . ignorance*] the soft
impression of which will, like an interpreter, give you the meaning which I
in my ignorance cannot give you.

70–3. *Here . . . gait*] There seems
little doubt that Shakespeare copied
down from North's *Plutarch* two epitaphs, each in a couplet, meaning to

Seek not my name. A plague consume you, wicked caitiffs left!
Here lie I, Timon, who, alive, all living men did hate.
Pass by and curse thy fill, but pass and stay not here thy gait.
These well express in thee thy latter spirits.
Though thou abhorr'dst in us our human griefs,   75
Scorn'dst our brains' flow and those our droplets which
From niggard nature fall, yet rich conceit
Taught thee to make vast Neptune weep for aye
On thy low grave, on faults forgiven. Dead
Is noble Timon, of whose memory   80
Hereafter more. Bring me into your city,
And I will use the olive with my sword,
Make war breed peace, make peace stint war, make each
Prescribe to other, as each other's leech.
Let our drums strike.   [*Exeunt.*   85

71. *wicked*] *F1*; *not in F2-4*.   72. *alive*] *F1*; *not in F2-4*.   73. *pass and*] *As F1*;
not in F2-4.   73. *gait*] *As Pope*; *gate Ff*.   76. *brains'*] *Dyce (ed. 2)*; *Braines F*;
brain's Steevens; *brine's Hanmer*.

omit one or the other (probably the first) on revision. As it is, they contradict each other ("Seek not my name", "Here lie I, Timon"). The first is said by Plutarch to have been composed by Timon himself, the second by the poet Callimachus. For the full passage, see Appendix A; and for the use of "caitiffs" in place of North's "wretches", see Introduction, Section 5. The second epitaph may well have suggested the famous one written for himself by W. B. Yeats: "Cast a cold eye / On life, on death. / Horseman, pass by!"

74. *latter*] more recent, belonging to the second half of your life.

76. *brains' flow*] tears ("our brains' flow" means the same as the following "droplets"—which is then used for the contrast between the small drops that are human tears and the vast flow of Neptune or the sea).

77. *niggard*] parsimonious—in that it cannot produce tears to compete with the sea.

rich conceit] ingenious or fruitful imagination.

79. *on faults forgiven*] Emendation merely to avoid the repetition of "on" is quite unacceptable, since the repetition seems to involve a deliberate quibble, which "over" in modern usage would preserve.

82. *use . . . sword*] i.e. show mercy even while being strong.

83. *stint*] check.

83-4. *make each . . . leech*] make each operate in such a way as to be for the good of the other, and so for the general good, as two physicians may prescribe for each other's ailments.

APPENDIX A

Antonius followeth the life and example of *Timon Misanthropos* the *Athenian*.
Plato and *Aristophanes* testimony of *Timon Misanthropos*, what he was.

Antonius, he forsook the City and company of his friends, and built him a house in the Sea, by the Isle of PHAROS, upon certain forced mounts which he caused to be cast into the Sea, and dwelt there, as a man that banished himself from all mens company: saying that he would lead *Timons* life, because he had the like wrong offered him, that was before offered unto *Timon*: and that for the unthankfulness of those he had done good unto, and whom he took to be his friends, he was angry with all men, and would trust no man. This *Timon* was a Citizen of ATHENS, that lived about the War of PELOPONNESUS, as appeareth by *Plato* and *Aristophanes* Comedies: in the which they mocked him, calling him a viper and malicious man unto mankind, to shun all other mens companies, but the company of young *Alcibiades*, a bold and insolent youth, whom he would greatly feast and make much of, and kissed him very gladly. *Apemantus* wondering at it, asked him the cause what he meant to make so much of that young man alone, and to hate all others: *Timon* answered him, I do it, said he, because I know that one day he shall do great mischief unto the ATHENIANS. This *Timon* sometimes would have *Apemantus* in his company, because he was much like of his nature and conditions, and also followed him in manner of life. On a time when they solemnly celebrated the Feast called Choæ at ATHENS (to wit, the Feasts of the dead where they make Sprinklings and Sacrifices for the dead) and that they two then feasted together by themselves, *Apemantus* said unto the other: O here is a trim Banquet *Timon*. *Timon* answered again: Yea, said he, so thou wert not here. It is reported of him also, that this *Timon* on a time (the People being assembled in the Market-place about dispatch of some affairs) got up into the Pulpit for Orations, where the Orators commonly use to speak unto the People: and silence

---

1. The text quoted is that of 1676. It has been checked against the First Edition and two minor errors have been silently corrected.

being made, every man listening to hear what he would say, because it was a wonder to see him in that place, at length he began to speak in this manner: My Lords of ATHENS, I have a little yard at my house where there groweth a Fig-tree, on the which many Citizens have hanged themselves: and because I mean to make some building on the place, I thought good to let you all understand it, that before the Fig-tree be cut down, if any of you be desperate, you may there in time go hang yourselves. He died in the City of HALES, and was buried upon the Sea side. Now it chanced so, that the Sea getting in, it compassed his Tomb round about, that no man could come to it: and upon the same was written this Epitaph:

> *Here lies a wretched corse, of wretched soul bereft:*
> *Seek not my name: a plague consume you wicked wretches left.*

It is reported that *Timon* himself, when he lived, made this Epitaph: for that which is commonly rehearsed, was not his, but made by the Poet *Callimachus:*

> *Here lie I* Timon, *who alive all living men did hate:*
> *Pass by and curse thy fill: but pass, and stay not here thy gate.*

Many other things could we tell you of this *Timon*, but this little shall suffice at this present.

APPENDIX B

From NORTH'S "LIFE OF *ALCIBIADES*"

(i)   And on a day as he came from the Council and assembly of the City, where he had made an excellent Oration, to the great good liking and acceptation of all the hearers, and by means thereof had obtained the thing he desired, and was accompanied with a great train that followed him to his honour: *Timon* surnamed *Misanthropos* (as who would say, *Loup-garou*, or the man-hater) meeting *Alcibiades* thus accompanied, did not pass by him, nor give him way (as he was wont to do to all other men) but went straight to him, and took him by the hand, and said: O, thou dost well my Son, I can thee thank, that thou goest on, and climbest up still: for if ever thou be in authority, wo be unto those that follow thee, for they are utterly undone. When they heard these words, those that stood by fell a laughing: other reviled *Timon*, other again marked well his words, and thought of them many a time after: such sundry opinions they had of him for the unconstancy of his life, and waywardness of his nature and conditions.

(ii)   *Alcibiades* called home from exile.

Wherefore those that were *Alcibiades* friends, being at that time the stronger and greater men in the Council in the Army of SAMOS:

they sent one *Pisander* to ATHENS, to attempt to alter the Government, and to encourage the Noblemen to take upon them the Authority, and to pluck it from the people: assuring them that *Tisaphernes* would give them aid to do it, by means of *Alcibiades*, who would make him their friend. This was the colour and cloke wherewith they served their turns, that did change the Government of ATHENS, and that brought it into the hands of a small number of Nobility: for they were in all but four hundred, and yet they called themselves five thousand. But so soon as they felt themselves strong, and that they had the whole authority of Government, without contradiction in their hands, they made then no more reckoning of *Alcibiades*, and so they made Wars more coldly and slackly then before. Partly because they mistrusted their Citizens, who found the change of Government very strange: and partly also because they were of opinion that the LACEDÆMONIANS (who at all times did most favour the Government of Nobility) would be better inclined to make peace with them. Now the common People that remained still in the City, stirred not, but were quiet against their wills, for fear of danger, because there were many of them slain, that boldly took upon them in open presence to resist these four hundred. But those that were in the Camp in the Isle of SAMOS, hearing these news, were so grievously offended, that they resolved to return incontinently again, unto the haven of PIRÆA. First of all, they sent for *Alcibiades*; whom they chose their Captain, then they commanded him straightly to lead them against these Tyrants, who had usurped the liberty of the People of ATHENS. But nevertheless he did not herein, as another would have done in this case, seeing himself so suddenly crept again in favour with the common People: for he did not think he should incontinently please and gratifie them in all things, though they had made him now their General over all their Ships, and so great an Army, being before but a banished man, a vagabond, and a fugitive. But to the contrary, as it became a General worthy of such a charge, he considered with himself, that it was his part wisely to stay those, who would in a rage and fury carelessly cast themselves away, and not suffer them to do it. And truly *Alcibiades* was the cause of the preserving of the City of ATHENS at that time from utter destruction. For if they had sudenly (according to their determination) departed from SAMOS to go to ATHENS: the Enemies finding no man to lett them, might easily have won all the Countrey of IONIA, of HELLESPONT, and of all the other Isles without stroke striking, whilest the ATHENIANS were busie fighting one against another in civil Wars: and within the compass of their own walls. This *Alcibiades* alone, and no other, did prevent, not onely by perswading the whole Army, and declaring the inconvenience thereof, which would fall out upon their sudden departure: but also by intreating some particularly apart, and keeping a number back by very force.

APPENDIX C

From LUCIAN'S DIALOGUE "TIMON THE MISANTHROPE"

(No English translation is known to have been available to Shakespeare. That given is by H. W. Fowler, from *The Works of Lucian*, Translated by H. W. Fowler and F. G. Fowler, Vol. 1, Oxford 1905.)

Timon. O Zeus . . . To leave generalities and illustrate from my own case—I have raised any number of Athenians to high position, I have turned poor men into rich, I have assisted every one that was in want, nay, flung my wealth broadcast in the service of my friends, and now that profusion has brought me to beggary, they do not so much as know me; I cannot get a glance from the men who once cringed and worshipped and hung upon my nod. If I meet one of them in the street, he passes me by as he might pass the tombstone of one long dead; it has fallen face upwards, loosened by time, but he wastes no moment deciphering it. Another will take the next turning when he sees me in the distance; I am a sight of ill omen, to be shunned by the man whose saviour and benefactor I had been not so long ago.

Thus in disgrace with fortune, I have betaken me to this corner of the earth, where I wear the smock-frock and dig for sixpence a day, with solitude and my spade to assist meditation. So much gain I reckon upon here—to be exempt from contemplating unmerited prosperity; no sight that so offends the eye as that. And now, Son of Cronus and Rhea, may I ask you to shake off that deep sound sleep of yours—why, Epimenides's was a mere nap to it—, put the bellows to your thunderbolt or warm it up in Etna, get it into a good blaze, and give a display of spirit, like a manly vigorous Zeus? or are we to believe the Cretans, who show your grave among their sights?

Zeus. Hermes, who is that calling out from Attica? there, on the lower slopes of Hymettus—a grimy squalid fellow in a smock-frock; he is bending over a spade or something; but he has a tongue in his head, and is not afraid to use it. He must be a philosopher, to judge from his fluent blasphemy.

Hermes. What, father! have you forgotten Timon—son of Eche-cratides, of Collytus? many is the time he has feasted us on unexceptionable victims; the rich *parvenu* of the whole heca-tombs, you know, who used to do us so well at the Diasia.

Zeus. Dear, dear, *quantum mutatus*! is this the admired, the rich, the popular? What has brought him to this pass? There he is in filth and misery, digging for hire, labouring at that ponderous spade.

Hermes. Why, if you like to put it so, it was kindness and generosity and universal compassion that ruined him; but it would be nearer the truth to call him a fool and a simpleton and a blunderer; he did not realize that his protégés were carrion crows and wolves; vultures were feeding on his unfortunate liver, and he took them for friends and good comrades, showing a fine appetite just to please him. So they gnawed his bones perfectly clean, sucked out with great precision any marrow there might be in them, and went off, leaving him as dry as a tree whose roots have been severed; and now they do not know him or vouchsafe him a nod—no such fools—, nor ever think of showing him charity or repaying his gifts. That is how the spade and smock-frock are accounted for; he is ashamed to show his face in town; so he hires himself out to dig, and broods over his wrongs—the rich men he has made passing him contemptuously by, apparently quite unaware that his name is Timon.

Zeus. This is a case we must take up and see to. No wonder he is down on his luck . . .

Zeus. (to *Plutus*) Come, be off with you; you will find Timon has much more sense nowadays.

Plutus. Oh, of course! he will not do his best to let me run out of a leaky vessel before I have done running in! oh no, he will not be consumed with apprehensions of the inflow's gaining on the waste and flooding him! I shall be supplying a cask of the Danaids; no matter how fast I pour in, the thing will not hold water; every gallon will be out almost before it is in; the bore of the waste-pipe is so large, and never a plug. . .

Poverty. (to *Hermes* and *Plutus*) Slayer of Argus, whither away, you two hand in hand?

Hermes. Zeus has sent us to Timon here.

Poverty. Now? What has Plutus to do with Timon now? I found him suffering under Luxury's treatment, put him in the charge of Wisdom and Toil (whom you see here), and made a good worthy man of him. Do you take me for such a contemptible helpless creature that you can rob me of my little all? have I perfected him in virtue, only to see Plutus take him, trust him to Insolence and Arrogance, make him as soft and limp and silly as before, and return him to me a worn-out rag again? . . .

Timon. Who are you, villains? What do you want here, interrupting a hired labourer? You shall have something to take with you, confound you all! These clods and stones shall provide you with a broken head or two. . .

Hermes. Now don't be foolish, Timon; cease overdoing the ill-tempered boor, hold out your hands, take your luck, and be a rich man again. Have Athens at your feet, and from your solitary eminence you can forget ingratitude. . . A misanthrope you may well be, after the way men have treated you; but with the Gods so thoughtful for you, you need not be a misotheist.

Timon. Very well, Hermes; I am extremely obliged to you and Zeus for your thoughtfulness—there; but I will not have Plutus.

Hermes. Why, pray?

Timon. He brought me countless troubles long ago—put me in the power of flatterers, set designing persons on me, stirred up ill-feeling, corrupted me with indulgence, exposed me to envy, and wound up with treacherously deserting me at a moment's notice. Then the excellent Poverty gave me a drilling in manly labour, conversed with me in all frankness and sincerity, rewarded my exertions with a sufficiency, and taught me to despise superfluities; all hopes of a livelihood were to depend on myself, and I was to know my true wealth, unassailable by parasites' flattery or informers' threats, hasty legislatures or decree-mongering legislators, and which even the tyrant's machinations cannot touch.

So, toil-hardened, working with a will at this bit of ground, my eyes rid of city offences, I get bread enough and to spare out of my spade. Go your ways, then, Hermes, and take Plutus back to Zeus. I am quite content to let every man of them go hang. . .

Plutus. You prostituted me vilely to scoundrels, whose laudations and cajolery of you were only samples of their designs upon me. . .

Timon. Come, spade, show your mettle; stick to it; invite Thesaurus to step up from his retreat. . . O God of Wonders! O mystic priests! O lucky Hermes! whence this flood of gold? Sure, 'tis all a dream; methinks 'twill be ashes when I wake. And yet—coined gold, ruddy and heavy, a feast of delight!

O gold, the fairest gift to mortal eyes!
be it night, or be it day,
    Thou dost outshine all else like living fire.

Come to me, my own, my beloved. I doubt the tale no longer; well might Zeus take the shape of gold; where is the maid that would not open her bosom to receive so fair a lover gliding through the roof?

Talk of Midas, Croesus, Delphic treasures! they were all nothing to Timon and his wealth; why, the Persian King could not match it. My spade, my dearest smock-frock, you must hang, a votive offering to Pan. And now I will buy up this desert corner, and build a tiny castle for my treasure, big enough for me to live in all alone, and, when I am dead, to lie in. And be the rule and law of my remaining days to shun all men, be blind to all men, scorn all men. Friendship, hospitality, society, compassion—vain words all. To be moved by another's tears, to assist another's need—be such things illegal and immoral. Let me live apart like a wolf; be Timon's one friend—Timon.

All others are my foes and ill-wishers; to hold communion with them is pollution; to set eyes upon one of them marks the day unholy; let them be to me even as images of bronze or stone. I will receive no herald from them, keep with them no truce; the bounds of my desert are the line they may not cross. Cousin and kinsman, neighbour and countryman—these are dead useless names, wherein fools may find a meaning. Let Timon keep his wealth to himself, scorn all men, and live in solitary luxury, quit of flattery and vulgar praise; let him sacrifice and feast alone, his own associate and neighbour, far from the world. Yea, when his last day comes, let there be none to close his eyes and lay him out, but himself alone.

Be the name he loves Misanthropus, and the marks whereby he may be known peevishness and spleen, wrath and rudeness and abhorrence. If ever one burning to death should call for help against the flames, let me help—with pitch and oil. If another be swept past me by a winter torrent, and stretch out his hands for aid, then let mine press him down head under, that he never rise again. So shall they receive as they have given. Mover of this resolution—Timon, son of Echecratides of Collytus. Presiding officer—the same Timon. The ayes have it. Let it be law, and duly observed.

All the same, I would give a good deal to have the fact of my enormous wealth generally known; they would all be fit to hang themselves over it. . . Why, what is this? Well, that is quick work. Here they come running from every point of the compass, all dusty and panting; they have smelt out the gold somehow or other. Now, shall I get on top of this knoll, keep up a galling fire of stones from my point of vantage, and get rid of them that way? Or shall I make an exception to my law by parleying with them for once? contempt might hit harder than stones. Yes, I think that is better; I will stay where I am, and receive them. Let us see, who is this in front? Ah, Gnathonides the flatterer; when I asked an alms of him the other day, he offered me a halter; many a cask of my wine has he made a beast of himself over. I congratulate him on his speed; first come, first served.

Gnathonides. What did I tell them?—Timon was too good a man to be abandoned by Providence. How are you, Timon? as good-looking and good-tempered, as good a fellow, as ever?

Timon. And you, Gnathonides, still teaching vultures rapacity, and men cunning?

Gnathonides. Ah, he always liked his little joke. But where do you dine? I have brought a new song with me, a march out of the last musical thing on.

Timon. It will be a funeral march, then, and a very touching one, with spade *obbligato*.

Gnathonides. What means this? This is assault, Timon; just let me find a witness! . . . Oh, my God, my God! . . . I'll have you before the Areopagus for assault and battery.

Timon. You'd better not wait much longer, or you'll have to make it murder.

Gnathonides. Mercy, mercy! . . . Now, a little gold ointment to heal the wound; it is a first-rate styptic.

Timon. What! you *won't* go, won't you?

Gnathonides. Oh, I am going. But you shall repent this. Alas, so genial once, and now so rude!

Timon. Now who is this with the bald crown? Why, it is Philiades; if there is a loathsome flatterer, it is he. When I sang that song that nobody else would applaud, he lauded me to the skies, and swore no dying swan could be more tuneful; his reward was one of my farms, and a £500 portion for his daughter. And then when he found I was ill, and had come to him for assistance, his generous aid took the form of blows.

Philiades. You shameless creatures! yes, yes, *now* you know Timon's merits! *now* Gnathonides would be his friend and boon-companion! well, he has the right reward of ingratitude. Some of us were his familiars and playmates and neighbours; but *we* hold back a little; we would not seem to thrust ourselves upon him. Greeting, lord Timon; pray let me warn you against these abominable flatterers; they are your humble servants during meal-times, and else about as useful as carrion crows. Perfidy is the order of the day; everywhere ingratitude and vileness. I was just bringing a couple of hundred pounds, for your immediate necessities, and was nearly here before I heard of your splendid fortune. So I just came on to give you this word of caution; though indeed you are wise enough (I would take your advice before Nestor's myself) to need none of my counsel.

Timon. Quite so, Philiades. But come near, will you not, and receive my—spade!

Philiades. Help, help! this thankless brute has broken my head, for giving him good counsel.

Timon. Now for number three. Lawyer Demeas—my cousin, as he calls himself, with a decree in his hand. Between three and four thousand it was that I paid in to the Treasury in ready money for him; he had been fined that amount and imprisoned in default, and I took pity on him. Well, the other day he was distributing-officer of the festival money; when I applied for my share, he pretended I was not a citizen.

Demeas. Hail, Timon, ornament of our race, pillar of Athens, shield of Hellas! The Assembly and both Councils are met, and expect your appearance. But first hear the decree which

I have proposed in your honour. 'WHEREAS Timon son of Echecratides of Collytus who adds to high position and character a sagacity unmatched in Greece is a consistent and indefatigable promoter of his country's good and Whereas he has been victorious at Olympia on one day in boxing wrestling and running as well as in the two and the four-horse chariot races—'

Timon. Why, I was never so much as a spectator at Olympia.

Demeas. What does that matter? you will be some day. It looks better to have a good deal of that sort in—'and Whereas he fought with distinction last year at Acharnae cutting two Peloponnesian companies to pieces—'

Timon. Good work that, considering that my name was not on the muster-rolls, because I could not afford a suit of armour.

Demeas. Ah, you are modest; but it would be ingratitude in us to forget your services—'and Whereas by political measures and responsible advice and military action he has conferred great benefits on his country Now for all these reasons it is the pleasure of the Assembly and the Council the ten divisions of the High Court and the Borough Councils individually and collectively THAT a golden statue of the said Timon be placed on the Acropolis alongside of Athene with a thunderbolt in the hand and a seven-rayed aureole on the head Further that golden garlands be conferred on him and proclaimed this day at the New Tragedies the said day being kept in his honour as the Dionysia. Mover of the Decree Demeas the pleader the said Timon's near relation and disciple the said Timon being as distinguished in pleading as in all else wherein it pleases him to excel.'

So runs the decree. I had designed also to present to you my son, whom I have named Timon after you.

Timon. Why, I thought you were a bachelor, Demeas.

Demeas. Ah, but I intend to marry next year; my child—which is to be a boy—I hereby name Timon.

Timon. I doubt whether you will feel like marrying, my man, when I have given you—this!

Demeas. Oh Lord! what is that for? . . . You are plotting a *coup d'état*, you Timon; you assault free men, and you are neither a free man nor a citizen yourself. You shall soon be called to account for your crimes; it was you set fire to the Acropolis, for one thing.

Timon. Why, you scoundrel, the Acropolis has not been set on fire; you are a common blackmailer.

Demeas. You got your gold by breaking into the Treasury.

Timon. It has not been broken into, either; you are not even plausible.

Demeas. There is time for the burglary yet; meantime, you are in possession of the treasures.

Timon. Well, here is another for you, anyhow.

Demeas. Oh! oh! my back!

Timon. Don't make such a noise, if you don't want a third. It
would be too absurd, you know, if I could cut two companies
of Spartans to pieces without my armour, and not be able to
give a single little scoundrel his deserts. My Olympic boxing
and wrestling victories would be thrown away.

Whom have we now? is this Thrasycles the philosopher?
sure enough it is. A halo of beard, eyebrows an inch above
their place, superiority in his air, a look that might storm
heaven, locks waving to the wind—'tis a very Boreas or Triton
from Zeuxis' pencil. This hero of the careful get-up, the solemn
gait, the plain attire—in the morning he will utter a thousand maxims, expounding Virtue, arraigning self-indulgence,
lauding simplicity; and then, when he gets to dinner after his
bath, his servant fills him a bumper (he prefers it neat), and
draining this Lethe-draught he proceeds to turn his morning
maxims inside out; he swoops like a hawk on dainty dishes,
elbows his neighbour aside, fouls his beard with trickling
sauce, laps like a dog, with his nose in his plate, as if he
expected to find Virtue there, and runs his finger all round the
bowl, not to lose a drop of the gravy.

Let him monopolize pastry or joint, he will still criticize the
carving—that is all the satisfaction his ravenous greed brings
him—; when the wine is in, singing and dancing are delights
not fierce enough; he must brawl and rave. He has plenty to
say in his cups—he is then at his best in that kind—upon tem-
perance and decorum; he is full of these when his potations
have reduced him to ridiculous stuttering. Next the wine dis-
agrees with him, and at last he is carried out of the room,
holding on with all his might to the flute-girl. Take him sober,
for that matter, and you will hardly find his match at lying,
effrontery or avarice. He is *facile princeps* of flatterers, perjury
sits on his tongue-tip, imposture goes before him, and shame-
lessness is his good comrade; oh, he is a most ingenious piece
of work, finished at all points, a *multum in parvo*. I am afraid
his kind heart will be grieved presently. Why, how is this,
Thrasycles? I must say, you have taken your time about
coming.

Thrasycles. Ah, Timon, I am not come like the rest of the crowd;
they are dazzled by your wealth; they are gathered together
with an eye to gold and silver and high living; they will soon be
showing their servile tricks before your unsuspicious, generous
self. As for me, you know a crust is all the dinner I care for; the
relish I like best is a bit of thyme or cress; on festal days I may
go so far as a sprinkling of salt My drink is the crystal spring;
and this threadbare cloak is better than your gay robes. Gold
—I value it no higher than pebbles on the beach. What brought

me was concern for you; I would not have you ruined by this same pestilent wealth, this temptation for plunderers; many is the man it has sunk in helpless misery. Take my advice, and fling it bodily into the sea; a good man, to whom the wealth of philosophy is revealed, has no need of the other. It does not matter about deep water, my good sir; wade in up to your waist when the tide is near flood, and *let no one see you but me*.

Or if that is not satisfactory, here is another plan even better. Get it all out of the house as quick as you can, not reserving a penny for yourself, and distribute it to the poor—five shillings to one, five pounds to another, a hundred to a third; philosophy might constitute a claim to a double or triple share. For my part—and I do not ask for myself, only to divide it among my needy friends—I should be quite content with as much as my scrip would hold; it is something short of two standard bushels; if one professes philosophy, one must be moderate and have few needs—none that go beyond the capacity of a scrip.

Timon. Very right, Thrasycles. But instead of a mere scripful, pray take a whole headful of clouts, standard measure by the spade.

Thrasycles. Land of liberty, equality, legality! protect me against this ruffian!

Timon. What is your grievance, my good man? is the measure short? here is a pint or two extra, then, to put it right.

Why, what now? here comes a crowd; friend Blepsias, Laches, Gniphon; their name is legion; they shall howl soon. I had better get up on the rock; my poor tired spade wants a little rest; I will collect all the stones I can lay hands on, and pepper them at long range.

Blepsias. Don't throw, Timon; we are going.

Timon. Whether the retreat will be bloodless, however, is another question.

APPENDIX D

"TIMON OF ATHENS"
ON THE ENGLISH STAGE[1]

It is a regrettable but perhaps not altogether surprising fact that between Shakespeare's day and the later nineteenth century,

1. Principal authorities include Genest, *Some Account of the English Stage from the Restoration in 1660 to 1830* (Bath 1832); F. W. Hawkins, *The Life of Edmund Kean* (London 1869); W. May Phelps and John Forbes-Robertson, *The Life and Life-Work of Samuel Phelps* (London 1886); H. A. Evans, notes to *Timon of Athens* in the "Henry Irving Shakespeare", vol. VII (London, [1890]); Stanley

Timon of Athens was known on the English stage only in adaptations.[1]

The first and best-known of these was Thomas Shadwell's *The History of Timon of Athens the Man-Hater*, played at Dorset Garden in 1678. The Dedication to the Duke of Buckingham includes the famous pronouncement that "it has the inimitable hand of *Shakespear* in it, which never made more masterly strokes than in this. Yet I can truly say I have made it into a Play". History has been less than fair to Shadwell as a dramatist, perhaps because of Dryden's unforgettable ridicule of him in *MacFlecknoe*; but his *Timon* certainly does him little credit. Even if he could be excused for giving Timon both a faithful mistress, Evandra, and an unfaithful one, Melissa, with the consequent triteness of plot, he can hardly be pardoned for the triteness of his language, so inadequate to the tragic theme. He is also far less wise than Shakespeare in his final scenes: in particular, he allows Timon to die on stage. Interestingly, however, he does bring out a final contrast between Timon and Alcibiades: Apemantus tells Alcibiades at the end of the play that his scourging of Athens is good but that his motives are nevertheless purely personal.

The cast included the great Betterton, presumably as Timon, while Harris played Apemantus[2]; but the play seems to have owed its later popularity rather to an added masque by Purcell. There were many revivals during the years 1701–37, at Drury Lane, Lincoln's Inn Fields, Covent Garden and the Haymarket: Mills, Powell, Keene, Booth, and Milward each played Timon several times. The play was revived on 20 March 1740 at Drury Lane for Milward's benefit performance (with Milward and Quin) and again on 20 April 1745 at Covent Garden for Hale's benefit (with Quin still as Apemantus).[3]

Genest also notes performances of a comic version of the Timon

---

T. Williams, "Some Versions of *Timon of Athens* on the Stage", *M.P.*, xviii (1920), 101–17 and C. B. Hogan, *Shakespeare in the Theatre 1701–1800* (Oxford, 1952, 1957).

1. Adaptations of Lucian's *Timon* and of Shakespeare's have also been known on the French and German stages since the late seventeenth century. The original Shakespeare play was produced in Dublin, in 1761.

2. One version of the cast reverses the roles: see Vickery's edition of the play in The Bankside-Restoration Shakespeare, p. 13.

3. A public performance of *Timon of Athens* by the Master and Children of the Charity School at Clerkenwell, on 7 February 1712, not only aroused the ire of the Society for the Promoting of Christian Knowledge but also caused the Bishop of Chester to cancel a sermon he had promised to deliver for the school. See A. H. Scouten, "The S.P.C.K. and the Stage", *Theatre Notebook*, xi. 2 (January–March 1957), p. 61.

story, *Timon in Love, or, the Innocent Theft*. This comedy in three acts, from the French and attributed to Kelly, was played at Drury Lane on 5 December 1733. In a reduced two-act form, it was apparently revived at Covent Garden on 23 March 1736. This version obviously traces back to Lucian, since the plot turns on Plutus' action in making the unwilling Timon rich, under orders from Jupiter.

A 1768 revision of Shadwell's *Timon* by James Love (James Dance) retained Evandra but restored more Shakespeare and is praised by Genest accordingly. It was followed by Richard Cumberland's version, first produced at Drury Lane on 4 December 1771, with Barry as Timon and Mrs Barry as Evanthe. Evanthe is Timon's daughter, with whom Alcibiades falls in love. It is she who now goes to Lucius seeking financial help for Timon, but although Lucius has previously made love to her, he refuses. At the end, after Athens has surrendered to Alcibiades, Timon throws off his misanthropy and lives long enough to give his daughter's hand to the conqueror. As befits the period of the "Sentimental Muse", the mistresses, Phrynia and Timandra, are omitted. In one respect only, as Genest points out, is Cumberland's version superior to Shadwell's: "in the original scenes which he retains, he seldom makes any change but omissions", whereas Shadwell constantly "adulterated".[1]

A further alteration of Shadwell's Shakespeare by Thomas Hull was produced at Covent Garden on 13 May 1786 (but never published). The first genuine attempt to get back to Shakespeare's play, however, was the version of *Timon of Athens* prepared for Edmund Kean by the Hon. George Lamb and acted at Drury Lane on 28 October 1816. This retained something of Cumberland's version in the last act, but the text for the most part was Shakespeare's, with omissions. Kean, who had long admired the play, gave a remarkable performance which has fortunately been captured in part for us by Leigh Hunt: "The finest scene in the whole performance was the one with Alcibiades. We never remember the force of contrast to have been more truly pathetic. Timon, digging in the woods with his spade, hears the approach of military music; he starts, waits its approach silently, and at last in comes the gallant Alcibiades with a train of splendid soldiery. Never was scene more effectively managed. First you heard a sprightly quick march playing in the distance,—Kean started, listened, and leaned in a fixed and angry manner on his spade, with frowning eyes and lips full of the truest feeling, compressed but not too much so; he seemed as if resolved not to be deceived, even by the

1. *Op. cit.*, v. 317.

charm of a thing inanimate;—the audience were silent; the march threw forth its gallant notes nearer and nearer, the Athenian standards appear, then the soldiers come treading on the scene with that air of confident progress which is produced by the accompaniment of music; and at last, while the squalid misanthrope still maintains his posture and keeps his back to the strangers, in steps the young and splendid Alcibiades, in the flush of victorious expectation. It is the encounter of hope with despair."[1] Other contemporaries praised particularly Kean's acting at the mock-banquet, in the delivery of the execrations throughout the last two acts, and in the final altercation with Apemantus.

The next great actor to attempt the role was Phelps, who produced the play at Sadler's Wells on 15 September 1851 and at least forty times between then and Christmas 1851 (followed by "Dibdin's Musical Farce of *The Waterman*"!). It was also successfully revived in 1856. Old theatregoers are alleged to have preferred Phelps's playing of the role to Kean's, and contemporary reviewers insist that although the costumes and the production were elaborate (there was a diorama showing Alcibiades' attack on Athens), it was the "human interest" of the play that most impressed them.[2] The *Morning Advertiser* significantly added: "We are never led to feel that Timon is right in his indiscriminating denunciations of mankind; but we cannot but mourn over a naturally noble nature thus upset."

The first performance at the Shakespeare Memorial Theatre at Stratford-upon-Avon was in 1892, under the direction of F. R. Benson, in a special version which arranged the play in three acts. Benson, like Kean, greatly admired *Timon*; and in view of their opinions and its previous history in the theatre, it is not easy to agree with Hudson that it is "singularly unsuited to the stage".[3] Benson's production of the tragedy, however, was apparently regarded rather as an interesting curiosity than as great drama in its own right. This attitude seems to have persisted throughout the twentieth century on the rare occasions when the play has been acted in England or America, from the production at the Court Theatre in 1904 to that at the Old Vic, with Sir Ralph Richardson as Timon, in 1956.[4] Only one critic of the latter production was honest enough to admit that the play was new to him; but reviews left the impression that it was new to most of the others also and that this performance had failed to make them understand either that *Timon*

1. Quoted from Hawkins, *op. cit.*, pp. 398–9.
2. Phelps and Forbes-Robertson, *op. cit.*, p. 121.
3. *Timon of Athens* (Harvard Edition xv), p. 185.
4. The Old Vic had previously produced the play in 1922 and 1952.

is not simply "a high-pitched scream of misanthropy" or that there is an experimental form even in the last two acts.

Somewhat paradoxically, *Timon of Athens* may have been the first Shakespearian play to be acted in modern dress at Stratford-upon-Avon. The production, in 1947, was by the Birmingham Repertory Theatre, and the special performance in the Conference Hall at Stratford followed several in the Company's own theatre in Birmingham. The play lent itself quite readily to modern dress, perhaps because it has so little of the "local colour" of Athens in it but perhaps also because of the timelessness of its theme.